International Perspectives on Forest School

Education at SAGE

SAGE is a leading international publisher of journals, books, and electronic media for academic, educational, and professional markets.

Our education publishing includes:

- accessible and comprehensive texts for aspiring education professionals and practitioners looking to further their careers through continuing professional development

- inspirational advice and guidance for the classroom

- authoritative state of the art reference from the leading authors in the field

Find out more at: **www.sagepub.co.uk/education**

International Perspectives on Forest School

Natural Spaces to Play and Learn

Edited by Sara Knight

Los Angeles | London | New Delhi
Singapore | Washington DC

Los Angeles | London | New Delhi
Singapore | Washington DC

SAGE Publications Ltd
1 Oliver's Yard
55 City Road
London EC1Y 1SP

SAGE Publications Inc.
2455 Teller Road
Thousand Oaks, California 91320

SAGE Publications India Pvt Ltd
B 1/I 1 Mohan Cooperative Industrial Area
Mathura Road
New Delhi 110 044

SAGE Publications Asia-Pacific Pte Ltd
3 Church Street
#10-04 Samsung Hub
Singapore 049483

Editor: Jude Bowen
Assistant editor: Miriam Davey
Production editor: Thea Watson
Copyeditor: Sharon Cawood
Proofreader: Salia Nessa
Indexer: Anne Solamito
Marketing manager: Lorna Patkai
Cover designer: Wendy Scott
Typeset by: C&M Digitals (P) Ltd, Chennai, India
Printed by: Henry Ling Limited, at the Dorset
Press, Dorchester, DT1 1HD

Library of Congress Control Number: 2013930591

British Library Cataloguing in Publication data

A catalogue record for this book is available from
the British Library

ISBN 978-1-4462-5913-9
ISBN 978-1-4462-5914-6

MIX
Paper from
responsible sources
FSC
www.fsc.org FSC® C013604

Dedication

This book is dedicated to the memory of my husband David (1943–2012), without whom this book would not have been created.

Contents

List of Figures

Acknowledgements

My grateful thanks are due to the huge number of international academics and practitioners who have given up their time and devoted their energies to write the chapters in this book, and to the groups they have worked with in giving their permission to tell their stories or share their photographs.

Chapter 8
The chapter author would like to thank the Director, Mary James (PHD ch), and the staff of LETCEE for their insightful discussions about the introduction of the veggie bag and for making the photographs available. The organisation has a strict protocol of using photographs of children participating in its programmes, and the pictures in this chapter are included with their permission and in accordance with that protocol.

Chapter 9
The director, parents and educators at the Westgarth Kindergarten were an inspirational group that fully supported the development of the Bush Kinder programme and the later evaluative study. The chapter author sincerely thanks them for their participation and for inviting her to share their journey. Further, she acknowledges the contribution of her colleague Dr Barbara Chancellor and the support of the Victorian Department of Education and Early Childhood Development and RMIT University for the evaluative study. Louise Dorratt, Doug Fargher and Ben Goodes kindly provided the photographs in this chapter; and our deepest thanks go to the children and parents involved in the photographs.

Notes on Contributors

The editor

Sara Knight is the course group leader for work-centred learning in the Department of Education at Anglia Ruskin University. As such, she oversees the undergraduate degrees awarded to all sectors of the Children's Workforce. A former nursery teacher in mainstream and special education, she contributed to the development of Forest School as an early years intervention across the UK. She has published several papers and three textbooks on this subject, and has been a keynote speaker at conferences in the UK, mainland Europe and Canada. Her chapter will link the importance of accessing and engaging with wilder spaces to laying the foundations for a lifetime of concern with sustainability and environmental issues.

The contributors

Eva Ärlemalm-Hagsér, PhD, has a background as a preschool teacher. Her main current interest is in early childhood education with a child-oriented approach, focusing on the lived curriculum. In previous years, she has focused on research on outdoor play, learning and gender and education for sustainability. Since 2008 she has been the convener for the Special Interest Group (SIG) Play and Learning in European Early Childhood Education Research Association (EECERA).

She also serves as the Stockholm president of Organisation Mondiale Sweden pour l'Éducation Préscolaire (OMEP).

Lori Driussi, an educator for 23 years, developed an interest in outdoor learning early in her career when she accompanied her 6th-grade class to Earthkeepers, a three-day camp designed to inspire a love of nature. Excited by students' deepened understanding and active involvement in sustainability projects, she became an Earth-keeper leader and trainer. Since then she has facilitated a variety of outdoor adventures for students and is now working to weave outdoor learning into students' everyday school experiences in urban environments. Lori has taught in elementary classrooms and as a Faculty Associate at Simon Fraser University. As Program Consultant K-12 in Burnaby, BC, she provided district direction and staff development in Literacy. Lori is currently the Principal at University Highlands Elementary in Burnaby, BC, Canada. University Highlands is a 'Learning in Depth' School where all students engage in inquiry-based learning. She is passionate about the role of outdoor learning and imagination in developing the whole child.

Dr Sue Elliott is a senior lecturer in early childhood education at the Australian Catholic University, Melbourne Campus. She has experience over many years as an educator in early childhood settings and as a tertiary lecturer. She is a long-term advocate of education for sustainability and, in particular, natural outdoor playspaces. Sue has completed doctoral studies investigating sustainable outdoor playspaces and is an acknowledged author in the early childhood field; in 2008 she edited *The Outdoor Playspace Naturally* (Pademelon Press Pty Ltd, 2007). Sue is the Convenor of the Australian Association for Environmental Education Early Childhood Special Interest Group and is currently engaged in research, publication and professional development regarding forest preschool approaches and education for sustainability in Australia.

Aida Figueiredo is Assistant Professor at the Department of Education, University of Aveiro, and a collaborator at the Research Center for Didactics and Technology in Teacher Education (CIDTFF), University of Aveiro, Portugal. She has a BA in Nursing and a degree and master's degree in Psychology. She lectures in disciplines related to practice supervision and health in early childhood. She has also been involved in several projects in early childhood and health. In recent years, she has developed interests in outdoor play and learning, and is developing her PhD in Psychology: 'Interactions between children and the outdoor environment during free play'.

Edson Grandisoli is a biologist with an MSc in the Ecology of Terrestrial and Aquatic Ecosystems from the University of Sao Paulo,

Brazil. He believes that nothing is better than hands-on experience to understand the world and all its complexity. Edson has been a high school teacher for more than 15 years and is the author of didactic and paradidactic book collections in Science, Biology and Environmental Education, which have been adopted in several different public and private schools in Brazil. As an independent consultant, he has recently collaborated on the diagnosis, development and implementation of Education for Sustainable Development (ESD) projects in different high schools in Sao Paulo.

Elizabeth Jackson-Barrett is a lecturer within the School of Education at Murdoch University. Libby has previously taught on Kulbardi's Aboriginal Tertiary Entrance Course (KATEC) at Murdoch University. She currently teaches in a variety of undergraduate courses within Murdoch University's School of Education Initial Teacher Education programme. As a Nyungar Yorga, Libby's research interests include exploring factors that promote and develop successful outcomes for Indigenous students in education and developing pathways into tertiary education for Education support workers. Libby has a particular interest in culturally relevant and critical pedagogy, diversity, inclusivity and Indigenous education issues. Currently, Libby is involved in *The Pilbara Aboriginal Health and Education Needs Analysis* for the Gumala Aboriginal Corporation; *Walliabup Connections* for Burdiya Aboriginal Corporation; and the *Northwest Early Childhood and Primary Teacher Workforce Development Strategy* for the WA Department of Education and Training.

Ithel Jones Ed.D. is a professor of early childhood education at Florida State University. He earned his bachelor's degree from the University of Wales, a master's degree from the University of Wisconsin, and a doctoral degree from the University of Georgia. Ithel was a primary school teacher and head teacher in Wales for several years. He has been a teacher educator at three universities in the USA. He currently teaches graduate and undergraduate courses in early childhood education. His research interests include early childhood education, science teaching and learning, and service-learning.

Mallika Kanyal is a Senior Lecturer at the Faculty of Health, Social Care and Education at Anglia Ruskin University, Chelmsford, UK. She teaches across a range of Early Childhood programmes and has been engaged in research around the areas of children's peer relationship, children's participation, blended learning in Higher Education and using the Virtual Learning Environment as a pedagogic tool in Higher Education. Mallika has received various research grants within the University and has successfully engaged undergraduate students in various research projects under her mentorship. She has written chapters for books and has organised workshops and presented research papers for both national and international conferences. Mallika's specialist area is the early years.

Mojca Kokot Krajnc is a researcher and PhD student. She works as a young researcher at the International Centre for Ecoremediations in the Faculty of Arts, University of Maribor. Her BSc is in geography and history, and her research work covers the sustainable development of brownfields, which is also the main topic of her PhD thesis. She is studying the advantages of and opportunities for using green infrastructure in urban and degraded areas. Her work also covers analysis of the quality of the water in Slovenia. She is also active in the pedagogical field, where she prepares exercises for experiential learning on learning polygons. In the polygons, she also guides groups, and, as a supervisor, participates in experiential learning on learning polygons.

Dr Libby Lee-Hammond is Associate Professor, Early Childhood Education, at Murdoch University. For the last 12 years, she has been involved in early years research and development in Australia, and is extensively published in journals and books. Her most recent book chapter is 'Big expectations for little kids' in Down and Smyth (eds) *Critical Voices in Teacher Education: Teaching for Social Justice in Conservative Times* (Springer, in press). She is currently Voluntary Co-ordinator of Ngarn Moort Noonook Moort (My Family to Your Family), a community project providing support for local Aboriginal families.

Vickie E. Lake is an Assistant Professor of Early Childhood Education at the University of Oklahoma. As a former teacher, staff developer and early childhood district coordinator, she has worked to further the efforts of high-quality education for young children and effective practices for educators and schools. She teaches courses in Mathematics Methods, Family and Community Connections, and Senior Capstone as well as doctoral courses. She has authored articles about service-learning with young children and preservice teachers, and has recently published a book entitled *Service Learning in the PreK-3 Classroom: The What, Why and How-to Guide for Every Teacher* (Free Spirit Publishing, 2011).

Theodora Papatheodorou, PhD, MEd, BEd, PGDip(SEN) and MBPsS is an international early childhood educator and researcher, and currently visiting professor at the University of the Free State in South Africa. Trained as a preschool teacher, she worked initially as a nursery teacher in Greece and then in higher education in various countries. Her teaching and research expertise are in preschool curriculum and pedagogy, educational and social inclusion, behaviour problems, multicultural pedagogy and bilingualism, and early childhood programme evaluation. She has extensive research experience in both qualitative and quantitative research, including participatory approaches to monitoring and evaluation and a strong background in research ethics. She is the author of *Behaviour Problems in the Early Years* (Routledge, 2005); co-author of *Child Observation for Learning and Research* (Pearson, 2011); editor of *Debates on Early Childhood Policies and Practices* (Routledge, 2012); and co-editor of *Learning Together in the Early Years: Exploring Relational Pedagogy* (Routledge, 2009) and *Cross-Cultural Perspectives on Early Childhood* (Sage, 2012).

Carlos Neto is the President of the Faculty of Human Kinetics, Technical University and Professor in the Department of Sport and Health where he coordinates the Masters in Child Development. For several years, one of his research interests has been outdoor spaces and children's motor development. He was behind the founding of the International Society for Child Studies (SIEC), of which he is president, and is the delegate for the International Play Association (IPA) in Portugal. In recent years, he has conducted several projects in cooperation with the Portuguese Language Countries in the area of graduate and postgraduate training. He teaches on several master's degree programmes in universities in Brazil in the fields of Children and Play, Motor Skills Development and Children and Sports. He is the author of several books and articles.

Gabriela Portugal is Associated Professor in the Department of Education at the University of Aveiro, Portugal, where she coordinates the training of early childhood teachers. A member of the Research Center for Didactics and Technology in Teacher Education (CIDTFF), her research interests unfold around questions of promoting the development and learning of children, considering their emotional well-being and involvement (experiential education), analysis of the ecology of development, the quality of educational settings, assessment, early childhood teacher training and, more recently, play and outdoor learning in the early years.

Pedro Sá-Couto is Assistant Professor in the Department of Mathematics at the University of Aveiro, Portugal. He is a collaborator in the Probability and Statistics Group of the Center of Research and Development in Mathematics and Applications (CIDMA) at the University. With a background in Applied Mathematics, Pedro has developed an interest in Biomedical Engineering, in the areas of physiological modelling for educational simulation and applied statistics in biology and health sciences. He has collaborated on a number of research projects at the Institute of Biomedical Engineering in Porto, Portugal, and is presently finishing his PhD thesis. In the Department of Mathematics at Aveiro, he lectures in numeric and statistical methods, and collaborates with the School of Health on applied statistics in health sciences.

Anette Sandberg is a Professor in Education at Mälardalen University, Sweden. She is a researcher focusing on early childhood education. Her interest in the preschool environment can be traced in most of them. She has several ongoing research projects, including Human Rights for Children and Language Environments in Preschool. She is also involved in two international research projects: Preschool Teacher's Views on Children's Learning and Participation and Support for Preschool Teachers' Professional Development. She is also involved in projects that focus on other fascinating areas of education, i.e. community and university partnerships. She is a contributing author to *Engaging Play* (Brooker and Edwards (eds), Open University Press, 2010); *Early Childhood Grows up: Towards a Critical Ecology of the Profession* (Springer, 2012); *Professionalism in Early Childhood Education and Care: International Perspectives* (Routledge, 2010).

Jochem Schirp has a degree in Political, Historical and Sports Sciences from the Philipps-University of Marburg, Germany. Since gaining his qualification, he has been involved in developing programmes that use adventure, nature, sports and other concepts of movement in the field of child and youth care. Jochem is the Director of the bsj Marburg, a non-profit youth and childcare organisation. He has been responsible for several innovative national and international pilot projects, and has authored and edited a range of publications in the context of education and social problems. Jochem has lectured at the Philipps-University of Marburg and the University of Kassel. He is a member of the board of the European Institute for Outdoor Adventure Education and Experiential Learning.

Martin Vollmar has a degree in Historical and Sports Sciences from the University of Marburg, Germany. Since gaining his qualification, he has been a researcher and lecturer at the University of Marburg. His main areas of interest are in the sociology of sports and outdoor and experiential education, especially issues concerning nature, experience, and child and youth development. Since 2009, Martin has worked at the youth and child care organisation, bsj Marburg, in its Center of Early Education. He is concerned with academic reflection on and the development and support of an early education approach dealing with nature. In particular, the current task is to support and research the bsj model project on the 'educational potential of nature for deprived children (of preschool age)', which is co-funded by the Land Hessen and the municipality of Marburg.

Ana Vovk Korže works as a professor in the Faculty of Arts at the University of Maribor. She is the founder and head of the International Centre for Ecoremediations. Ana received her first PhD in the field of pedogeography and her second in the field of environmental protection. Her research work covers the sustainable development of region, and the fields of ecoremediations and pedagogy. She studies and forms systems on a national level – for example, how can small local areas connect to common regions with the goal to provide common development of the area and to ensure the sustainability of such an area? She also contributes to the development of the curriculum for the study of environmental education. Ana has created learning polygons in Slovenia for students and pupils to learn about nature, sustainability and environmental problems.

Jane Waters is the Head of Initial Teacher Education and Training at Swansea Metropolitan University, part of the South West Wales Centre of Teacher Education. Having worked initially as a primary classroom teacher and, more recently, as Director of an undergraduate Early Childhood Studies programme, she now works most closely with postgraduate students training to be teachers. Jane lectures in outdoor play and learning, early years education and the ethics of research with young children. Jane's research interests lie in early childhood education; young children's agency and voice; and young children's experiences of outdoor spaces. Current research projects include working with international colleagues to consider pedagogical intersubjectivity in early education contexts in different countries. This project is an extension of Jane's doctoral research which focused on adult–child interaction, sustained shared thinking and the affordance of different educative spaces.

Christian Winterbottom is an assistant professor at Ohio State University. He earned his BA degree in English at the University of Bedfordshire in England, and a master's and PhD in Early Childhood Education at Florida State University. He has taught preschool and elementary children in Japan and worked with preschools and Head Start programs in Florida. He teaches undergraduate and graduate courses in child development and in social studies. His research is primarily on ethnic minority children and families in early education, both in the USA and the UK, and in working with pre-service teachers and children in service-learning.

Tingting Xu is a doctoral candidate and an instructor in early childhood education at Florida State University. She earned her bachelor's degree from the Nanjing University of Finance and Economics in China, and her master's from Florida State University. Tingting worked as a preschool teacher for several years and is currently a graduate teaching assistant at Florida State University. In addition to teaching undergraduate courses in early childhood education, she is engaged in research concerning issues related to children's health, physical activity, and physical and nutrition education.

Introduction

Sara Knight

Across the world, professionals from many disciplines are becoming concerned for the future health and well-being of both our children and the planet. We recognise that more children are obese or overweight, and that more of them spend a greater part of their time indoors, often on screen-based activities. Fewer children understand where their food comes from, or have an appreciation of the importance of their environment to their future. 'Education for Sustainability' has traditionally been the privilege of older and more able children in developed countries. However, there is a growing recognition that the younger you engage children with their outdoor spaces, the deeper their understanding will be. Perhaps the future of the planet lies in this recognition and in this understanding.

In this book, academics and professionals from many different countries recount ways in which various groups of people are trying to counter the problems associated with a disconnection from nature. Many of them are working with our youngest children, echoing the old Jesuit maxim 'Give me a child until he is seven and I will give you the man'.

1

The Impact of Forest School on Education for Sustainable Development in the Early Years in England

Sara Knight

Chapter overview

The chapter contextualises Forest School, with reference to its origins and its unique development in the UK. It goes on to describe recent developments of Forest School in the UK, and in England in particular. This includes the establishment of a national Forest School Association, and the chapter considers some of the impacts that this will bring to the sector. In particular, the debate around the core principles and ethos of the Forest School movement are discussed, and the chapter describes some new research in this area. The chapter goes on to consider the importance for young children of accessing and engaging with wilder spaces through a Forest School experience, and how this will lay the foundations for a lifetime of concern with sustainability and environmental issues. This chapter will link the delivery of Forest School to children in the Foundation Stage of the English curriculum.

Forest School in the UK

Forest School was developed in the UK in the mid-1990s as a response to observed practice in Denmark by a group of early years tutors and trainees on a field trip from Bridgwater College in Somerset. However, Forest School in the UK is not the same as the practice observed in Denmark. Practitioners who visit Denmark expecting to see exactly the same way of working with young children outside as happens in Forest School in the UK may be confused. Danish preschools will often have opportunities for wilder outdoor experiences, but they are predicated on different cultural and educational expectations, expectations that are closer to those in the other Scandinavian countries, which all share a historical-cultural concept that was called 'Friluftsliv' by the playwright Henrik Ibsen in 1859 (Dahle, 2003). Forest School in the UK is also used by groups other than preschool children, a phenomenon you are unlikely to see in other countries as yet.

'Friluftsliv' expresses the idea that the citizens of Scandinavian countries will wish naturally to connect with their environment in many different ways and as often as possible. When I lived in Norway in the 1970s, it was usual for families to go out at the weekends to walk or ski, light a fire to make a hot drink, collect berries in their season, hunt, fish and generally be in tune with their surroundings. Babies in backpacks or towed in pulks (like a cradle on skis; for an example, see http://www.orscrosscountryskisdirect.com/kindershuttle-ski-pulk.html) and older people in their eighties all participated. At the school where I taught, Wednesday afternoon was given over to taught outdoor activities. I visited the University of Umeå in Sweden in 2008 and observed trainee teachers being taught how to teach these activities, which included how to dig a snow hole to keep the children safe if stranded outdoors.

I include this description to highlight the difference between the cultural backgrounds of Scandinavia and the UK. In the more rural parts of the UK, there may be communities who still maintain this level of engagement with the world outside their door, just as inner-city life in Stockholm, Oslo and Copenhagen may preclude it, but the underlying assumptions hold good. Where Friluftsliv is an assumed norm, it is not necessary to define the taxonomy of Forest School, and to analyse what makes it successful and worthwhile. It may be that increasing urbanisation will erode the quality of outdoor experiences in some areas of Scandinavia, and in that case they may look at what we are doing and invent something similar. But it will not be the same, as it will be predicated on different cultural and educational expectations. While space is available for the majority of citizens, it will hopefully remain an expectation that young children at least will be outside for long periods of time interacting with wild spaces.

Space: By way of comparison, compare the population data collected by the World Bank in 2011 (see http://data.worldbank.org/indicator/SP.POP.TOTL). England would fit into Finland roughly 2.5 times. The population of Finland is roughly two thirds that of London.

Forest School in England

Since its inception, Forest School has spread rapidly. For example, in 2012 in the county of Essex there were more than 250 groups participating in Forest School (see http://www.essexfei.co.uk/index.php/about-us). Essex is one of 83 administrative counties in England, indicating the possibility of over 2000 groups across the country. Initially, funding and support were provided by the education arm of the Forestry Commission, the Forest Education Initiative, but unfortunately this ended in England in 2011.

Of these groups, the majority are working with children between the ages of 3 and 7 years. In England, most children start primary school in their fourth year. Many will attend some form of preschool provision before that, and it was in these settings and in classes for children in the first two years of their schooling that the Forest School idea spread the quickest. The reasons may be various. There is certainly more flexibility in the Foundation Stage curriculum for children under the age of 5, and also recognition of the importance of a play-based curriculum in the training of practitioners with these age groups. The influence of theorists such as Steiner and Rousseau can also be seen in the ready acceptance by many of those practitioners of the Forest School ethos.

In 2007 UNICEF published a report that put the UK at the bottom of a chart of children's well-being in industrialised countries (UNICEF, 2007). Whilst some academics have criticised the findings, even if it was only partially true it makes uncomfortable reading (UNICEF, 2007). The impact of this report also assisted the spread of Forest School, as one of the key outcomes does seem to be that it provides children with more robust self-esteem and confidence (O'Brien and Murray, 2007).

The situation in Wales and Scotland has been even better, with the support for Forest School being shared between the Forestry Commission and regional government. Chapter 2 looks at one such project in Wales. Whilst developments in Northern Ireland were slower to get started, there are now a healthy number of Forest School groups operating there. However, in this chapter I will focus on the picture in England where a differentiation is appropriate, as this is the most crowded part of the UK and thus at most risk of 'nature deficit disorder' (Louv, 2010).

Forest School coming of age

In 2012 the Forest School Association (FSA) was formed, with representatives from all four countries of the UK on the Executive Board.

Funding was obtained for a development officer, and work began to formalise the sector (Wellings, 2012). This succeeded the Forest School Special Interest Group (FSSIG), which was a part of the Institute for Outdoor Learning (IOL). IOL continued to support the FSA as it grew, with both advice and administrative assistance.

This is timely. As Forest School has spread, it has run the risk of losing its identity. Indeed, there are examples in England of groups purporting to be Forest Schools which do not subscribe to the principles and ethos agreed by the majority of practitioners in the field. In 2010 and 2011, the FSSIG consulted with the wider Forest School community and drew up a definition of the ethos and the principles that were included in the FSA Business Plan, and which can be seen in Box 1.1 below. Readers will see that these principles are applicable to a wide range of groups, reflecting practice across the UK, where Forest School is being used with all ages, often therapeutically (Knight, 2011a).

Participation in the consultation was invited as widely as possible, being advertised by IOL, FEI and the FSSSIG, as well as through informal networks and visits to key stakeholder groups, but it is probable that there will be dissenting voices. Forest School is a way of working that engenders strong passions amongst practitioners. In an effort to unpick possible misunderstandings, I have begun an analysis of the chapters in my book *Forest School for All* (Knight, 2011a), which I refer to again below. The chapter authors were largely self-selected, and represent practice from across Scotland, Wales and England with a wide range of groups (Knight, 2011b).

Forest School practitioners

Alongside the creation of the Forest School Association, work has been going on within the Forest School Training Network GB (2011) to draw up National Occupational Standards for practitioners. It is hoped that these will be agreed and accepted for placement on the Government's Qualifications Framework for England and Wales in 2013. Once this has been done, it will be easier to ensure that trainees receive the appropriate standards of training.

As you will see from point 5 of the Ethos/Definition below, members of the Association agree that training in Forest School is important, and leaders should be qualified to Level 3. In England, qualifications are given levels that indicate the academic standard of the award, and Level 3 is equivalent to the academic standard required for A-levels, Diplomas and Higher Certificates. It is common practice, and in some situations a legal requirement, that adults working with children can only be left in sole charge of a group if they have a Level 3 award in an appropriate subject. The award must also include an element where practice is observed. Thus, a Forest School practitioner has received a minimum training in human development, bushcraft, outdoor first aid and the Forest School ethos. In addition, they should have been observed carrying out a Forest School session.

Box 1.1   Ethos/Definition

Forest School is an inspirational process that offers *all* learners regular opportunities to achieve, develop confidence and self-esteem, through hands-on learning experiences in a local woodland or natural environment with trees.

Forest School is a specialised approach that sits within and complements the wider context of outdoor and woodland learning.

Principles with criteria for good practice:

1 Forest School (FS) is a long-term process with frequent and regular sessions in a local natural space, not a one-off visit. Planning, adaption, observations and reviewing are integral elements:

- FS takes place regularly, ideally at least every other week, over an extended period of time, if practicable, encompassing the seasons.
- An FS programme has a structure which is based on observations and joint work between learners and practitioners. This structure should clearly demonstrate progression of learning.
- The initial sessions of any programme establish physical and behavioural boundaries, as well as making initial observations on which to base future programme development.

2 Forest School takes place in a woodland or natural wooded environment to support the development of a relationship between the learner and the natural world:

- Whilst woodland is the ideal environment for FS, many other sites, some with only a few trees, are able to support good FS practice.

(Continued)

(Continued)

- The woodland is ideally suited to match the needs of the programme and learners, providing them with the space and environment in which to explore and discover.
- An FS programme constantly monitors its ecological impact and works within a sustainable site management plan agreed between the landowner/manager and the practitioner and the learners.
- FS aims to foster a relationship with nature through regular personal experiences in a local woodland/wooded site to help develop long-term environmentally sustainable attitudes and practices in staff, learners and the wider community.
- FS uses natural resources for inspiration, to enable ideas and encourage intrinsic motivation.

3 Forest School aims to promote the holistic development of all those involved, fostering resilient, confident, independent and creative learners:

- Where appropriate, the FS leader will aim to link experiences at FS to home, work and/or school/education.
- FS programmes aim to develop, where appropriate, the physical, social, cognitive, linguistic, emotional, social and spiritual aspects of the learner.

4 Forest School offers learners the opportunity to take supported risks appropriate to the environment and themselves:

- FS opportunities are designed to build on an individual's innate motivation, positive attitudes and/or interests.
- FS uses tools and fire only where deemed appropriate to the learners, and is dependent on completion of a baseline risk assessment.
- Any FS experience follows a risk–benefit process managed jointly by the practitioner and learner that is tailored to the developmental stage of the learner.

5 Forest School is run by qualified Forest School practitioners who continuously develop their professional practice:

- FS is led by qualified Forest School practitioners, who are required to hold a minimum of an equivalent Level 3 qualification.

- There is a high practitioner/adult-to-learner ratio.

- Practitioners and adults regularly helping at Forest School are subject to relevant checks into their suitability to have prolonged contact with children, young people and vulnerable people.

- Practitioners need to hold an up-to-date first aid qualification which includes paediatric and outdoor elements.

- FS is backed by working documents which contain all the relevant policies and procedures required for running FS and establish the roles and responsibilities of staff and volunteers.

- The FS leader is a reflective practitioner who sees themselves as a learner too.

6 Forest School uses a range of learner-centred processes to create a community for development and learning:

- A learner-centred pedagogical approach is employed that is responsive to the needs and interests of learners.

- Play and choice are an integral part of the FS learning process, and play is recognised as vital to learning and development at FS.

- FS provides a stimulus for all learning preferences and dispositions.

- Reflective practice is a feature of each session to ensure learners and practitioners can understand their achievements, develop emotional intelligence and plan for the future.

- Practitioner observation is an important element of FS pedagogy. Observations are used to 'scaffold' and tailor learning and development at FS.

- The practitioner models the pedagogy which they promote during their programmes through careful planning, appropriate dialogue and relationship building (Wellings, 2012: 9).

Many practitioners bring other skills to their Forest School sessions. The research study I mentioned above (Knight, 2011b) identified that while seven of the 16 authors could primarily be classified as teachers and nine as outdoor educators, some were also artists (two), therapists (three), Forest School trainers (three) or had strategic roles (two).

My analysis of the book chapters has shown recurring themes:

Conceptual category	Key words used
Respect/love of environment	Awareness of weather, seasons, connectedness, valuing
Time, repeated occurrences	All expressed negatively, as in <u>not</u> rushed, <u>not</u> interrupted, <u>not</u> tidied away
Trained leaders	CPD plus skills, empathy, sharing
Calm, serenity, de-stressing	
Establishing a base camp	Belonging needs, ownership
Importance of fire	
Freedom to be in unsafe places	Personal responsibility, independence
Importance of wild natural spaces	Nurturing nature
Leader-led relationship	Trust, attachment, interdependency, role model
Learner-initiated/learner-led	Rights, responsibilities, decision-making, negotiated, open-ended
Magic, mystery, spirituality of nature	Awe and wonder, imagination, fantasy, creativity
Natural activities with real purpose	Dens, bushcraft skills
Preventing/remediating social exclusion	Group cohesion, interdependency
Healthy habits	Exercise, food
Holistic learning opportunities	Natural curiosity, learning, attainment
Brain processes, neural pathways	
Parental partnerships, community links	Inclusion, participation, societal links

Figure 1.1 Recurring themes

In the original paper, they are listed in alphabetical order, but here I have grouped them according approximately to the frequency in which they are mentioned in the different chapters, which could be an indicator of their value in Forest School, although I have not taken the next step which will help me to verify this thought. Whether the sequence is substantiated or not, the themes that recur in the chapters seem to place the 'internal' personal development of the individual in respect of their well-being alongside the 'external' relationship that they are developing with the environment. It is this theme that I wish to explore further.

Forest School and Education for Sustainable Development (ESD)

The UNESCO ESD website states that ESD 'requires participatory teaching and learning methods that motivate and empower learners to change their behaviour and take action for sustainable development' (UNESCO, 2012). In Figure 1.1, practitioners identify participation and behaviour change as concepts central to Forest School. The participation comes from empowering the participants to take a leading role, with rights and responsibilities, and the opportunity to negotiate and make decisions. This applies to all, even the youngest children, where the emphasis is on facilitating their choices and following their interests.

The behavioural changes are those which Forest School practitioners link to repeated occurrences of the Forest School experience. We know that repetition reinforces learning; what it does is create and reinforce neural pathways in the brain (Geake, 2009), which create the habits of speech, behaviour and attitudes. At different ages the brain is more plastic than at others, and so I have taught 4-year-olds fluent in three languages, whilst I as a young adult struggled to master a second, and my grandmother only regained partial speech following a stroke. Two of the chapters refer to this process, one (Partridge and Taylor, 2011: 198) referring to the importance of the high level of plasticity of the brain of preschool children, and the other (Cree, 2011: 111) to the opportunity to take advantage of the adolescent period of plasticity. The important point here is that when Forest School is offered to groups where brains are less plastic, it will take longer to effect lasting change, and yet it is in the younger age groups that we are seeing the possibilities for years of Forest School opportunities.

This is an excellent thing, as it will help to form global citizens who are aware of, engaged with and committed to their environments; where children do not have these opportunities, their heartfelt commitment to ESD may be lessened to a purely intellectual engagement. The key words identified in Figure 1.1 of ownership, responsibility, awareness, awe and wonder are developed as a response to an emotional engagement, and this takes time.

Another emotional element on the list is de-stressing. One colleague reported that this is as effective for the teachers as it is for the children that she takes out. Jakins identifies how stress inhibits learning (2012: 153); other important elements of ESD are fostering flexibility and critical thinking, to enable the next generation to be prepared for the unknowns they may have to deal with, and creativity, also recognised as an integral part of many Forest School events.

The UNESCO statement above talks about taking 'action for sustainable development', and to do this requires an understanding of what sustainable development is. The UN Earth Summit in Rio in 1992 led to the writing of 'Agenda 21: the United Nations Programme of Action from Rio' (United Nations, 1992). This listed 27 aspirational principles of sustainability, the first of which is 'people are entitled to a healthy and productive life in harmony with nature' (UNESCO, 2012). If these aspirations are to become reality, then Forest School should be acknowledged as part of the UK programme to create a new generation of world citizens.

Further reading

Knight, S. (2013) *Forest School and Outdoor Learning in the Early Years*, 2nd edn. London: Sage.
Since its first publication in 2009, this book has been popular across the world with all those interested in Forest School. It has been updated to incorporate new developments in the UK, including information from the Forest School Association and The Trainers Network.
Milchem, K. and Doyle, J. (2012) *Developing a Forest School in Early Years Provision*. Salisbury: Practical Preschool Books.
Both authors are highly respected Forest School practitioners who have invested time and energy in inspiring and supporting others to develop their Forest School provision. They have now transferred that shared knowledge into a handbook for practitioners.
Siraj-Blatchford, J. and Pramling, I. (2013) *Education for Sustainable Development in the Early Years*. London: Routledge.
This book is a collaboration between a well-respected UK academic and researchers from the University of Gothenburg in Sweden, and as such will offer practitioners ideas and information about developing the attitudes and values of our youngest children.

Information for practice

Settings interested in starting up Forest School can contact the Forest School Association at fsa@outdoor-learning.org. The first two books above include additional links to trainer and support networks.

For early years settings who feel that Forest School may be beyond them at the moment, there are many texts that can advance outdoor practice towards wilder activities, including *Risk and Adventure in Early Years Outdoor Play* (Knight, 2011c), which was runner-up for a Nursery World award in 2011.

References

Cree, J. (2011) 'Maintaining the Forest School ethos while working with 14–19-year-old boys', in S. Knight (ed.), *Forest School for All*. London: Sage, pp.111.

Dahle, B. (2003) Norwegian 'Friluftsliv' – 'Environmental Education' as a Lifelong Communal Process. Seventh World Wilderness Congress symposium, USDA Forest Service Proceedings RMS-P-27 [online]. Available at: http://www.fs.fed.us/rm/pubs/rmrs_p027.html

Forest School Training Network GB (2011) Guidance Note 4: History of the Forest School Training Network [online]. Available at: http://www.foresteducation.org/images/uploads/GN4_-_History_of_Forest_School_Training_Network.pdf

Geake, J. (2009) *The Brain at School*. Maidenhead: Open University Press.

Jakins, A. (2012) 'Learning and teaching styles', in P. Beckley (ed.), *Learning in Early Childhood*. London: Sage, pp.153.

Knight, S. (ed.) (2011a) *Forest School for All*. London: Sage.

Knight, S. (2011b) 'Forest School as a way of learning in the outdoors in the UK', *International Journal for Cross-Disciplinary Subjects in Education (IJCDSE)*, Special Issue, 1(1): 590–595 [online]. Available at: http://infonomics-society.org/IJCDSE/Contents%20Page%20Special%20Issue%20Volume%201%20Issue%201,%20 2011.pdf

Knight, S. (2011c) *Risk and Adventure in Early Years Outdoor Play: Learning from Forest Schools*. London: Sage.

Louv, R. (2010) *Last Child in the Woods*, 2nd edn. London: Atlantic Books.

O'Brien, L. and Murray, R. (2007) 'Forest School and its impact on young children: case studies in Britain', *Urban Forestry and Urban Greening*, 6: 249–265.

Partridge, L. and Taylor, W. (2011) 'Forest School for families', in S. Knight (ed.), *Forest School for All*. London: Sage, pp. 198.

United Nations (1992) Earth Summit Agenda 21: The United Nations Programme of Action from Rio [online]. Available at: http://www.un.org/esa/dsd/agenda21/ (accessed 29 November 2012).

UNESCO (2012) Education for Sustainable Development [online]. Available at: http://www.unesco.org/new/en/education/themes/leading-the-international-agenda/education-for-sustainable-development/ (accessed 29 November 2012).

UNICEF (2007) 'Child poverty in perspective: an overview of child well-being in rich countries', *Innocenti Report Card 7*. Florence: UNICEF Innocenti Research Centre.

Wellings, E. (2012) *Forest School National Governing Body Business Plan 2012*. Cumbria: Institute for Outdoor Learning. Also available at: http://www.outdoor-learning.org/Portals/0/ForestSchoolAssociation/FS%20NGB%20FINAL%20BP%20 2012%5B1%5D.pdf

2

Talking in Wild Outdoor Spaces: Children Bringing Their Interests to Their Teachers in Wales

Jane Waters

Chapter overview

This chapter reports the findings from a research study that considered the child-initiated interactions that took place between children and their teachers in both indoor (classroom) and outdoor (natural country park) spaces in three early years and Key Stage 1 classes in South Wales (Waters, 2011). These classes are for children from 4 to 7 years old, described in Wales as the 'Foundation Phase'. The chapter presents data that suggests the natural outdoor space better supported the children in initiating interaction with their class teachers than the indoor space. Further, the content of the child-initiated interactions when outside was more likely to include enquiry-based questions and lead to longer periods of interaction between child and teacher, including episodes of sustained shared thinking (Sylva et al., 2003). The exploratory and essentially child-led nature of the outdoor learning observed in the study challenges approaches to learning outdoors that are limited by pre-planned learning outcomes, adult direction or children playing with pre-defined materials without adult interaction. Essentially, the observed practice offers an alternative model of outdoor learning that addresses the priorities established in the Foundation Phase framework for 3–7-year-olds in Wales (DCELLS, 2008), namely the requirement for child-initiated activity and learning, development of curiosity, and engagement in questioning and sustained shared thinking. This chapter promotes the value of children spending time regularly in wild, natural spaces with their teachers; the study suggests this is particularly valuable for children's cognitive engagement with, and enquiry about, the world around them.

The study

The research was undertaken in a large inner-city primary school in South Wales. Three classes of children (Reception: 4- to 5-year-olds, Y1: 5- to 6-year-olds and Y2: 6- to 7-year-olds) and their teachers were involved. Each class visited a local country park for an afternoon four times across the school year. This activity, initiated as part of an Outdoor Learning Project (OLP; Waller, 2006), had been part of the children's school experience for four years. The visits involved the children putting on appropriate protective clothing (wet weather trousers, padded waterproof jackets and Wellington boots) as needed, and walking for 15 minutes or so along pavements through a housing development to reach the country park. The park itself was situated surrounding the summit of a hill, and incorporated a variety of geomorphic features such as shallow and steep terrain, wooded areas, open scrubland and heavily covered vegetation, grassed space, puddles and swampy ground, trees and panoramic views. A popular area for local dog walkers and used by local youths for recreation, there were often aspects of the space that required care and children's attention to avoid (e.g. broken glass, faeces, litter), as well as aspects that provided further variety for children's use and/or attention (e.g. abandoned rope, lengths of wood, a mattress, a rusting car). The children and teachers usually negotiated between them where, within the park, they would go on any particular visit. The ratio of adults to children was usually 1:2 or 1:3, as a result of support from student volunteers and, occasionally, parents or additional adults from school.

For the duration of one school year, the interaction between the teacher and the children was captured using digital audio and video devices during each of the four outdoor visits per class. An equivalent amount of time was spent recording interaction within the classroom while children undertook a range of play-based and teacher-directed activities. The teacher wore a microphone so that all instances where children initiated interaction with the teacher were recorded. The video footage was taken on a hand-held video recorder from an optimal distance of 3–5 metres. Every episode of interaction that began with a child initiating talk with the teacher was transcribed; the content of the child's talk and the type of interaction were categorised.

Findings

The key findings of the study, pertinent to this chapter, included the relative proportion of child-initiated interaction taking place indoors and outdoors and the features of the environment that created opportunities for prolonged adult–child interaction. While indoor and outdoor observation sessions varied only slightly in terms of duration, it is notable that substantially fewer child-initiated interactions were recorded for the indoor sessions compared to the number recorded in the outdoor environment for each class. The Y2 children initiated over six times more interactions with the teacher when outside than when inside; the Y1 and Reception children initiated three times more. That the outdoor environment appeared to offer more opportunity for children to initiate interaction with their teachers than the indoor environment could be explained by the relative novelty of the activity and the inherent interest that the outdoors holds for young children (e.g. Hart, 1979; Moore, 1986; Titman, 1994; see Box 2.1). However, when the content and duration of these child-initiated interactions are also considered, we find that the nature of the interactions is different too. When indoors, children did not initiate any interaction with the teacher that was about the space they were in; that is, they did not talk about any recalled events related to their classroom, did not open conversation about the classroom and did not offer any information about their classroom during the observations. Only the Reception children drew the teacher's attention to any object indoors; this was infrequent and related to the product(s) of teacher-directed activity. The children in the two older classes did not draw their teacher's attention to anything in their classroom space. However, when outdoors about a third of all child initiations were to an element within the environment. A further third of all initiations outdoors were *indirectly* related to the environment (this was when the child's initiation was related to being outside but not directly focused on a specific element in the environment; see also Waters and Maynard, 2010). Not only did children bring what interested them to the teacher when outdoors, but also the teachers engaged in many more prolonged interaction sequences when outdoors. Indeed, only one episode of 'sustained shared thinking' (Sylva et al., 2003; see Box 2.2) occurred indoors but 31 were observed outdoors. It appeared that children's interest in features of the environment, and loose parts in the natural outdoor space, created opportunities for prolonged, engaging adult–child interactions that were centred on the child's interests.

Box 2.1   Seminal works – Titman, 1994; Moore, 1986; Nicholson, 1971

Elements and features of the outdoor space in this study reflect some of those in which children have consistently reported

(Continued)

(Continued)

their interest over time (e.g. Hart, 1979; Moore, 1986; Titman, 1994). In Titman's (1994) study, for example, children reported that their ideal outdoor space associated with school was a space for doing, thinking, feeling and being – ideally simultaneously. Signifiers of such 'ideal' environments were a natural landscape, livings things, colour diversity and change, features that can be used for seating/shelter, and private spaces and materials that can be changed or used in an imaginative way. It is pertinent to recognise the convergence of these reported signifiers with the elements of the outdoor space to which children repeatedly draw teachers' attention in this study. Indeed, all the signifiers identified by Titman's work are features of the outdoor environment in this study.

Similarly, Moore (1986) records in his study of children's use of their environments in the mid-1980s, how children made use of 'found objects' (p. 78), including flowers, seeds, nuts, berries and 'loose parts', e.g. abandoned seats and 'collecting things' such as rocks, toadstools and leaves; he also looked at how they made use of these in conjunction with 'landscape features' (p. 80) such as pools, hills and streams. Moore's work reflected the interests of children in their middle years, recording what they did in their neighbourhoods, usually without supervisory adults, in informal play situations. Again, the elements of the environment that the children in Moore's study commented on and valued are reflected in what the children in the current study are drawn to in their outdoor environment. It appears that flexible, natural environments inherently offer opportunities for capturing children's interest. The theory of loose parts, put forward by Nicholson (1971), suggests that: 'In any environment, both the degree of inventiveness and creativity, and the possibility of discovery, are directly proportional to the number and kind of variables in it' (p. 30).

The loose parts appear to inspire awe and wonder as evidenced by children's attention to minute detail, colour, shape and their exclamations made about various found objects. The loose parts appear to inspire responses from the children in this study that Nicholson predicted in his theory; particularly inventive and creative responses (see Waters, 2011).

Box 2.2   Theoretical links – sustained shared thinking

Sustained shared thinking has been defined as: 'an effective pedagogic interaction, where two or more individuals 'work together' in an intellectual way to solve a problem, clarify a concept, evaluate activities, or extend a narrative' (Siraj-Blatchford, 2010: 3; Siraj-Blatchford et al., 2003; Sylva et al., 2003). The term 'sustained shared thinking' 'emerged as an analytic node ... in the process of qualitative research' (Siraj-Blatchford, 2009: 78). The research in question was part of the large-scale longitudinal project Effective Provision of Preschool Education (EPPE) (Sammons et al., 2002, 2003) and the extension Researching Effective Pedagogy in the Early Years (REPEY) (Siraj-Blatchford et al., 2003; Siraj-Blatchford and Sylva, 2004). The EPPE project tracked the developmental trajectories of 3,000 children from randomly selected preschool (or home) settings in England as they progressed through school. Outcomes for the children were assessed in terms of cognitive, social and behavioural measures. The 12 preschool settings considered the most effective as a result of these measures were taken as case studies for the REPEY project. This project sought to identify the practice(s) associated with the observed high quality outcomes and emergent sustained shared thinking. Siraj-Blatchford claims the importance of the 'evidential basis for sustained shared thinking' (2010: 162) and describes how the term:

> came to be defined as sustained shared thinking because research respondents and observers specifically referred to the sharing of thinking, and to the particularly sustained nature of some of the interactions identified in effective (in terms of child outcomes) preschool settings.
> (2010: 1)

Findings from the projects indicated that sustained shared thinking 'was most likely to occur when children were interacting 1:1 with an adult or with a single peer partner. Freely chosen play activities often provided the best opportunities for adults to extend children's thinking' (Siraj-Blatchford, 2010: 158).

Case study: Burnt trees

The case study that follows takes the form of a transcript and commentary: this is the first visit to the country park for the Y2 class, in October. The class have been taking regular trips such as this for two years. The class are walking past a bank that slopes away from them where some burnt logs are lying flat on the ground. The outdoor space allows Omar to express his interest, solve a problem and extend his solution into a playful episode. It is interesting to note that Omar withdraws from interaction with the teacher when this becomes 'teacherly', and re-enters the interaction when he has a resolution to offer. The engagement of the teacher in the subsequent play episode indicates Omar's solution has been respected.

Key for the following transcript:

TEA: teacher

OMAR: focus child

CHB: other child (boy)

CHG: other child (girl)

CB2: second additional child (boy)

XXX: inaudible speech

<>[?]: uncertain transcript

Bold text: commentary

OMAR: Miss, look, the tree's been cut down.

OMAR draws attention to something of interest in the environment.

TEA: I wonder why?

TEA responds congruously – seeking to explain the observed phenomenon.

OMAR: 'cos it's coming Autumn.

OMAR offers an explanation for the phenomenon.

TEA: Joel, can you come and join us on the path?

TEA is distracted.

OMAR: Miss! I know why they're cutting the tree down!

(Continued)

(Continued)

OMAR returns to the problem of explaining this phenomenon; his first explanation may not have been sufficient to satisfy his enquiry.

TEA: Why do you think?

OMAR: To make more paper!

OMAR offers further explanation.

TEA: Good plan, Stan.

This is an evaluative comment that could 'close' the interaction.

TEA: What do you need paper for?

This 'teacherly' question may narrow the interaction, though it does potentially extend OMAR's contribution and explanation.

CHB: To write on?

TEA: Something else?

This request reinforces the 'teacherly' pattern; TEA is asking the children to give more answers to her question.

OMAR: For the newspaper!

OMAR contributes a response in this routine interaction.

TEA: Yes, something else?

This is a closed 'teacherly' move. Note: OMAR appears to have withdrawn.

CHB: Um, I dunno.

CB2:   I been over your house.

The interaction appears to have moved on and away from OMAR's interest in the trees.

TEA: J! We're carrying on and we're going round the corner.

CHB: Miss <look at those>[?] trees.

Another child draws attention to the trees again [pointing out another feature – that they are not only cut down but burnt].

TEA: Do you think someone naughty has burnt those trees down?

TEA addresses a social agenda in this leading question.

CB2:   XXXX.

TEA: I know. Why are they burnt?

(Continued)

(Continued)

CHB: I dunno.

TEA: Do you think somebody naughty's done that?

TEA reinforces the social agenda in this repeat question. OMAR takes no part in the preceding judgement of the burning of trees.

OMAR: Aha! Somebody's been camping!

OMAR engages again: this utterance explains the observed phenomenon. He is excited by this idea.

TEA: Do you think so? [laughs] And had an enormous campfire.

Congruous response; TEA accepts OMAR's explanation and extends it.

OMAR: Yeah.

OMAR: Or a bonfire!

OMAR accepts TEA's extension and adds to it.

TEA: Yeah.

Congruent conclusion between OMAR and TEA; observed phenomenon is explained.

This episode is followed 30 minutes later by a playful episode in which Omar extends his ideas into a play situation and the teacher appears, in turn, to extend this further by developing the narrative through briefly joining this play.

OMAR: Miss! Miss! I'm having a campfire.

OMAR draws attention to the current play theme. This centres around the solution to his previous enquiry to explain the observed cut and burnt trees. He is using sticks to pile up a 'fire'.

TEA: What are you cooking?

This is a possible extension to the play since OMAR has not indicated that he is cooking on the 'fire'.

OMAR: XXX.

TEA: Pine cones? Can I have a t – can I have a cooked pine cone please?

TEA responds congruously, joins the play and extends it by joining as a new member.

(Continued)

(Continued)

CHB: [screams]

TEA: er F!

TEA: Omar's make – Omar's got a campfire there and he's making us some food.

TEA invites others to join the play.

OMAR: Here's your pine cone!

OMAR continues the play.

CB2:   Do you want to come to the pine cone shop?

CB2 asks TEA to join the related play theme.

TEA: Can I have two pine cones, please?

CB2:   There you go.

TEA: Cooked.

OMAR: I only had one.

OMAR continues with the original play narrative.

TEA: OK, I'll wait for the next one to be cooked.

CHG: I got one!

TEA: Oh I – can you cook it for me on the barbie?

TEA introduces different vocabulary and brings the two play themes together.

OMAR: Here's the cooking! Here's the cooking!

OMAR continues with the play narrative.

TEA: Oh, thank you.

OMAR: Here's the cooking!

TEA: Thank you <I'll have that now>[?].

Congruous conclusion of play episode.

Discussion

Wood (2007) is concerned that children's interests and needs do not necessarily generate a problem or activity space but, as the data reported above and the case study here demonstrates, on occasion what children identify and bring to the teacher for consideration can do just that. In the co-construction of cognitive problems that occasionally result from child-initiated interaction in the study, an enquiry space (Wood, 2007) is established in which teachers and children intersubjectively engage to find solutions. Such a space is created by the outdoor visits in this study and it is of concern that the indoor space did not support any child-initiated enquiry. Indeed, this position may reflect Brooker's concern that despite the rhetoric to take seriously children's interests in UK early education policy, what adults tend to do is offer a 'diet of activities dependent on specially produced learning materials with [an] inbuilt curriculum' (2011: 146). In this setting, the outdoor visits provide children with encounters with the *unknown and unpredictable* (Dahlberg, 2010) to which they thoughtfully respond and often choose to share this response with their teachers. This study, therefore, indicates that offering the unplanned, the new or unfamiliar in the form of a changing natural environment provides opportunities to respond to the requirements in early years curricula (e.g. the Framework for the Foundation Phase in Wales; DCELLS, 2008) to attend to children's interests.

The outdoor environment appears to be an effective stimulus for children's interest and enquiry because it is flexible, natural and contains many varied, fixed and loose elements. The indoor environment, by contrast, does not appear to stimulate children's activity and enquiry in the manner observed outside. It might be suggested that this implies the indoor environment is sterile and uninteresting for the children but Bang's work (2008), in which she considers the affordance (see Box 2.3) of aspects of the classroom environment for children's action, allows a richer explanation. Bang shows that objects in any environment cannot be thought of as 'neutral environmental elements' (p. 126), since they have a functional significance that is mediated by context. For example:

> different objects in the classroom have different properties; therefore they may afford different activities which are all part of a culturally developed pattern of activities. The objects in the classroom contribute to the overall idea of what it means to 'go to school'. They are artefacts invented by humans … and they help to organise and regulate the activities of the setting. They enable the child to participate in particular activities; at the same time they serve to frame the actions of the child. (2008: 126)

Associated with the physical features of any space, then, are the reified (Wenger, 1998; Aasen et al., 2009) and culturally established ways in which children enact interaction with objects. Outdoors, children in this study enact interaction with objects in a manner that supports enquiry, interest and wonder. That they do not interact with objects inside the classroom in this way does not necessarily imply that the objects there are dull or uninteresting; rather that, in this setting, children are not encultured to interact with objects in this way when indoors.

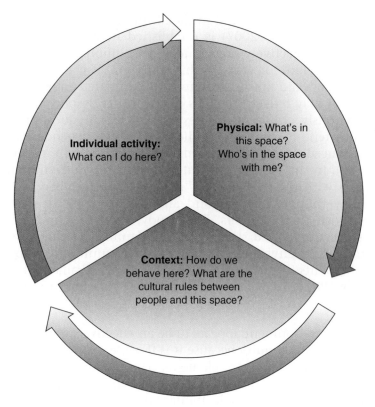

Figure 2.1   Individual, physical and contextual aspects of a space

The term 'affordance' is often used to describe the possibilities for action that a physical object or space offers to a particular individual, but, as the foregoing suggests, any such interaction between object and individual is mediated by the cultural context in which the meeting takes place (see Box 2.3). In order to fully appreciate spaces and what they offer, then, we need a model that allows us to conceptualise the contextual as well as the physical space in which an individual acts; Figure 2.1 represents these aspects of a space.

Box 2.3   Affordance

Gibson's (1977, 1979) theory of affordance was developed as an ecological approach to the consideration and understanding of

(Continued)

(Continued)

visual perception. This theory was a significant move away from previous psychological conceptualisations of perception, based on information-processing models, in which objects were considered to be perceived by a process of discrimination of their properties or qualities (colour, texture, size, shape, elasticity, and so on); Gibson's theory suggested that 'what we perceive when we look at objects are their affordances, not their qualities ... what the object affords us is what we normally pay attention to' (1979: 134).

> The fact that a stone is a missile does not imply that it cannot be other things as well. It can be a paperweight, a bookend, a hammer, or a pendulum bob. It can be piled on other rocks to make a cairn or a stone wall. These affordances are all consistent with one another. The differences between them are not clear cut, and the arbitrary names by which they are called do not count for perception. If you know what can be done with a graspable detached object, what it can be used for, you can call it whatever you please. The theory of affordances rescues us from the philosophical muddle of assuming fixed classes of objects, each defined by its common features then given a name ... you do not have to classify and label things in order to perceive what they afford. (Gibson, 1979: 134)

Gibson introduced the word 'affordance': 'I have made it up. I mean by it something that refers to both the environment and the animal in a way that no existing term does. It implies the complementarity of the animal and the environment' (1979: 127).

It is this complementarity between animal and environment that Gibson was at pains to point out. The location of the affordance lies neither with the animal nor with the environment but between them, within the perception by the animal of its environment. The fact that affordances are perceived by the animal might suggest that they exist 'external to the perceiver' (p. 127), and yet it is only when perceived by the animal that they come into being for the animal. 'The affordances of the environment are what it offers the animal, what it provides or furnishes, either for good or ill' (p. 127). The same environment may offer different animals different affordances. Gibson gives the example of the affordance for support of an animal by different types of ground surface with different physical properties. This affordance needs to be considered in relation to the animal – and is unique to the animal. For example, a

(Continued)

(Continued)

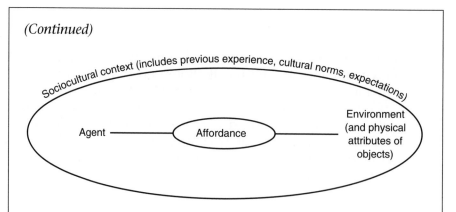

Figure 2.2 A model to conceptualise affordance within a sociocultural context

mosquito may land on the surface of a garden pond and be afforded support but a cat would sink. It is therefore not possible to measure affordance 'as we measure [physical properties] in physics' (Gibson, 1979: 128).

However, we cannot conceptualise affordance without acknowledging the sociocultural context within which the animal – or 'agent' – and 'environment' meet. Figure 2.2 represents Gibson's positioning of affordance as situated between the 'agent' and 'environment', and allows us to acknowledge the sociocultural context of such meetings.

It is suggested here therefore that while the outdoor space in this study inherently provided features and objects that drew the children's interest, stimulated their enquiry and caused them to call for the attention of the teacher, the culturally reified practices associated with being outdoors compared with being indoors in school also contributed to the observations made.

The physical space – *what is available to talk about* – is mediated by the sociocultural context through the culturally accepted practices associated with the spaces and objects through which humans enact interaction. In this study, the culture of the outdoor activity supported interaction with objects in ways that were child-initiated and/ or enquiry-based.

Further reading 📖

Nicholson, S. (1971) 'How NOT to cheat children: the theory of loose parts', *Landscape Architecture* 62(1): 30–34.
Nicholson's seminal paper sets out clearly why the *bits and pieces* inherent in natural and wild spaces are so good for children, their creativity and their development.
Waters, J. and Maynard, T. (2010) 'What's so interesting outside? A study of child-initiated interaction with teachers in the natural outdoor environment', *European Early Childhood Education Research Journal* 18(4): 473–483.
This article documents the specific aspects of the natural outdoor space that drew children's attention in the study reported in the chapter.
White, J. (2008) *Playing and Learning Outdoors: Making Provision for High-Quality Experiences in the Outdoor Environment.* Abingdon: Routledge.
Jan White provides clear and accessible advice on how to provide for young children's outdoor experiences without the dramatic and expensive development of natural areas.

Information for practice

The Welsh inspectorate, Estyn, in its evaluation of outdoor learning in the Foundation Phase (Estyn, 2011) found that children under 5 generally improve their well-being, behaviour, physical development, knowledge and understanding of the world through learning outdoors. But inspectors found that in about a third of the sessions they observed, some children's learning experiences were too adult-directed, lacked challenge or did not make the most of the facilities available. The report recommends that local authorities provide more training for leaders and managers to help them to identify good practice, challenge shortcomings and make more cost-effective decisions on improving outdoor facilities. This study suggests that the artificial 'development' of outdoor spaces for the purposes of supporting children's learning might be considered with a note of caution; the study supports the notion that wild outdoor spaces may be more valuable for capturing children's interest, developing their curiosity and thinking skills than adult-designed spaces aimed at meeting curricular targets (see also White, 2008).

References

Aasen, W., Grindheim, L.T. and Waters, J. (2009) 'The outdoor environment as a site for children's participation, meaning-making and democratic learning: examples from Norwegian kindergartens', *Education 3–13* 37(1): 5–13.
Bang, J. (2008) 'Conceptualising the environment of the child in a cultural-historical approach', in M. Hedegaard and M. Fleer (eds) *Studying Children: A Cultural-Historical Approach.* Maidenhead: McGraw-Hill Education, pp. 126.
Brooker, L. (2011) 'Taking children seriously: an alternative agenda for research?', *Journal of Early Childhood Research* 9(2): 137–149.

Dahlberg, G. (2010) *Something in the World Forces Us to Think*. Keynote speech to the 20th Annual Conference of the European Early Childhood Education Research Association, 5–9 September, Birmingham, UK.

DCELLS (2008) *Framework for Children's Learning for 3–7 Year Olds in Wales: The Foundation Phase*. Cardiff: DCELLS.

Estyn (2011) *Outdoor Learning: An Evaluation of Learning in the Outdoors for Children under 5 in the Foundation Phase*. Cardiff: Estyn.

Gibson, J.J. (1977) 'The theory of affordances', in R. Shaw and J. Bransford (eds) *Perceiving, Acting, and Knowing: Toward an Ecological Psychology*. Mahwah, NJ: Lawrence Erlbaum, pp. 127–134.

Gibson, J.J. (1979) *The Ecological Approach to Visual Perception*. London: Lawrence Erlbaum.

Hart, R. (1979) *Children's Experience of Place*. New York: Irvington.

Moore, R.C. (1986) *Childhood's Domain: Play and Space in Child Development*. London: Croom Helm.

Nicholson, S. (1971) 'How NOT to cheat children: the theory of loose parts', *Landscape Architecture* 62(1): 30–34.

Sammons, P., Sylva, K., Melhuish, E.C., Siraj-Blatchford, I., Taggart, B. and Elliot, K. (2002) *The Effective Provision of Preschool and Primary Education (EPPE) Project: Technical Paper 8a*. London: DfES/Institute of Education, University of London.

Sammons, P., Sylva, K., Melhuish, E.C., Siraj-Blatchford, I., Taggart, B. and Elliot, K. (2003) *The Effective Provision of Preschool and Primary Education (EPPE) Project: Technical Paper 8b*. London: DfES/Institute of Education, University of London.

Siraj-Blatchford, I. (2009) 'Conceptualising progression in the pedagogy of play and sustained shared thinking in early childhood education: a Vygotskian perspective', *Educational and Child Psychology* 26(2): 77–89.

Siraj-Blatchford, I. (2010) 'A focus on pedagogy', in K. Sylva, E. Melhuish, P. Sammons, I. Siraj-Blatchford and B. Taggart (eds) *Early Childhood Matters*. London: Routledge, pp.1–3.

Siraj-Blatchford, I. and Sylva, K. (2004) 'Researching pedagogy in English preschools', *British Education Research Journal* 30(5): 713–730.

Siraj-Blatchford, I., Sylva, K., Taggart, B., Sammons, P., Melhuish, E. and Elliot, K. (2003) *The Effective Provision of Preschool Education [EPPE] Project: A Longitudinal Study Funded by the DfES (1997–2003), Technical Paper 10. Intensive Case Studies of Practice across the Foundation Stage* (October). London: Institute of Education, University of London.

Sylva, K., Melhuish, E., Sammons, P. and Siraj-Blatchford, I. (2003) *The Effective Provision of Preschool Education [EPPE] Project, Technical Paper 10*. London: Institute of Education/DfES.

Titman, W. (1994) *Special Places, Special People: The Hidden Curriculum of School Grounds*. Godalming: World Wide Fund for Nature/Learning through Landscapes.

Waller, T. (2006) '"Don't come too close to my octopus tree": recording and evaluating young children's perspectives on outdoor learning', *Children, Youth and Environments* 16(2): 75–104.

Waters, J. (2011) A Sociocultural Consideration of Child-initiated Interaction with Teachers in Indoor and Outdoor Spaces. Unpublished PhD thesis, Swansea University.

Waters, J. and Maynard, T. (2010) 'What's so interesting outside? A study of child-initiated interaction with teachers in the natural outdoor environment', *European Early Childhood Education Research Journal* 18(4): 473–483.

Wenger, E. (1998) *Communities of Practice: Learning, Meaning and Identity*. Cambridge: Cambridge University Press.

White, J. (2008) *Playing and Learning Outdoors: Making Provision for High-Quality Experiences in the Outdoor Environment*. Abingdon: Routledge.

Wood, E. (2007) 'Reconceptualising child-centred education: contemporary directions in policy, theory and practice in early childhood', *FORUM* 49(1–2): 119–133.

3

Nature, Adventure and Early Education: A Regional Approach in Germany

Jochem Schirp and Martin Vollmar

Chapter overview

In Germany, the Zentrum für Frühe Bildung (ZFB) (Centre for Early Education), founded by the bsj Marburg in 2009, has been using wild outdoor spaces to encourage early years education. This chapter explores why such outdoor learning is important, and how it takes place. The work is carried out both directly with groups of children and also with practitioners who can take the work forward in their own centres.

The preschool stage

As a consequence of the many studies that have been conducted in German education since the beginning of the last decade, much attention is being paid – in parallel to the nationwide drive to increase the number of child day-care facilities – to the education of children of preschool day-care age and particularly to the transitional phase between preschool and primary school. These studies have clearly shown that successful promotion of early education correlates very closely with a lasting successful educational career. Risks and breaks later in educational life – and thus the risk of social exclusion – correspond to a large degree with educational shortcomings at the preschool stage (Rauschenbach, 2011). These discussions are embedded in complex economic and socio-political discussions, such as how the demands of work and family can be reconciled with each other, as well as the role of family in general, and how to make the best possible use of human resources in the face of prognoses of demographic trends (Fthenakis, 2010; Rossbach and Riedel, 2011). What critics see as problematic in this debate is its largely 'technocratic and economic' bias (Rittelmeyer, 2007: 101ff.).

Thus, a fierce debate on fundamental principles has ensued about how to answer questions such as what form education should take in the various forms of care at the preschool stage, which educational areas are relevant in the context of this stage, how individual educational plans should be developed which will also take into account the socio-cultural backgrounds and living conditions that shape children's socialisation, how the education, training and professionalisation of pedagogical staff can be made to match these demands, and what the basic understanding of education should be in answering all these questions, a debate which is far from concluded (see the analysis of early education discourse in Grochla, 2008). Therefore, to develop practices in preschool facilities there is a continued need for practice innovation, for individual projects that may serve as models and for systematic, scientific reflection, even though the dynamics of development in early education have been moving comparatively fast.

Until the beginning of the past decade, the existing educational scenario at preschool facilities had been described in rather gloomy colours: the average German day-care facility was said to provide insufficient support for children's urge to explore the world. What is more, this urge was said to be often ignored or even sometimes hindered. It was said that the staff working there did not understand what was going on in children's heads, what urged children on, what knowledge they had and what they took in. Parents and even pedagogues still believed that the concept of education and upbringing consisted of drumming knowledge into what were perceived to be the empty heads of children.

Within the space of only a few years, the ministries responsible for the preschool area in almost all German Federal States have reacted to educational policy and the urgency of the issue by developing educational plans for day-care facilities for children. Thus, frameworks for the necessary quality development processes differ from state to state – this is in contrast to the great number of European and non-European countries that have opted for the introduction of an obligatory curricular framework (Oberhuemer, 2010: 359ff.).

In the face of large-scale criticism of the 'state of education' in pre-school facilities, the Federal States and a great number of universities have also intensified their efforts to provide an appropriate academic qualification for pedagogical staff. A number of bachelor and master's degree programmes have been created, entitled, amongst other things, 'Education in Childhood', 'Early Education', 'Early Childhood Education' and 'Childhood Research and Education'. The adoption of this terminology from the Anglo-Saxon language shows quite clearly that other European and non-European countries had recognised much earlier which aspects of children's education and learning should be given more weight.

At present, therefore, we can attest to the existence of a broad pre-school educational movement with a great number of initiatives and exciting individual academic as well as practical projects, which, despite differences in their initial conceptual position or thematic focus, seem to have one central concern that serves as a common denominator: what didactic form might preschool education take which places the 'rich' learning potential of children (Dahlberg, in Oberhuemer, 2010: 371) at its centre, and how can the implementation of this didactic focus in preschool facilities be promoted? A regional attempt to find theoretical and practical answers to this can be found at the ZFB (Centre for Early Education), founded by the bsj Marburg in 2009 (http://www.bsj-marburg.de). With regard to the necessary transfer of competence and knowledge, the ZFB focuses on target groups of teams and trained staff in preschool and primary school education, and at the same time also implements educational projects with children in natural spaces. This child and youth welfare institution also operates nationwide and throughout Europe and has been working for about 25 years in physical and movement-related education, particularly with children and families from disadvantaged backgrounds. This means that it has recently intensified its cooperation with child day-care facilities, primary schools, after-school care centres and social institutions in the area of early education. By establishing the Centre, it has been possible to concentrate on these activities, the strength of which lies in the close connection between educational practice, counselling and further education. Principle considerations about this will unfold in this chapter.

In the spotlight: early education

Are children little scientists, who, born as competent babies, should be acquainted with the existing volume of knowledge from an early age? Or would it be more appropriate to grant children as long as possible an independent life phase, which resists societal trends for ever-increasing acceleration? Such questions, which are obviously rather pointed, seem to force themselves on us in the face of the present system of re-classification and re-orientation in the area of early education, and at the same time also make more demands on the institutional pedagogical field. There is, however, unanimity that children need stimulating spaces and arrangements, that they need opportunities for creativity and play and that these need to be fostered, and, finally, that it is essential for children to actively explore and discover the world by themselves and on their own terms – under the guidance of attentive and supportive adults or teachers – in order to go through a successful educational process. Simply extending school education into day-care facilities is just not enough.

This connection between increased attention to and increased demands on early education at local and regional level found its expression in the establishment of the ZFB. As a mobile service, it offers counselling, further education and practice, and intends to support day-care facilities and other educational institutions in the town of Marburg and the surrounding region to extend or accentuate and lay conceptual foundations for the content and methods of their pedagogical approaches. The ZFB sees itself as an external partner of these institutions, offering them new perspectives for their everyday work by giving them a stimulating objective view and by developing projects together with them.

For this, the Centre falls back on the many years of pedagogical experience that the bsj has in the area of conceptual and practical educational initiatives in early education. The great significance for children of kino-sensory references to the world, of physical and movement-based activities and of adventurous, aesthetic and nature-orientated approaches is the leading consideration. Thus, experiences are always also physical and connected with obstacles, and with open-ended and surprising situations.

Natural and nearly natural spaces offer small children enormous potential for development and learning. These spaces are both attractive and full of stimuli, the continuity as well as the constantly changing and open character of which structurally fit with children's general curiosity and development very well. The focus of the educational concept of the ZFB is to foster this curiosity, this spirit of exploration and discovery and this open attitude, especially in these particularly sensitive early education phases. On the basis of these ideas, which relate to the concepts of nature pedagogy and adventure and experiential learning, the ZFB tries to cooperate with child day-care centres, non-governmental social organisations and after-school care centres as well as with primary schools and to help them take new paths. These paths are joint practical projects carried out by the Centre together with the cooperating institutions, and always lead into the outdoors. The landscape in and around Marburg offers two kinds of natural space suitable for experiences with nature that the ZFB has been using in recent years: the woods and the river.

In addition to this, the staff at the Centre offer further education seminars as well as counselling and ideas workshops for teachers and parents. The Centre also holds public lectures and plans comprehensive model projects, supported by the Institut für Sportwissenschaften und Motologie der Philipps-Universität Marburg.

Forming spaces: the woods

The great increase in wood-pedagogical approaches and their implementation in many child day-care facilities all over Germany shows that the wood theme has greatly enriched preschool education, but also that there is still much potential to be developed. The latter is especially true for schools. But what exactly is it that makes the woods such an outstanding space for this experience?

First of all, one characteristic feature is that the woods are in contrast to our everyday world. If we leave behind the safety and pleasantly even temperatures of our houses and our over-regulated streets, and if we move through cultivated fields and cross the border into the woods, a new world opens itself up at a sensory level. It is cooler there and darker, our eyes can only make out the immediate vicinity, which is, however, not closed in by thick walls. Here it is mighty, sky-high trees that block the view and let in mysterious noises from far away. The ground in the woods is as soft as it is uneven, and is composed of uncountable leaves, needles, stones and crawling creatures. If we expect to see the well-known animals of the woods, we mostly only find their tracks or hear the sounds they make.

This shows what sensory richness the woods have to offer, and how different they are compared to the spatial formations we are used to. The wood is not a space that is pedagogically structured and complete with ready-made interpretations. However, it is, and perhaps exactly for this reason, a highly interesting space from a pedagogical point of view. As 'near wilderness', it has the air of something challenging, sometimes frightening, but also of something that is comforting and protective, in which one can hide and settle down. This dual character meets very well the fundamental needs of children for something new, on the one hand, and something that is familiar and comforting, on the other. For children to explore and take possession of the woods means that besides physically following their curiosity in the form of proving themselves and making conquests, they also direct their curiosity for knowledge at the multitude of forms and characters, living creatures and connections, with which they can become increasingly familiar through patient engagement.

The ZFB thematises the woods as a space that holds valuable opportunities for children to experience and confront what is strange and unfamiliar, surprising and unplanned. The woods are to be taken seriously as a space for education and learning. Nature in the woods does not only serve as a backdrop for play and experiences, but its specific characteristics and themes are also explored, for example the sensory qualities of its forms and colours (light and shadow, the form of trees or leaves) or natural science topics (plants, roots, growth, gravity). There is always room for small adventures and daring activities, such as balancing and climbing, but also bigger adventures and journeys. 'Forming spaces' also means that one can actually shape and create spaces. The woods offer a lot of opportunities to do so, such as building dens and hiding places, setting up balancing situations, using natural materials in creative work or opening up fictitious natural spaces (wood tales).

For school education and curricular learning, those developments and projects are especially relevant; this has been established in the form of outdoor schools (Uteskole) in Scandinavia for quite some time. The ZFB considers it very important that prior experiences and the actual conditions of the day-care facility, school, public club or social organisation, are taken into account when planning the project together.

Forming spaces: the river

Whenever most children approach a puddle or see a stream at a distance, their hearts beat faster. They are fascinated by this liquid element. Its formlessness and its varied manifestations are irresistible. Water can flow, stand, reflect, splash, bubble, make a waterfall and fall from the sky. It always seeks its way down. One can make it murky, clear it, dam it up, make waves with it or make it meander, and there is no end to what else one could do with it.

In the river, water takes a spatial form that consists of more than just the liquid element. In Marburg, it is the river Lahn and its bordering landscape that can be explored as educational and learning space in an unusual form. Since 2009 the bsj has been operating a raft for children as a floating educational place on the Lahn river, which is available for child day-care centres and other institutions for projects lasting one or more weeks. It is designed for groups of 15 children, who can explore living creatures and plants in, on and along the river, on the water, on the river banks and in the meadows along the river. Experience with the projects and feedback from them bear out the chapter authors' assumption that this natural landscape offers a wealth of stimulation for children. The children quickly get used to the unusual ride on the raft and are soon involved in what is happening in the water and on the riverbanks. They have tools at their disposal, such as fishing-nets, magnifying cups, filters, straws, pipes or even an aquarium in the middle of the raft. During the extended periods they spend on land, the children intensively explore the riverbank areas.

An essential focus of the Centre's river projects lies in initiating and reinforcing experience with nature study, which is carefully guided and stimulated. For this, it is necessary that the pedagogues in attendance have a profound knowledge of the living creatures and plants and their physical connections, such as in regard to water. This knowledge is used in a sensitive way to develop children's learning through their own and self-directed discoveries.

Further education practice

These projects in natural spaces in cooperation with partner institutions provide interesting activities well-suited to give trained staff practice-integrated training and qualifications, professional colleague-to-colleague advice on methodological and didactic planning, as well as to convey the relevant practical knowledge *en passant*, but by no means unintentionally or randomly. The aim is to ensure immediate support on the spot and thus to guarantee the sustainable implementation of the new conceptual approaches. Furthermore, the ZFB offers open courses which factually connect further education for trained staff in early learning to the focus of nature. In these courses, emphasis is placed on meeting with various natural spaces and their phenomena which introduce the adventurous, mysterious, enigmatic, stimulating or contemplative side of nature into the theoretical educational foundation of pre-school and elementary school education. They deal with, for example, various activities which represent their own approaches and attitudes to the world. The range of further education courses offered takes its orientation, among other things, from a spectrum of approaches such as adventurous exploration and experimentation, play fighting, and creating and building. Further courses offered consider issues such as the development of language skills in nature and of the recognition and interpretation of educational processes in children and the reflection of pedagogical actions.

In these further education courses, which are for trained staff from child day-care facilities, communal initiatives, after-school day-care and schools, and also for parents, the focus and aim is to:

- extend the personal approach and the action repertoire of participants on the basis of their own experiences

- increase participants' sensitivity to processes typical of children, to interpret and understand them in order to be able to guide or initiate possible reinforcement and extension

- provide or develop feasible ideas for practical implementation

- place activities in nature appropriately, relevant to the children's stage of development (supporting knowledge)

- impart the knowledge necessary to carry out activities (technical knowledge, legal and ecological principles).

The basic ideas of these further education courses, which relate to different attitudes and approaches to nature, can be summarised as follows:

1 The course 'Little designers … and their natural materials' tries to work out the functions and learning-relevant aspects of creative play and of artistic design in natural environments such as the woods and to provide ideas for small or large building projects. Such processes are important, in fact even essential, for the development of children. The fine-motor demands required when crafting artistic designs helps children gain increasing control of their hands. This motor component is accompanied by valuable opportunities for children to gain experience in expressing themselves alone or together with others aesthetically and creatively, and to experience themselves as creative constructors. This course combines the participants' own engagement with and experiences in nature with theoretical reflections, such as in relation to guiding and initiating such processes in practice.

2 The focus of the course 'Little adventurers … in nature' is on a movement-oriented approach to nature which will make children

feel they are adventurers. The course deals with what adventure and daring mean to little and big people and how pedagogues can design, stimulate and carry out adventurous, age-appropriate activities with children. The relevant supporting theoretical and practical knowledge, as well as the participants' own processes of experience, make the adventure-pedagogical approach fruitful for the preschool and primary education field.

3   An approach to nature governed by curiosity can be investigated and experienced in the course 'Little explorers ... and the secrets of nature'. It deals with the way participants' own delighted amazement, explorative drive and persistent inquiry into the objects and relationships of natural spaces automatically prompt children to ask questions and formulate hypotheses. Why does one's breath turn white in winter? How does the earthworm breathe underground? What is the wind doing when it is not blowing? Question over question for which there are no simple answers. The didactic methods of nature study offer interesting approaches to initiate and foster self-directed insights. Furthermore, the course teaches selected experiments and how they can be implemented with simple materials. The knowledge focus for interpretation relates particularly to two exciting, interconnected aspects: explanations that are based on the facts of natural science and on a spirit that is typical for children of a young age.

4   The course 'Little players and fighters ... in nature' deals with games that are physically intensive and may stretch over a large area, such as playing hide and seek, other games that use landscape and smuggling games, thus the kind of games which are particularly inspired by the unstructured spaces that nature offers. The course focuses on the theoretical significance of games and play fighting in the development of children, as well as on their pedagogical potential. Play fighting is of particular importance in this course. As in all courses, the reflective examination of a playful fighting approach to the world is carried out on the basis of the participants' own processes of experience. This is designed to extend the action repertoire of the participants and to overcome possible barriers as regards these issues. One rule governs all games: everything is allowed that does not cause pain! Wrestling with each other always remains contained by playful togetherness.

Institutional and regional embeddedness

The Centre for Early Education is a model attempting to set up a supportive regional infrastructure for the further education and professionalisation processes in early education institutions. Since, due to lack of personnel, the ZFB cannot work with all facilities that express an interest – the town of Marburg alone has about 50 child day-care facilities and crèches – it has to make a choice as regards work plans. Priority is given first of all to those facilities that actively make contact with the ZFB and show a willingness to develop a stance based on the new educational focus, so that a productive cooperative relationship can be fostered.

The partner institutions are actively involved in the planning and practical execution of the project as well as in the evaluation of it. They wish for their staff to gain further education in the course of the project and support their participation in the proposed courses. For the duration of the individual project, binding cooperation agreements are put in place. The ZFB can enter into intensive practical project work with about 20 facilities in the course of one year. In addition to this, further facilities can participate in the courses offered by the ZFB. Each year, the ZFB works out a detailed plan outlining its envisaged projects and activities with individual partners, as well as a programme of further education courses.

Due to the fact that the Hessischer Bildungs- und Erziehungsplan (the education plan for the State of Hessen) covers not only the preschool but also the primary school stage, activities are also directed at interested regional primary schools and after-school care facilities as well as parents. The ZFB sees itself as a partner and not as a competitor to specialist counsellors of responsible public authorities and private agencies, and tries to pick up and support other initiatives.

At the same time, the ZFB would like to stimulate greater openness of preschool and primary school facilities within the local community. Other regional institutions could well become actively involved in an educational network that may extend according to demand (environmental groups, such as Greenpeace, youth wood hostels, nature projects, forestry departments, etc.). Thus, the Centre sees itself as one building block in the communal educational landscape of Marburg.

This concept of communal educational landscapes, which has gradually developed in the educational debates in Germany in recent years, is based on the consideration that education is not exclusively the concern of schools. Education and learning take place in formal, non-formal and informal places; a great number of actors are involved, who all have an influence on and give structure to the educational journey of individuals. Furthermore, education is more than the purely reproductive acquisition of immediately useful knowledge from books; it is a complex, lifelong process, the aim of which is to develop individual autonomy that proves lastingly reliable. Against the background of constant change, successful educational careers – also from the perspective of balancing social disadvantages – are increasingly important. In order to meet the complexity of these challenges, there is a demand for a consistent overall system of education, learning and care (BMFSFJ, 2005), a 'collaboration between all institutions and organisations on the local level that are responsible for education and learning', in order to overcome the 'separating division of responsibility in the local area', and to ensure the multi-dimensional quality of a 'holistic understanding of education' (Deutscher Verein, 2007: 1; see also AGJ, 2006). These considerations are taken up by the idea of implementing local educational landscapes, in which 'on the basis of an overall local educational policy the various opportunities and places for education, learning and care are institutionally and bindingly dovetailed' (DV, 2007: 9).

The educational and developmental processes of young people in their very early years are often discussed in outlines of local educational landscapes as children are particularly dependent on the resources of their direct environment. Against this background, the ZFB sees itself as a regional partner in this testing of structured cooperation between different actors: child day-care facilities, parents, public authorities, primary schools, non-governmental youth care agencies, and so on.

Further reading

Becker, P., Schirp, J. and Vollmar, M. (2013) *Abenteuer, Natur und frühe Bildung.* Opladen and Farmington Hills: Verlag Barbara Budrich.
The edition includes different contributions that focus on structural, developmental, historical, practical and international aspects of early education. Based on different pedagogical and psychological perspectives, the chapters contribute profound theoretical and practical knowledge to a concept of early education that is orientated towards adventure and natural pedagogical ideas.

Gebhard, U. (2009) *Kind und Natur: Über die Bedeutung der Natur für die psychische Entwicklung,* 3rd edn. Wiesbaden: VS Verlag für Sozialwissenschaften.
In this publication, Gebhard presents his eco-psychological approach to the relationship between child and nature. Thus, this book is a standard work for the German-speaking area about the relevance of natural spaces for the development of children.

Schäfer, G., Alemzadeh, M., Eden, H. and Rosenfelder, D. (2008) *Natur als Werkstatt.* Kiliansroda: Verlag das Netz.
This book is based on a large research project, which conceptualises and discusses nature as a workshop to engage the child's curiosity and experience. From the authors' perspective, the nature workshop is not primarily a space to teach about nature or even about the natural sciences, but a space to stimulate children to explore in terms of a 'wild exploration'.

Information for practice

The work experiences of the ZFB have shown that playful engagement in challenging and adventurous natural situations offers children a multitude of opportunities to develop an open and exploratory attitude, to acquire emotional and social competences and to dovetail experimental physico-sensory experiences in nature with forms of basic education in nature study that are appropriate to children's developmental stage. This is not primarily about following the laws of one discipline but about following children's curiosity and being action-based. Pedagogically framed experiences in natural spaces open up options to develop a set of dispositions which could also be called 'basic competences', 'fundamental skills, abilities and personality characteristics', which represent 'the basis of the children's physical and mental health, well-being and quality of life' (HSM/HKM, 2007: 47). These dispositions are also the essential prerequisites for the concept of resilience, which forms the basis of the 13th Children and Youth Report of the Federal Government (BMFSFJ, 2009), as well as of diverse educational plans.

Using natural spaces in preschool education is, of course, not new. The movement of wood and nature kindergartens (with about a thousand existing facilities in Germany) is a good example. One can also observe numerous nature-related activities in the work of traditional child day-care facilities. However, from what trained counsellors report about their practice, it becomes clear that there is still no generally satisfactory link between these increasingly popular opportunities and everyday practice, that the teachers can normally only draw on very limited reflections of practical experiences and, most of all, that their work is rarely integrated into a productive didactic overall concept. Most activities are often based on a multitude of sometimes implicit rather than explicit conceptual justifications. Thus, natural opportunities run the risk of being used as a form of pedagogy on sale, to be consumed and easily reproduced, which may take place or may be cancelled, 'depending on the weather'. But day-care facilities must make up their minds now whether they 'want to be content with just providing recreational activities and care for children of preschool age' (Laewen and Andres, 2002: 65), or whether they want to take their educational mandate seriously.

In the recent practice of the ZFB, the great willingness of child day-care and after-school care facilities to implement this change in perspective does not only show through an enormously increased demand for outdoor projects. Teams of staff and teachers take up joint practice opportunities with the staff of the ZFB in order to gain more mastery in their actions in a pedagogical field that they may have only briefly encountered, guided by their 'natural common sense'. Bit by bit, these pedagogues acquire the knowledge necessary for their actions and for more methodological didactic approaches; pre-scientific knowledge is increasingly turned into

(Continued)

(Continued)

reflected experience. What was previously done intuitively can now be transformed into planned educational practice based on well-reasoned factual decisions, supported by ideas derived from their own personal experience. This not only reduces the risk that opportunities to work in natural spaces are entered as events or fashionable accessories into the calendars of day-care centres, but helps ensure that they accompany the individual educational journeys of children, are linked with everyday practice, are integrated into work with parents, and so on.

Pedagogical arrangements in natural spaces – as the experiences of the ZFB so far show emphatically – open up stimulating settings for participating children and thus offer them 'educational opportunities in which they are confronted with a multitude of habits, skills, knowledge, concepts, opinions, attitudes, emotions, so that they can fully develop their potential in dealing with them', which Fried et al. (2003: 61) demand should be the standard quality of education in child day-care facilities. Pedagogical arrangements in natural spaces would make a 'complexity' and an 'imposition of topics' possible (Laewen and Andres, 2002: 50ff.), without which the educational journey of the children and the trained pedagogical personnel would come to a standstill. The institutional educational process, the development from day-care centres to educational institutions can 'not take place without accessing the counselling and transfer systems which make sure that the preschool area keeps up with the research resources and the international scientific progress in the relevant fields' (2002: 67). The Centre of Early Education sees itself as a part of this counselling and transfer system, on the one hand, in the sense that it carries out its own innovation transfer to early education facilities, but, on the other hand, in the sense that it is also a learning organisation, which receives essential interaction with other institutions and guidance from international scientific discussions in the field.

References

Arbeitsgemeinschaft für Kinder- und Jugendhilfe (AGJ) (ed.) (2006) *Handlungs- empfehlungen zur Kooperation von Jugendhilfe und Schule.* Berlin.
BMFSFJ (2005) 12. *Kinder- und Jugendbericht.* Berlin: BMFSFJ.
BMFSFJ (2009) 13. *Kinder- und Jugendbericht.* Berlin: BMFSFJ.
Deutscher Verein (DV) für öffentliche und private Fürsorge (2007) *Diskussionspapier des Deutschen Vereins zum Aufbau kommunaler Bildungslandschaften.* Berlin.
Fried, L., Dippelhofer-Stiem, B., Honig, M.-S. and Liegle, L. (2003) *Einführung in die Pädagogik der frühen Kindheit.* Weinheim, Basel, Berlin: Beltz.
Fthenakis, W. (2010) 'Implikationen und Impulse für die Weiterentwicklung der Bildungsqualität in Deutschland', in W. Fthenakis and P. Oberhuemer (eds) *Frühpädagogik international: Bildungsqualität im Blickpunkt, 2.* Auflage. Wiesbaden: VS Verlag, pp. 387–402.
Grochla, N. (2008) *Qualität und Bildung: Eine Analyse des wissenschaftlichen Diskurses in der Frühpädagogik.* Berlin: LIT Verlag, Dr. W. Hopf.

HSM/HKM (2007) *Bildung von Anfang an: Bildungs- und Erziehungsplan für Kinder von 0 bis 10 Jahren in Hessen*. Wiesbaden. See http://www.bep.hessen.de/irj/BEP_Internet

Laewen, H.J. and Andres, B. (2002) *Künstler, Forscher, Konstrukteure*. Weinheim, Basel, Berlin: Beltz.

Oberhuemer, P. (2010) 'Bildungskonzepte für die frühen Jahre in internationaler Perspektive', in W. Fthenakis and P. Oberhuemer (eds) *Frühpädagogik international: Bildungsqualität im Blickpunkt, 2.* Auflage. Wiesbaden: VS Verlag, pp. 359–386.

Rauschenbach, T. (2011) 'Aufwachsen unter neuen Vorzeichen', *DJI Bulletin* 1: 4–7.

Rittelmeyer, C. (2007) *Kindheit in Bedrängnis: Zwischen Kulturindustrie und technokratischer Bildungsreform*. Stuttgart: Kohlhammer.

Rossbach, J. and Riedel, R. (2011) 'Mehr Plätze alleine reichen nicht: Beim Ausbau der Kinderbetreuungsangebote ist die Qualität entscheidend', *DJI Bulletin* 1: 10–12.

4

Outdoor Play in a Swedish Preschool Context

Eva Ärlemalm-Hagsér and Anette Sandberg

Chapter overview

This chapter presents a broad overview of outdoor play and learning in a Swedish early childhood educational context. We present historical and pedagogical perspectives that view nature as gender-neutral and the European Romantic Movement's un-problematized view of the child as deeply intertwined with nature (Rousseau, 1892), as well as some perspectives critical of these ideas, along with two case studies from preschools. Before we discuss this further, some background needs to be given about the Swedish preschool's administrative and management structures.

The Swedish preschool

The Ministry of Education and Science (2010) is responsible for the educational system in Sweden, where preschool teachers work with children aged 1–6 years. In 2010, 86 percent of all children in the age group 1–5 attended preschool. In 2003, universal preschool was introduced for 4- and 5-year-olds. 'Preschool class' is a specific form of schooling for 6-year-old children, while compulsory school begins at the age of 7; 95 percent of 6-year-olds were enrolled in preschool class and 3 percent in compulsory school. There are two staff categories in

Swedish preschools: preschool teachers and day-care attendants. Over half of all preschool staff members hold a university degree in early childhood education. The day-care attendants have a vocational qualification at the post-secondary level (Swedish National Agency for Education, 2010). Early childhood education has its own curriculum in the form of a regulatory framework. The overall national goals are set out by the Swedish Parliament and Government in Parliamentary Education Acts and are set out in the curriculum steering document The National Curriculum for the Swedish Preschool (2010). These documents emphasize the importance of preschool as the first step in a lifelong process of learning.

A historical overview of outdoor play and learning

When Swedish preschool pioneers opened the first kindergartens and day-care institutions in Sweden in the mid-1850s, they were inspired by Friedrich Fröbel (1782–1852) and his ideas about children and nature (Fröbel, 1887). Outdoor learning through exploration and play, nature studies and gardening were seen as important components, together with the idea that the child's encounter with the outdoors would instil a sense of responsibility toward living things. The encounter with nature was seen as an important vehicle for teaching the traditional Swedish value of respect for nature. To this end, at the beginning of the 1900s, kindergarten teachers organized excursions for city children to forests and farmlands with the goal of strengthening their relationship with nature. This relationship was lost as a result of the industrialization and migration that characterized the late 19th century, when children moved with their families from the countryside to cities (Hatje, 1999).

For the past 60 years, outdoor play and nature have been significant components of Swedish educational policy documents for early childhood education. The contents can be summarized as follows: Outdoor play can serve as a vehicle for promoting children's development and the use of all five senses to learn, especially in and around natural settings. It can help them cultivate a relationship with and caring attitude toward nature and the natural world and develop environmentally friendly behaviour.

In the revised National Curriculum for the Swedish Preschool (Swedish National Agency for Education, 2010), there is a shift toward a greater emphasis on learning. The natural sciences are one of the teaching areas with new ambitious goals to develop children's interest in and understanding of nature, science and natural interrelationships, as well as knowledge about plants, animals, chemical processes and physical phenomena.

In a preschool context, play has served an important function linked to education. Although theories of children's learning have changed throughout history, play is now accorded the same importance as formal learning in Sweden, and is regarded as necessary for making sense of the surrounding world. Nevertheless, outdoor learning is not explicitly highlighted in the curriculum, but has been inherited from past pedagogical practice at Swedish preschools, as we will show below.

Figure 4.1   In rain and shine

'Skogsmulle' and 'In Rain and Shine' schools

When describing the history of the Swedish preschool in relation to outdoor play and learning, we also must mention some features of great importance for this development. Outdoor play and learning, as a pedagogical practice in preschools, has been strongly influenced by the Skogsmulle school. The 'Skogsmulle' or 'Mulle' school was started in the late 1950s by Gösta Frohm and the Association for the Promotion of Outdoor Life. The fundamental principles of Mulle pedagogy were as follows: children learn about nature and the environment in the forest; children's play, discovery and curiosity are the basis for learning in the forest; and outdoor play in the forest is a natural way for children to develop an interest in outdoor life, to cultivate environmental awareness and to lay the foundations for a healthy lifestyle (Rantatalo, 2000).

Since the 1970s, preschool staff have been offered training to become Skogsmulle leaders, and preschools have worked with Mulle pedagogy.

In addition to its use in after-school activities, Mulle schools are organized by the Association for the Promotion of Outdoor Life.

This Mulle school movement was the origin of the forest schools in Sweden, which were developed in 1985 and are called 'In Rain or Shine' or 'All Weather' schools (in Swedish, 'I Ur och Skur' [IUoSk]). The pedagogical approach in an IUoSk preschool is based on the idea that children's needs in terms of knowledge, development, activity and togetherness can be fulfilled by their spending time and playing in a natural outdoor environment. Children learn to understand the interconnections in nature, to act carefully and to protect nature. All this knowledge and these skills are to be acquired by having fun together with peers and adults in the forest or in a variety of habitats in natural settings such as fields, mountains or lakes, in all kinds of weather, all year round. This method of educating children outdoors has spread to other countries throughout the world – to Finland, Norway, Germany, Latvia, Japan, Russia, the Lebanon, England, Wales and Scotland (The National Association for the Promotion of Outdoor Life, 2012).

Memories of outdoor play during childhood

A Swedish study (Sandberg and Vourinen, 2006) that investigated adults' memories of childhood play environments from the 1940s to date found that children's play and access to different environments changed in the latter part of the 1900s. The oldest participants, who grew up in the 1940s, describe playing in environments in the countryside more often than younger participants. For example, they mention haylofts and farms as environments for play. Typical of older participants' statements is that they primarily refer to outdoor play, often in environments that were not explicitly intended for play. Environments for play were often large stones, hills or dens built in the forest, with or without the help of adults. Furthermore, in rural areas play took place near adults' places of work. Some of the participants had grown up in towns and played on the streets or in nearby wooded areas.

Case studies: Outdoor play in a Swedish context

Swedish preschool children spend about 1.5 to 3 hours on the preschool playground each day and go to wooded areas in the neighbourhood on a weekly basis (Ärlemalm-Hagsér, 2008). To illustrate contemporary outdoor play and learning in the Swedish preschool, we will describe two preschools, from different places and environments, and show how they structure their outdoor play and learning programs.

Case study 1: Tallkottens Preschool (set in a small town in central Sweden)

Our preschool has an inviting outdoor environment for children to play in and explore. The preschool grounds have several pieces of play equipment such as a climbing frame, swings, sandboxes and water, but also a wooded area to explore year-round and to pick blueberries in, in the autumn. We usually spend an hour outside before lunch, and also one or more hours in the afternoon. On the preschool grounds, children often play together and develop their play in interaction with each other, and find others from different units to play with. Children have opportunities to move freely over large areas of the preschool grounds and ride bikes or the 'mooncar', a pedal car that you control with adjustable levers. Playing outside, moving and doing physical activities, and breathing in fresh air are things we think are important for children's health.

Another healthy thing – the youngest children always sleep outside after lunch in their strollers in the shade under a roof. They sleep outside for approximately 1–2 hours every day; it's a year-round activity, including in the winter.

We go to the forest for at least half a day every week. We explore our environment and look at and follow nature's subtle changes. In the forest, children have the opportunity to test their abilities in challenging activities such as climbing and balancing. We have begun to work with mathematical concepts in the forest such as long–short, big–small, and also arithmetic. The forest offers many opportunities, and lots of materials are available to explore and play with, such as sticks, pine cones, rocks and leaves, among many other things. (Preschool teacher, working with children aged 1–4)

 ## Case study 2: Granens Preschool (set in a municipality close to a large city)

In the forest, we can easily and inexpensively integrate all curriculum goals, and we are in a healthy environment without the usual interruptions that otherwise happen when we are inside. We have our nature/outdoor day on Wednesday and the cook prepares our food. We usually have pasta salad with sausage or ham, Russian pasties, or crêpes or pancakes. If we take the portable stove, we may have soup or bread dipped in melted cheese.

(Continued)

(Continued)

Even if we have already planned some activities, the children and the weather decide. Self-esteem and cooperation are strengthened, and when it comes to gender questions, the forests are not so gender-coded. Everyone is dressed in long trousers, boots and rain clothes.

What we do is as follows:

One of the children takes responsibility for the group; she or he chooses the path we should take to get to our meeting place – a large rock where there are cups, water and fruit. We climb with ropes up on the mountain, in easy places and then more difficult ones. We build dens and climb trees. We pretend that branches are dragons, horses or other things. We pick and talk about mushrooms, blueberries and lingonberries, and lily of the valley berries (they are poisonous). We pick rosehips, dry them and make a drink out of them. We taste wood sorrel and resin and other plants from the forest, and go 'fishing' in ponds. We talk about the water cycle; follow tracks, both natural and human-made; pick up rubbish; take care of 'abandoned animals' (soft toys); collect natural things and then organize them by different shapes and colours; the children jump from boulders, and so on.

During all this, we weave maths into all the activities: who goes first and last; who's in the middle; high up in a tree; measure the height of the tree; a heavy stone; a light stick. 'Get a thick stick and thin pine-needles!' 'Add two leaves and one stone, put them beside each other, and repeat the pattern!' 'How many grapes do you think we have today? Seven, ok, let's divide ... no, we have seven and this many are left', 'What should we do now?', 'How do we do this?'. On forest days, conflicts between children are much less frequent than on other days.

Our playground at the preschool has some woods: some parts are paved; we have walkways, playhouses, a hill, sandboxes, a train to play on, large and small treehouses and a barbecue. We also used to have a spinning swing to play on. But now the municipal regulations are getting stricter, so some things that the children played with before are no longer allowed, and we are waiting for 'replacement tools' though it has been over two years now.

We spend at least two hours outdoors every day, morning or afternoon, but on forest days (Wednesdays) we are outside for 4–5 hours.

The children's parents are very satisfied with our forest day and we feel that it is a meaningful and worthwhile thing to do. (Preschool teacher, working with children aged 5)

Critical perspectives on outdoor play: the 'good' nature as rhetoric

In recent years, the indoor preschool environment has been the focus of a lively discussion on how the environment can stimulate and challenge a competent, active and meaning-making child (Björklid, 2009). This is a perspective that permeates both preschool teachers' narratives in the case studies. The children are described as active and at Granens Preschool the children's participation and agency are visible.

Thus, the outdoor environment and outdoor play and learning at Swedish preschools have not been empirically studied to any great extent (for a few exceptions, see, for example, Mårtensson, 2004; Änggård, 2011; Mårtensson et al., 2011). As seen above, both preschool teachers speak of outdoor play and learning as an important component of the daily activities at the preschool. Play is mostly described as free play: playing on the playground with different equipment, together with friends, or in the forest, climbing and jumping, and using natural materials.

Outdoor play is often seen as a space for freedom and just being a child, as good, healthy and stimulating without any critical questioning or problematizing about whether this is a naïve concept (Halldén, 2009, 2011); and the unreflected-on pedagogical, didactic and ethical dilemmas this practice involves need to be brought to light. Here, we notice the first blind-spot in the narratives as neither teacher mentions any critical dilemmas in relation to outdoor play: no power structures, no reflections about the outdoors as being unequal and no ethical or didactical dilemmas. However, the Granens Preschool teacher does mention that there are fewer conflicts among the children outdoors.

Play and learning outdoors in the forest and other natural settings provides children with a range of different experiences (Niklasson and Sandberg, 2010; Hellman and Ärlemalm-Hagsér, 2011). The preschool teachers connect outdoor play and learning with several curriculum goals, in particular those regarding natural science, the identification of local flora, seasonal changes and their nuances, the water cycle and mathematics. They also stress physical play, as it gives the children opportunities to take risks, test their abilities and discover places. Practising gross motor skills, breathing in fresh air and sleeping outside are described at Tallkottens Preschool as promoting good health. The second blind-spot can be seen here, as outdoor play and learning are described as taking place in a neutral and context-free zone.

Figure 4.2   Matching and sorting outside

It is important to be aware that outdoor spaces, like other places, should not be seen as lacking power structures and ethical dilemmas, or as gender-neutral. The National Curriculum for Preschool in Sweden (Swedish National Agency for Education, 2010) states that gender equity should be embedded in all preschool activities. The goal is to counteract traditional gender patterns and roles, and offer preschoolers access to alternative ways of being girls and boys without gender limitations (Sandberg and Ärlemalm-Hagsér, 2011). In a recent research project (Ärlemalm-Hagsér, 2010) rhetoric about improving gender equity was common among the project participants, and outdoor play was described in the first discussions as gender-neutral.

Interpretations of the outdoor environment can just as well give gender-equal as gender-*un*equal structures (Ärlemalm-Hagsér, 2010; Ärlemalm-Hagsér and Sandberg, 2011), because the natural environment and natural materials are seldom pervaded by prevailing gender codes that would ascribe girlish or boyish qualities to the children. At Granens Preschool, the teacher also talks about gender issues, and her interpretation is that outdoor play is relatively gender-neutral; when children look alike in their outdoor clothes, gender becomes less relevant. This can be seen as the third blind-spot, as gender always needs to be reflected on, to avoid inequality and inequity.

When children describe their fantasy play in the forest, it clearly emerges that play themes differ between genders, which has previously been noted in other research on children's play (Ärlemalm-Hagser, 2010, 2008; Änggård, 2011) but also challenged (Hellman and Ärlemalm-Hagsér, 2011; Ärlemalm-Hagsér and Hellman, in press). Sandberg and Vuorinen (2008) show that boys of preschool age prefer to play outdoors in the yard and in the forest. Preschool-age girls primarily prefer to play indoors. One issue that is unavoidable is whether it is possible for all children to choose the environment they wish to access. This observation is also made by Mårtensson (2004) who shows that boys and girls play differently outdoors. Boys move physically over most of the preschool grounds, while girls are more place-bound.

To understand the meanings of play and learning in different educational places and contexts and the consequences for children's learning about themselves, others and the environment, a number of blind-spots have to be scrutinized. For example, working with equity in preschools seems to be a gender-blind practice. However, the children themselves display a wide range of positions in different situations (Ärlemalm-Hagsér, 2010; Ärlemalm-Hagsér and Pramling-Samuelsson, 2009; Eidevald, 2009; Hellman and Ärlemalm-Hagsér, 2011; Sandberg and Sandström, 2012). Sharing knowledge and understanding within the preschool team about how gender and power structures are constructed is one way to form a practice offering possibilities for children to deviate from stereotyped gender norms. All these studies show that children's outdoor play is a highly complex whole, including elements of gender, position and power, and in this gender choreography 'doing gender' influences children's and adults' structural, symbolic and individual understanding, and the possibilities for children to understand themselves and their positions (Thorne, 1993).

Further reading

Fröbel, F. (1887) 'The Education of Man', in D.N. Robinson (ed.) (1977) *Significant Contributions to the History of Psychology 1750–1920*. Washington D.C: University Publications of America, Inc.
Read the original words that inspired so much of the development of early education in Northern Europe.
Halldén, G. (2011) *Barndomens skogar: Om barn och natur och barns natur* [Forests of childhood: Children and nature and children's nature]. Stockholm: Carlsson.
Read in Swedish or use a translation tool to gain a flavour of the discussions taking place in Swedish preschool education.
Sandberg, A. and Ärlemalm-Hagsér, E. (2011) 'The Swedish National Curriculum: play and learning with the fundamental values in focus', *Australasian Journal of Early Childhood* 36(1): 44–50.
This is an examination of the revised preschool curriculum in Sweden.

Figure 4.3   Confident climbing

Information for practice

One thing for which Swedish preschools are known is that they take children outdoors no matter what the weather. This is probably because of the common belief that children are healthier when they spend time outdoors, as we saw in the narratives. But children's outdoor play has changed (see, for example, Sandberg and Vuorinen, 2006; Sandberg, 2012). Nowadays, preschool-age children have a more limited play space than older children, and their ability to go out on their own is restricted, for instance because of safety reasons. In recent years, the play equipment in outdoor areas has been a topic of safety concerns and new regulations at Swedish preschools. These regulations sometimes hinder children's creative play and can also be frustrating for preschool staff, as we saw at Granens Preschool.

How does a child think about outdoor play and its effects? Does it change in accordance with how preschool teachers teach? It is essential to make children's perspectives visible, since this can contribute to research and cause adults to look at preschool activities with 'new' eyes. Hopefully, it will become more common to reflect upon what can be considered quality from children's points of view.

(Continued)

(Continued)

Because researchers and childcare personnel contribute to conveying opinions, attitudes and values regarding outdoor environments, it is important to be aware of which attitudes are being conveyed, both in terms of what kinds of outdoor activities are encouraged and what verbal expressions are conveyed and mediated.

From our point of view, it is important to reflect upon the ethical perspectives on nature – anthropocentric and ecocentric – that are implicitly transferred through language and mindsets.

All these latter areas need further research, in order to better understand contemporary issues in outdoor play and learning in the Swedish preschool, and to ensure that the activities provided in preschool are meaningful, enjoyable and instructive for all children. It is also important that teachers support children's outdoor play and practice using an inclusive approach, so that all children in preschool have the opportunity to develop through play with peers of both genders. This may eventually contribute to less polarizing views on boys' and girls' play and give children the opportunity to develop even more skills and attributes through play. Hopefully, this can generate further development of the play environment and of this pedagogical activity for children.

References

Änggård, E. (2011) 'Children's gendered and non-gendered play in natural spaces', *Children, Youth and Environments*, 21(2): 5–33.

Ärlemalm-Hagsér, E. (2008) 'Skogen som pedagogisk praktik ur ett genusperspektiv', in A. Sandberg (ed.), *Miljöer för lek, lärande och samspel* [Environments for play, learning and communication]. Lund: Studentlitteratur, pp. 107–136.

Ärlemalm-Hagsér, E. (2010) 'Gender choreography and micro structures: early childhood professionals' understanding of gender roles and gender patterns in outdoor play and learning', *European Early Childhood Education Research Journal* 18(4): 515–526.

Ärlemalm-Hagsér, E. and Hellman, A. (in press) 'Boys struggling socially and geographically for equity and participation in the Swedish preschool', *Children in Europe*.

Ärlemalm-Hagsér, E. and Pramling-Samuelsson, I. (2009) 'Många olika genusmönster existerar samtidigt i förskolan [In preschool many gender patterns exist simultaneously]', *Pedagogisk Forskning i Sverige* 14(2): 89–109.

Ärlemalm-Hagsér, E. and Sandberg, A. (2011) 'Sustainable development in early childhood education: in-service students' comprehension of the concept', *Environmental Education Research Journal* 17(2): 187–200.

Björklid, P. (2009) *Lärande och fysisk miljö en kunskapsöversikt om samspelet mellan lärande och fysisk miljö i förskola och skola*. Stockholm: Skolverket.

Eidevald, C. (2009) Det finns inga tjejbestämmare: att förstå kön som position i förskolans vardagsrutiner och lek [There are no girl decision-makers: understanding gender as a position in preschool practices], School of Education and Communication, Jönköping University. Dissertation No 4. Jönköping: ARK Tryckare AB.

Fröbel, F. (1887) 'The Education of Man', in D.N. Robinson (ed.) (1977) *Significant Contributions to the History of Psychology 1750–1920*. Washington D.C, University Publications of America, Inc.

Halldén, G. (2009) *Naturen som symbol för den goda barndomen [Nature as representation for the good childhood]*. Stockholm: Carlsson.

Halldén, G. (2011) *Barndomens skogar: om barn och natur och barns natur [Forests of childhood: children and nature and children's nature]*. Stockholm: Carlsson.

Hatje, A. (1999) *Från treklang till triangeldrama: barnträdgården som ett kvinnligt samhällsprojekt under 1880–1940-talen*. Lund: Historiska media.

Hellman, A. and Ärlemalm-Hagsér, E. (2011) 'Demokrati och jämställdhet på förskolegården [Democracy and equity at the preschool ground]', *KRUT* 141(1): 31–40.

Mårtensson, F. (2004) *Landskapet i leken: en studie av utomhuslek på förskolegården*. Alnarp: Swedish University of Agricultural Sciences, Agraria 464.

Mårtensson, F., Lisberg Jensen, E., Söderström, M. and Öhman, J. (2011) Den nyttiga utevistelsen? Forskningsperspektiv på naturkontaktens betydelse för barns hälsa och miljöengagemang, Naturvårdsverket rapport. See http://www.naturvardsverket.se/

Ministry of Education and Science (2010) *Förskola i utveckling: bakgrund till ändringar i förskolans läroplan [Preschool in development: the background to the changes in the preschool curriculum]*. Stockholm: Ministry of Education and Science.

National Association for the Promotion of Outdoor Life, The (2012) 'In Rain or Shine or All Weather School' [in Swedish I Ur och Skur (IUoSk)] [online]. Available at: http://www.vindeln.friluftsframjandet.se/skogsmullestiftelsen/32 (accessed 14 May 2012).

Niklasson, L. and Sandberg, A. (2010) 'Children and the outdoor environment', *European Early Childhood Education Research Journal* 18(4): 485–496.

Rantatalo, P. (2000) 'Skogsmulleskolan [Skogsmulleskolan-outdoor education]', in K. Sandell and S. Sörlin (eds) *Friluftshistoria*. Stockholm: Carlsson, pp. 138–155.

Rousseau, J. (1892) *Emil eller Om uppfostran [Emile and education]*. Göteborg: Wald, Zachrissons boktryckeri.

Sandberg, M. (2012) *De är inte ute så mycket: den bostadsnära naturkontaktens betydelse och utrymme i storstadsbarns vardagsliv ['They are not outdoors that much': nature close to home – its meaning and place in the everyday lives of urban children]*. Göteborg: University of Gothenburg.

Sandberg, A. and Ärlemalm-Hagsér, E. (2011) 'The Swedish National Curriculum: play and learning with the fundamental values in focus', *Australasian Journal of Early Childhood* 36(1): 44–50.

Sandberg, A. and Sandström, M. (2012) 'Genuspraktik hos förskollärare', in A. Sandberg and M. Sandström (eds) *Kritiska händelser för lärande i förskolan*. Lund: Studentlitteratur, pp. 75–92.

Sandberg, A. and Vuorinen, T. (2006) 'From hayloft to own room – girls' play environments', in J. Brodin and P. Lindstrand (eds) *Interaction in Outdoor Play Environments: Gender, Culture and Learning*. Stockholm: Stockholm Institute of Education. Research Report no. 47, pp. 1–22.

Sandberg, A. and Vuorinen, T. (2008) 'Barndomens lekmiljöer: förr och nu', in A. Sandberg (ed.) *Miljöer för lek, lärande och samspel*. Lund: Studentlitteratur.

Swedish National Agency for Education (2010) *Curriculum for the Preschool: Lpfö 98*. Stockholm: Fritzes.

Thorne, B. (1993) *Gender Play: Girls and Boys in School*. Buckingham: Open University Press.

5

Increasing Experiential Learning Using Ecoremediations in Slovenia

Mojca Kokot Krajnc and Ana Vovk Korže

Chapter overview

Environmental problems, which appear as key challenges in the 21st century, require different approaches to solve them. Education and learning for sustainable development are at the heart of experiential education, and the most efficient setting for this is the classroom in nature. Learning polygons are classrooms in nature, which are made up of different natural learning environments, where students are set up in the real environment with real causes and effects of the interactions between nature and people. This chapter presents two learning polygons in nature, which are unique in the educational system in Slovenia. They present space in nature, where students of different ages, particularly those from primary and secondary schools, can, in interdisciplinary and empirical ways, acquire different skills for life and learn the importance of their responsibility to the environment and society. In learning polygons, students engage with experiential learning to meet different learning goals and come up with new knowledge about the natural, social and technical environment.

The importance of nature in experiential education for sustainable development

Slovenia has, like other European countries, engaged with Education for Sustainable Development (ESD). In the guidelines for ESD from preschool to university education (Slovenia Ministry of Education, 2010), it has been determined that the main required competencies for ESD are to acquire skills for life and to learn to take responsibility for the environment and society; and to become independent in decision-making and personal growth through responsible actions that will develop positive interactions in society.

If we want our children to acquire the skills to live, to learn to be independent and act responsibly towards the environment and society, they need to take an active role in a skills-based education. They can easily develop their competencies and skills in a direct learning process in nature, where, upon the acquisition of practical experience, they develop their relationship with nature (Praterious, 2006; Sharon and Wright, 2000).

The most appropriate way to educate learners to become responsible people is in the introduction of experiential learning into the learning process, based on 'what I do that I remember' (Gentry, 1990). In experiential education, learners first identify the problem, seek appropriate solutions and then ultimately establish the impact of the specific solutions for a concrete example. Experiential education or 'learning by doing' promotes changes in thinking and behaviour, which improves safety, health, well-being and quality of life (Vovk Korže and Sajovic, 2010).

Experiences in nature are crucial for effective environmental education. Children show greater interest in environmental issues when in nature, and develop a positive attitude and concern for the wider environment (Maynard and Waters, 2007). In nature, children gain direct experience, and if experiential activities are properly planned then children will come up with new knowledge on the basis of all their senses, experiences and emotions. This is the best way to permanently acquire knowledge that can be transferred to other environments. For such an education, outdoor classrooms can't be beaten. In this chapter, we call them 'learning polygons in nature'.

The natural classroom: a good example for experimental learning

In natural classrooms, students learn about real environmental problems and through problem- and research-based activities come up with new knowledge. This requires direct experience of nature. The purpose of such learning is that the problems touch each individual and they begin to think about them and look for the most suitable solutions. With this form of education, young people can decide on direct experience in favour of nature and the environment, and with their knowledge and decisions they can make substantial contributions to sustainable development in their local environments.

A key purpose of the polygons in nature is to develop skills for lifelong learning with the integration of knowledge from different fields and with that, the development of skills for solving different problems. Following this, students' generic skills can be developed as they work on the learning polygon: the ability to collect information, the ability to analyze and organize work, the ability to work independently and in team work, organization and planning of work, verbal and written communication, the ability to interpret, the ability to synthesize conclusions, the ability to solve problems, and, very important, the ability to transfer theory into practice. At the same time, the learning environment in nature helps strengthen cooperative learning, teamwork, deep learning and innovation.

Learning polygons allow the development of key dimensions of students' competencies (Vovk Korže and Sajovic, 2010; Vovk Korže, 2011a, b), namely:

- cognitive competence – this is about acquiring quality knowledge, based on an understanding of processes and events, and using these skills in different situations or to solve different problems

- emotional competence – by learning about environmental problems and solving them, learners develop a positive attitude towards nature – what is good and what is bad for nature and the environment

- competence of action – this encourages learners to transform internal knowledge and values into concrete actions, with which an individual can contribute to environmental protection.

Students try via the polygons to develop individual learning points which identify key environmental issues in the region through various measurements, analysis, data processing, and performance comparisons. On this basis, learners can individually, and/or with the help of the teacher, uncover the causes and consequences of environmental problems and based on the data collected, seek solutions to problems.

The learning polygon for ecoremediations

The learning polygon for ecoremediations is a complex learning environment in nature with the most important natural and anthropogenic forms of ecoremediation, which are crucial in environmental education. Ecoremediations are methods by which we solve, with the help of nature, degradation problems, and hence prevent further pollution, and preserve and improve the environmental situation. Ecoremediations are an innovation in the Slovenian education system, and they help raise awareness of the environment. They also have a view to solving many environmental problems such as the improper management of running and standing water, waste water, soil erosion, soil and air pollution. The basic functions of ecoremediations, which are used for educational purposes, are to create large buffer regions, with a self-cleaning ability and the creation of habitats.

The natural characteristics of the polygon are varied, as an interweaving of different landforms, and the area is very rich in both standing and flowing water. Because of this, there is also much plant and animal diversity as the polygon itself has some protected animal and plant species. The polygon environment is appropriate for the sensory and emotional experience of nature and is a suitable place for experimental teaching (Vrhovšek and Vovk Korže, 2009; Vovk Korže and Sajovic, 2010).

The learning polygon of ecoremediations is designed so that students can learn about the environment and ecosystem units through experiential learning with a problem-based research approach, and can be aware of the consequences of their actions and their occasional intervention in the environment. Therefore, the learning polygon

Figure 5.1   The learning polygon of ecoremediations

enables comprehensive learning by engaging all the senses and places an emphasis on connections and relationships between appearances, and not so much on individual knowledge and facts. In the learning polygon, children at both primary and secondary school can gain knowledge about environmental issues and topics in the fields of environmental protection, biology, chemistry and geography. Trainee teachers of geography and social science, and technology students can also be educated. All tasks carried out by the learner are problem-based, designed to build on curriculum integration and the use of interdisciplinary knowledge.

The learning polygon for ecoremediation enables students to use their own experiences to develop an understanding of the polygon through their own activities. The most common methodology is a form of project work, where the group explores an environmental problem, discusses it and then provides a variety of possible solutions to the problem. For research work at the learning polygon, the following learning points are established that perform a variety of learning functions and thus meet the specific learning objectives of different subjects:

- Areas with natural ecosystems (pond, marsh, stream, and coniferous plantations, dry and wet meadow, forest edge)

Natural ecosystems are learning environments where learners get to know their basic features through their senses and various data acquisition (measurement of the air temperature, of water temperature, of the moisture in the soil, of evaporation, transpiration and photosynthesis, of the amount of oxygen and carbon dioxide in the air). The direct monitoring of ecosystem services can also be experienced. The exercises are interdisciplinary and meet various learning objectives. Along with learning about the natural ecosystem of the forest, knowledge about which tree species are typical for moist coniferous and deciduous forests can be acquired, as can knowledge of how the moisture in the soil and the air temperature are changing. At the forest edge, it can be determined by counting plants that this is one of the most diverse ecosystems in the area of the polygon. Through a comparison of wet and dry meadow, students can learn about the characteristics of vegetation and identify the differences in soil, air temperature and soil moisture. The swamp as a learning point is highlighted because it is a diverse ecosystem, where students can learn about the characteristics of plants which are adapted to moisture, and about the characteristics of amphibians that live in these swampy areas.

Figure 5.2 Experimental learning about water ecosystem functions and services

The stream and pond are examples of running and standing water ecosystems. In both the stream and pond, physical and chemical analyses of water can be carried out, through which students learn about the characteristics of these aquatic ecosystems. Combining experiential learning with teaching about natural ecosystems, students come to learn about the characteristics of each natural ecosystem, and about the functioning and services of different parts in each ecosystem.

- Ecoremediation learning models (constructed wetland and sand filters for water treatment, plant models designed for cleaning groundwater)

Ecoremediation learning models are aimed at solving two environmental problems: waste water and erosive surfaces. Learners are first confronted with the problem of waste water. With the help of their senses (smell and sight), plus physical and chemical analysis, students can determine the composition of the waste water which is formed in the area of the polygon. In the next phase of work, they encounter two ecoremediation models for waste water treatment: wetland and sand filter, where they examine their composition, function and the process of treatment. Both systems work in the ecoremediation learning polygon, so the students can, with the use of simple chemical analyses, verify the performance of these two models. Further, learners can produce their own sand filters to check the success of the filtering treatment of water. In most cases, exercises about waste water treatment are carried out with children over 12 years old in the form of project work. The conclusion of this work, in most cases, involves a presentation of the project on the studied topic, where students provide the acquired data, their analyses and then discuss and evaluate alternative waste water treatment solutions.

- Other learning points in the polygon, such as a room for experiments, a garage with a green roof, an observatory for animals, standing book profiles, a learning point for waste and a relaxation area

In the ground, there are different types of soil. We can dig a soil pit and set up standing books by them for individual or group learning projects about different soil types using our senses. Learners can come to appreciate the characteristics of each soil type. These exercises are appropriate for children of all ages, including the very youngest, who learn that sand soils contain a lot of sand, are dry and that with them we cannot create anything, whilst clay soil is more moist and can easily be formed into a variety of structures. The educational facilities offer independent or guided learning and teaching on the principles of and processes that occur in nature (the ecosystem). This is a basis for understanding the complex nature conservation and environmental content.

All the activities in the learning polygon about ecoremediations are based on experiential problems, because only when a student goes through a set of possibilities will s/he find a correct solution and gain knowledge, while at the same time learning to evaluate and defend the results obtained. This is essential knowledge for the future – students will continue their formal and informal learning, and can draw on this when making future decisions.

A learning polygon develops and gives strength to the individual's ability to recognize and understand the processes which are taking place in nature and the environment. Based on their findings, learners are able to design their vision and devise several alternative proposals for solving many environmental problems. They can also make assessments and decisions that will support sustainable development. Thus, students acquire skills and abilities to prevent and resolve problems and conflicts, and they also improve their abilities to reason and engage in critical thinking. The knowledge and experiences which are acquired on the learning polygon can be transferred to their local environment, and with these experiences they can identify local environmental problems and know how to find appropriate solutions. In this, we actually fulfill the key principles of the strategy for ESD.

The learning polygon for self-sufficiency

The permaculture polygon at Dole was established with the aim of dealing with the issue of food self-sufficiency in Slovenia. Slovenia currently produces only about half of its own food; the rest is imported. Based on data from Eurostat, Slovenia is 24th among EU countries in the extent of its arable land (The European Commission Statistics database). About 11 acres of land are destroyed daily for house-building. At the same time, we know that Slovenia has relatively unfavourable conditions for intensive agricultural production (unfavourable statutes, inappropriate land-property structures, deforestation, natural disasters, etc.). The purpose of the learning polygon is to show students the possibilities for self-sufficiency in traditional and innovative ways; there is also the chance to establish a permaculture garden on unfavourable ground conditions, such as infertile soil or a steep slope. The methods of self-sufficiency are environmentally friendly, because their design is based on a symbiosis of individual elements; self-sufficiency promotes the consumption of home-made food, which is much healthier and safer, both for our own bodies and for the environment.

A good example of sustainable agriculture and sustainable land use in practice is permaculture, which doesn't appear in Slovenian education. Permaculture is based on ethical design systems, which are suitable for food production, land use and house-building (Praterious, 2006).

With the vision that young people should become more responsible consumers of food and should understand the importance of home-grown food, as well as appreciate that there are limited natural resources, we established the learning polygon for self-sufficiency at Dole, which is based on the principle of permaculture and the sustainable use of natural energy sources. The polygon itself is located on a steep slope; there are perfect conditions for the use of wind and solar energy, but the area itself has limited water. Despite the fact that the soil is of good quality, the territory has been set aside due to the high slope. This natural environment has enabled us to present some alternative ways of living in today's consumer-driven world.

In the polygon, the students use experiential methods, often through games that make use of their senses, and learn to plan living spaces, where we plan to put natural resources for the optimal utilization of space for living. For example, they can use their senses to search for the most warm and suitable place to build a house.

The centre of the polygon is a yurt, a traditional dwelling used by Mongolian nomadic tribes and which can be used for education all year round. A solar trap is placed before the yurt, which creates a warm microclimate, and helps with heating the area in the colder parts of the year. The solar trap consists of shrubs, small trees and

Figure 5.3 A yurt, which is the centre of the polygon for self-sufficiency

larger trees and is south-facing, so it protects the environment from the wind and creates warmth in front of the yurt, which then consumes less energy. Alongside the yurt is the water storage, which has – as has everything in permaculture – more than one function. In the colder parts of the year, the water acts as a mirror and thereby contributes additional passive solar resistance. In summer, the water during the day cools the surrounding area due to evaporation, and at night warms it due to its higher temperatures. A greenhouse is attached to the last part of the yurt for seedlings, with a small kitchen and bathroom.

The place itself helps students in an experiential way to learn how to identify suitable land for farming through games with the soil. They determine the characteristics of the various soil types, and learn to produce plans for their own permaculture garden. Experiential learning is derived from the principles of permaculture. Students learn that those plants which are most needed in the household and which need more of our care are placed close to home, while plants that do not need that much care and are more adaptable to weather conditions are placed further away from the home. Furthermore, learners on the polygon realize that each thing and its function are interrelated, which is fundamental to designing permaculture gardens. For example, one permaculture garden is called 'three sisters'; this consists of an interplanting of corn, beans and pumpkins. Students can see that the corn is used to support the beans, and the beans enrich the soil with nitrogen which is needed to grow the corn, and the pumpkins are needed to make mulch, which helps to increase the soil moisture, and in turn benefit from the shade of the other two plants.

With these findings, students can create their own plans for a permaculture garden that can be set in the immediate vicinity of their school. The plans are very specific; learners plan where to put the school permaculture garden so it can use the maximum energy that nature can offer them. They decide which permaculture garden will be built and which natural laws must be taken into account. In the next step, they name all the tools they will need to build their own permaculture garden and they write down a list of plants that will be planted. In most cases, the students decide to create raised permacultural beds, where they will grow vegetables, and hence they will be looking for good vegetable neighbours which can be planted together. The final step in creating a plan for a permaculture garden is writing down the care instructions for the garden. This task is suitable for children aged 10 years and over. Here, learners recognize that permaculture gardens require little work, since most of the work is done by nature itself and so the gardens produce healthy food.

A key finding is that students learn in a concrete way and see that it is possible to live on renewable energy sources alone, which are limited in extent, and if we consider certain laws of nature, we do not need to do much to provide ourselves with safe, healthy food.

This knowledge, which is acquired in the learning polygon for self-sufficiency, can be transferred to students' own environments, where they can spread their awareness about the importance of permaculture. Permaculture can achieve a long-term impact on sustainable agriculture and sustainable spatial planning in Slovenia; it can increase interest in a self-sufficient population, so that each of us can produce high-quality, healthy food and appreciate locally grown food. This would also ensure a clean environment and protect soil quality and natural sources of energy.

In order to achieve sustainability and a good quality of life, lifestyles have to be adapted to nature. This means that we have to protect

Figure 5.4   Experimental work on the polygon for self-sufficiency – developing a different permaculture garden

ecosystems and their operation, and take into account their internal borders; in our development programmes, we have to adjust to these constraints. The best way to achieve this is through experiential education in nature, because students learn through their own experiences how to properly deal with nature to maintain ecosystem functions and services, which enable us to improve our quality of life.

Further reading

Kokot, M., Križan, J., Vovk Korže, A. and Globovnik, N. (2011) 'Ecoremediation educational polygons in Slovenia as good examples of experiential learning of geography', *Literacy Information and Computer Education Journal* 3(2): 481–490.

Vovk Korže, A. (2012) 'The ecoremediation educational polygon: a "classroom in nature"', *Geography* 97(2): 95–99.

Vovk Korže, A., Križan, J., Kokot Krajnc, M. and Globovnik, N. (2011) 'Learning about ecoremediations and sustainability on the new education polygon in Modraže, Slovenia', *International Conference: The Future of Education* 1: 338–342.

Information for practice

Many settings use gardening to help children understand where their food comes from, and to encourage a healthier diet. Permaculture is a way of growing more with less effort in a smaller space, which you might like to investigate further. Wildlife spaces in your grounds can give you opportunities to try out some of the other suggestions provided in this chapter.

References

European Commission Statistics database, see http://epp.eurostat.ec.europa.eu/portal/page/portal/eurostat/home

Gentry, J.W. (1990) *What is Experiential Learning? Guide to Business Gaming and Experimental Learning.* London: Nichols/GP, pp. 9–20.

Maynard, T. and Waters, J. (2007) 'Learning in the outdoor environment: a missed opportunity?', *Early Years* 27(3): 255–265.

Praterious, P. (2006) 'A permaculture school garden', *Teaching Green* 78: 6–10.

Sharon, T. and Wright, A. (2000) 'No more pencils ... no more books? Arguing for the use of experiential learning in the post secondary environmental studies classroom', *Electronic Green Journal* 1(13). Available at: http://escholarship.org/uc/item/77c882jt (accessed 15 June 2012).

Slovenia Ministry of Education (2010) Guidelines for Education for Sustainable Development from Preschool to University Education in Slovenia [online]. Available at: http://www.coe.int/t/dg4/education/standingconf/Rapports%20des%20Etats/MED-23-35%20SLOVENIA.pdf (accessed December 2012).

Vovk Korže, A. (2011a) 'Vzpostavitev izvedbenih pogojev za izkustveno izobraževanje za trajnostni razvoj', *Trajnostni razvoj v šoli in vrtcu* 5(1): 9–17.

Vovk Korže, A. (2011b) 'Ucilnica v naravi: tudi v Sloveniji izkustveno izobraževanje za trajnostni razvoj', *Didakta* 21(148): 54–56.

Vovk Korže A. and Sajovic, A. (2010) 'Ucni poligon v Modražah v obcini Poljcane', *Geografski obzornik* 57(2): 22–27.

Vrhovšek, D. and Vovk Korže, A. (2009) *Ecoremediations*. Maribor: Faculty of Arts, University of Maribor.

6

Early Outdoor Learning in Portugal

Aida Figueiredo, Gabriela Portugal, Pedro Sá-Couto and Carlos Neto

Chapter overview

Outdoor spaces, which are critical for children's development and learning, are hardly used by Portuguese early childhood teachers. Play activities taking place outside, endorsing active interaction and exploration of open spaces, are not reinforced. Outdoor spaces are generally conservative (due to the homogeneity of spaces, materials and equipment), thus are not conducive to the practices of exploration, challenge and adventure, which are extremely important in childhood.

Since there are no empirical studies on this subject, a doctoral research plan was implemented in order to better understand how Portuguese early childhood outdoor spaces are used. We selected four kindergartens: two of them located in the city of Aveiro and two in the city of Coimbra. Nineteen early childhood teachers, working with children aged between 3 and 6 years, completed a form from February to May 2011 each time they went out with the children, taking notes about the period of day (morning/afternoon), the time spent outside and the weather conditions. The results seemed to indicate that Portuguese children don't go outside every day and that the length of time spent outdoors is between 30 and 60 minutes. That time is spent in both free play and in adult-directed activities. In this chapter, we will reflect on the research results and look to recommend that children spend more time outdoors in free play.

Box 6.1   Normative framework of outdoor spaces in childhood education in Portugal (childhood education in Portugal covers nursery (0–3 years) and preschool (3–5 years))

Since 1997, preschool education has been considered the first stage of basic education and the Curriculum Guidelines for Preschool consider quality education as an ultimate goal, educators having the chance to reflect upon their situation, and to choose the most appropriate practices considering their work context and each group of children.

Outdoor spaces are mentioned in some official documents, including the Curriculum Guidelines for Preschool Education (Ministério Educação, 1997a) where they are assumed to be educational spaces, where consideration is given to the opportunities and potential they can offer. Exterior spaces are highlighted as promoting exploratory activities and permitting children to recreate and reorganize those spaces. The educator's role is also considered in the planning of these spaces, along with the suitability of the equipment for playspaces and children's recreational needs for movement, exploration and testing of physical capabilities. In article 11 of D.L. no. 119/2009 (Ministério Educação, 2009), it is mentioned that the planning and conception of playspaces should take into consideration the environment, the goals and use of playful activity. Ministerial Order no. 258/97 of 21 August (Ministério Educação, 1997b) underlines the suitability of the equipment in playspaces for children's needs of movement, exploration and physical exertion.

Box 6.2   The importance of quality outdoor spaces in the development and learning of children

Several studies demonstrate the importance of permanence in outdoor spaces in the development and learning of children. Carlos Neto (nd: 1) states that 'without the immunity that is conferred by spontaneous play, by the encounter with other children in a free space, playing with the soil, inventing games,

(Continued)

(Continued)

living adventures, the child will reveal less defense capability and adaptability to new circumstances'.

According to Kittä (2003), when a child plays outside, s/he gradually establishes a relationship with the environment. However, this relationship is only achieved if there is an active interaction with it. When the mobility and activities of children in the environment are compromised or non-existent, the child has no opportunity to get acquainted with the environment through the use of his/her own body.

The idea that the quality of the outdoor space is decisive is emphasized by Van der Speck et al. (cited in Arez and Neto, 2000: 35) when pointing out the importance of a stimulating outdoor space permitting different types of activities – children having access to a wide variety of experiences, being highly involved, investigating and solving problems.

A rich space in opportunities to experience and discover, with unconventional materials and activities, enabling active exploration, according to Laevers, gives rise to intense mental activity, and consequently promotes the development of the child (Laevers and Sanden, 1997). In the same way, Neto (1980) tells us that there should be a concern to facilitate children's action, through access to diverse experiences of movement and in stimulating the direct exploration of space and materials. Arez and Neto (2000: 23) confirm the interdependence of these factors, stating that movement and mobility, space and child development are closely interrelated.

The potential for Portuguese outdoor spaces and the perspectives of early childhood teachers

 Case study 1

In the context of a PhD project, we conducted an exploratory study in order to understand how, when and in what weather conditions outdoor space is used by early childhood educators in the context of Portuguese kindergartens and nurseries (Figueiredo et al., 2011).

(Continued)

(Continued)

For this purpose, we selected four kindergartens from the centre of the country: two in the city of Aveiro and two in the city of Coimbra. The four childhood contexts were quite different in terms of the characteristics of their outdoor space. We created a register form, completed by 19 educators (three educators working in nurseries and 16 with preschool children). Data collection was conducted from February to May 2011. For the purpose of the study, we used two software programmes: SPSS, version 17.0, for quantitative analysis; and the WebQDA programme, version 1.0, for qualitative analysis.

After analysing the data obtained through the grid records of the 19 Portuguese kindergarten teachers, the results showed a slight tendency to use the outdoor spaces in the kindergarten and nursery. Of note, the small sample size and its non-probabilistic selection do not allow for generalization across the Portuguese system as a whole.

For greater understanding, we will use the results to answer the research questions in this study.

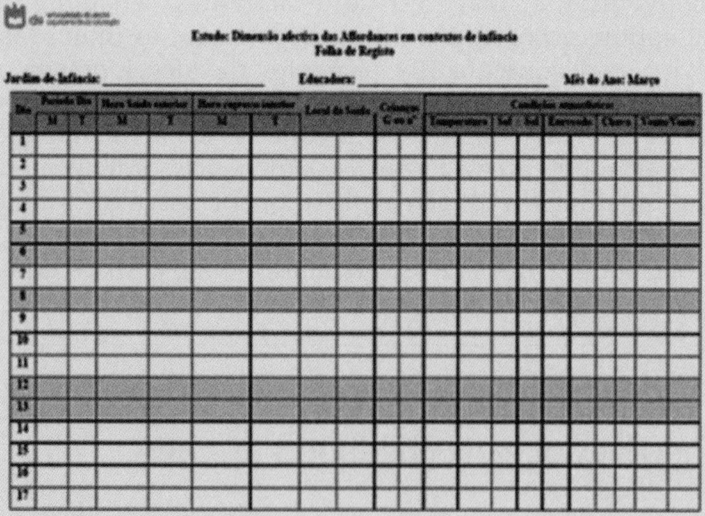

Figure 6.1 Register form

Question 1: How often do children play in outdoor spaces?

Looking at Figure 6.2, we can see that the number of children's outdoor playtime sessions in the four kindergartens is somewhat

(Continued)

(Continued)

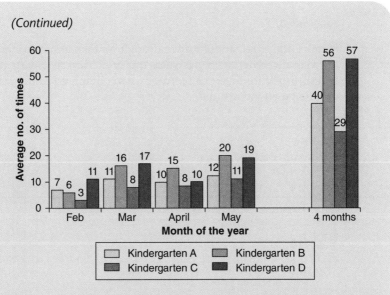

Figure 6.2 Average number of times children go to outdoor spaces per month

lower than expected, reaching an average of between 3 and 20 per month. Kindergarten C had a lower average than this in the four months of registration and kindergartens B and D each showed a higher average (between 11 and 20). These results seem to indicate that there are days when children do not go outdoors at all, staying inside all day.

By analysing data on the nursery (Figure 6.3), we found that children under the age of 1 year rarely go outdoors, having been outside only twice in a four-month period.

Question 2: How long do children remain outdoors?

Given the previous results, it seems important to understand how long children remain outside. The results, as can be seen in Figure 6.4, show a higher frequency of time spent outside of between 16 and 30 minutes (12%); this is similar to what happens in primary school. The results also indicate that they stay up to 1 hour quite frequently (10% and 9%).

Performing data analysis on the effective time spent by children outdoors, we found that the percentage values obtained were low (between 6% and 14%), as seen in Figure 6.5. If we compare these results with the study by Moser and Martinson (2010), carried out in 117 Norwegian kindergartens, a marked difference

(Continued)

(Continued)

in percentage becomes more relevant if we take into consideration the climatic differences between the two countries, with winter and spring more severe in Norway when compared to the warmer weather seen in Portugal.

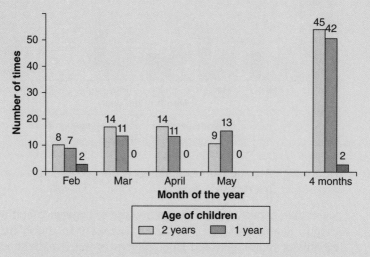

Figure 6.3   Number of times children under 3 years go to outdoor spaces per month

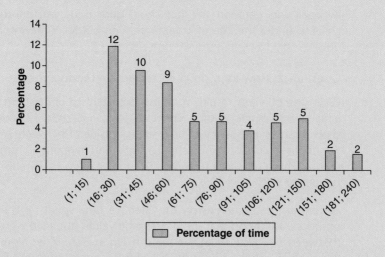

Figure 6.4   Percentage of length of time spent outdoors (in minutes)

(Continued)

(Continued)

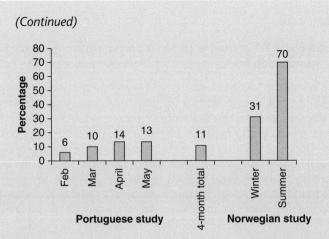

Figure 6.5 Percentage of total time spent outdoors

| | | Period of day | |
| | | Morning (Length, min) | Afternoon (Length, min) |
Kindergarten	Type of activity	Mean	Mean
A	Free play	39	42
	Oriented activity	58	60
	Mixed activity	53	0
B	Free play	49	64
	Oriented activity	76	70
	Mixed activity	68	77
C	Free play	31	59
	Oriented activity	38	0
	Mixed activity	0	53
D	Free play	50	59

Figure 6.6 Mean length of period of time spent outside (in minutes) by type of activity and period of the day in different kindergartens

(Continued)

(Continued)

Question 4: What do the children do during the time they spend outdoors?

In three of the four kindergartens, children go outdoors, not just for free play, but also to engage in large group activities directed by adults, and also for mixed activities (where a small group of children develops an activity organized by an adult, while the other children play freely; small groups are rotatable and are overseen by the adult). Figure 6.6 shows the results by type of activity in the morning and afternoon periods, by kindergarten. In the morning, we found that kindergartens A, B and C spend more time in directed activities. In the afternoon, it is the same situation for kindergartens A and B. Note that the children, on average, play freely for between 30 and 60 minutes a day, with the longest free-play session in the afternoon. It should also be noted that kindergarten D only uses outdoor spaces for free play.

 ## Case study 2

From March to May 2012, as part of a curricular unit of the Elementary Education Course, we conducted a case study (Figueiredo et al., 2012a, b, unpublished) in which structured interviews were prepared for seven early childhood teachers, five in rural contexts and two in urban contexts. The early childhood teachers were all female, aged between 34 and 50 years and with differing professional experience, ranging from 12 to 30 years of service. All elements of the sample had kindergarten functions in their institutions, and four of them had childcare facilities. The purpose of this case study was to establish the teachers' perception of Portuguese outdoor spaces in general, and, specifically, their perception of their own kindergarten's outdoor space.

Question 1: What do they think about the outdoor spaces in kindergartens and childcare facilities in Portugal?

The answers to this question are essentially based on the experience of only seven educators, with differing opinions. Six of the seven participants (86%) reported that outdoor spaces either do not exist or are unattractive, limit the creativity of children, are little suited to the age of users and have dubious safety levels. However, one of the respondents considered them pleasant, good and exciting. Three participants (43%) believed that the natural elements, namely soil, sticks and stones, were deliberately removed from these spaces. They

(Continued)

(Continued)

also stated that in designing outdoor spaces, the major concern seems to be the aesthetic aspect rather than its functional aspect.

Question 2: How would they describe the outdoor space in the kindergarten where they work?

This question elicited a variety of responses ranging between 'satisfactory', 'good', 'excellent' and 'exciting'. Comments given included: 'very well equipped', 'plenty of space', 'some fixed structures (swing, slide, playground)', 'different floors (paths, patio, playfields, grass)' and 'of different natural elements (soil, flowers, trees)'. Using a Likert scale to classify the outdoor space (as 'not very stimulating', 'stimulating' or 'very stimulating'), five of the participants (71%) rated their space as 'stimulating' and two (29%) as 'very stimulating'.

Question 3: Would they like to change anything about the outdoor space in the institution where they work?

Six of the seven participants (86%) reported that they would change something, although the proposed changes were relatively simple, such as planting fruit trees for shade and relaxation, adding grass and/or marking the floor for playing traditional games.

In order to understand the notions that these educators had in relation to outdoor spaces, we posed the following question:

Question 4: For you, what is the relevance of play in outdoor spaces in the development and learning of children?

The responses coincided and all agreed that outdoor spaces are very important for the development of gross motor control and excellent for children's diversified learning, allowing exploration, discovery of the world, sharing of knowledge and experiences. Also mentioned was the importance of children's contact with nature.

Question 5: If children were given the opportunity to choose to play outdoors or indoors, which would be their choice? Why?

On this question, four of the seven participants (57%) said that children would choose the outdoor space, since this allows jumping, running, screaming, releasing energy and tension, and discovering nature. However, one participant (14%) said that the educator must balance the children's interests with what is 'most useful and necessary'.

Given the importance of outdoor spaces for the development and learning of children and their preferences, a last question was posed:

(Continued)

(Continued)

Question 6: How often does your group of children go outside on a daily basis, and for how long?

The answers given by the participants seem to corroborate with the results of Case study 1. All seven participants (100%) reported that when the weather is bad (rainy/cold) they do not go outside, and one of them (14%) stated that when there is a lot of work to do in the classroom they 'do not have time to go outside'. Regarding the time spent outside, again the results coincide with those of the first study: the mean length of the stay outside is about 30 minutes up to 1 hour following the afternoon break.

Examples of Portuguese situations in childcare centres and kindergartens

The following examples of experiences in childcare centres and kindergartens allow for illustrations of some of our results.

The impact of the weather conditions on adults' and children's behaviour

Example 1 – The early childhood teacher and the assistant are talking. The teacher suggests that the children could go to play outside. The weather is overcast, with some periods of light rain. Daniel, having heard the conversation, says, 'It's raining, we cannot go outside'.

Example 2 – A group of 12 children is preparing to go and visit the 'Culture House' to see a film. There are four adults going with the group of children and the distance between the two buildings is about 800 metres. The thermometer indicates that the temperature is 11°C, the sky is overcast and there are occasional periods of light rain. All the children are ready to go and are sitting waiting for the adults. Because of the weather, the adults seem very anxious and look through the window, wondering whether it is a good idea to go outside. After a few minutes, they decide to go. During the session, the adults become concerned that the children don't get wet, so they repeatedly say to them, 'do not touch the bushes' and 'do not walk in puddles'. However, the children are not very well dressed for the rain: only two of them are wearing Wellies. All the children demonstrate some motor difficulties, including climbing stairs as well as little autonomy in dressing.

What children say about being outdoors for a long time

Example 1 – The children play freely outside from 9.50 a.m. to 11.45 a.m. When they return indoors, we hear the follow dialogue:

Daniel: 'Today we spent a lot of time outside, didn't we?'

Caroline: 'Yes, we did!'

Daniel: 'It was a fantastic day! Until my trousers got dirty!'

Adult: 'Today we have been outside for a long time, so we must wash our hands very carefully with soap.'

The adult's role and children's creativity, self-organization and free initiative

Example 1 – Some children are in pretend play and have two tricycles. One of them decides to go inside to fetch two skipping ropes. The adult supervising the playground observes what the child is doing. The child ties the end of one rope to a tricycle and starts tying the other end to another tricycle. Observing the child, the adult gets up and says, 'The ropes are for skipping, not to tie tricycles.'

Example 2 – The children are preparing to go and play outside. They put their hats and coats on. Some children want to carry equipment, including balls. Robert addresses the adult and asks: 'Florence, can I carry a ball?'

Example 3 – At 11.20 a.m. a group of children goes to the playground, after being inside from 9.00 a.m., accompanied by an adult. When the children arrive at the playground, there are already other groups of children there. The newly arrived group spreads across the playground and starts to play. At 11.35 a.m. the adult responsible for the group starts calling children, in small groups, to wash their hands to have lunch. After washing their hands, the children have orders to sit on a step near the bathroom and wait for the rest of the group. There are some children who sit there for longer than the time they had to play. At 11.45 a.m. there aren't any children in the playground.

Children and nature

Example 1 – Five girls are sitting around and talking. Some of the girls get up and gather sticks and dry leaves. Another girl walks through the space and picks up a plastic bag lying in a flower bed. She takes it and goes to meet two girls proposing to make a nest for a chicken. The three girls begin looking for natural materials: sticks, leaves and stones to make the chicken's nest. Another group sits around with sticks and leaves and decides to make a necklace for the adults in the group.

Example 2 – Two boys are digging in a flower bed with the aid of sticks and stones. The task is sporadically interrupted by the arrival of other children who observe what the boys are doing. One of the boys is concentrating very hard on digging with a stone, without interruption, when he suddenly finds a stick. He gets up and screams with joy and delight: 'Look what I found, a treasure!'

Example 3 – A group of children is exploring a repository of hacked natural material (grass, tree branches, soil and leaves), sharing all the interesting discoveries they make. They shake their sticks in the air and run after the 'bad guys'. At one point, we observe the following dialogue: Tim – 'Look what I found', waving a stick; At the same time, Adam approaches the group by dragging a large palm leaf. Tim, when he sees the leaf, says, 'It is quite large!' and repeats 'It's really big!', displaying surprise and excitement. 'It's a dinosaur and that is his horn', he says, pointing to the sharp edge of the leaf.

Example 4 – Six boys have a pretend play fight against the 'bad guys', flapping sticks in the air. They run from one side to the other and say, 'Come on, is there another one?', while raising sticks and all running in the same direction. The pretend play continues with periods of dialogue between the boys and fighting against 'the bad guys'.

Example 5 – A group of children is outside on a large lawn. Two adults develop an activity with some members of the group. The other children play freely. Next to the work table is a bucket of water. The weather is hot (21°C) and the sun is shining. Two girls move closer to the bucket and wet their hands. The play continues for several minutes. More children come close and join in with the play. The children start to wet their faces and then throw water at each other. The adult observes the play and calls out to the children when they begin to throw water at each other, giving orders to stop playing with the water. The children continue to play, and two of them get wet, including their clothes. Then the adult interrupts the children's play and the children have to go inside to change their clothes.

The adult and nature

Example 1 – Some children are close to a forbidden area which has a slight slope. The adults supervising the group are having doubts about letting the children play in this area. After some indecision, the children slowly invade the forbidden area and wait for the adults' reaction. The adults remain silent and the children move forward, first slowly and then with excitement, testing their limits and capabilities. Now, the adults are very anxious and observe the children carefully, but the children are excited by the possibility of exploring a new space.

Example 2 – Six boys have a pretend play fight against the 'bad guys', flapping sticks in the air. They run from one side to the other and say, 'Come on, is there another one?', while raising the sticks and all running in the same direction. The adult who is in the area observes the boys carefully, demonstrates some anxiety and looks intently at the sticks in the air and at the distance the boys are from him (approximately 50 metres). Since we have asked for the minimum adult intervention during free play, the adult tries not to intervene, but he can't help himself, and asks the boys to approach and be careful with the sticks.

Example 3 – A group of 16 children and two adults is in an open space with grass and a slight slope. The weather is cloudy with some sunny periods and the grass is wet. The children play freely. One of the adults rolls down the slope and two children immediately do the same. Another child approaches and tries to go down on their hands and knees.

Conclusion

We are aware that these case studies have some investigative limits, including size and sample selection, which do not allow for generalization across the Portuguese population of kindergartens and nurseries. However, it seems that early childhood teachers show a positive inclination towards the idea of outdoor spaces and their impact on children's development and learning in the first years of life. It is apparent though that the use of outdoor spaces is rare and the length of stay in these spaces is short. And yet, due to the constraints mentioned above, other studies should be carried out in order to confirm the data obtained from these pilot case studies.

Further reading 📖

Figueiredo, A., Portugal, G. and Neto, C. (2011) 'Emotional dimensions of affordances in childhood contexts', *EECERA*. Genève (unpublished).

Figueiredo, A., Portugal, G. and Neto, C. (2012) 'Children's interaction with the outdoor environment during free play', *ICCP.* Tallinn, Estonia (unpublished).

Figueiredo, A., Portugal, G. and Neto, C. (2012) 'Outdoor play in early childhood contexts', *Child in the City.* Zagreb, Croatia (unpublished).

Information for practice

The literature stresses that outdoor spaces are important for children's learning and development. But how do we know that in practice? Observations and reflection on children's free play and their well-being and involvement levels should be done in a systematic way. Moreover, the results of a recent study carried out at Aveiro University show that the role of the adult during children's free play is crucial for the quality of the interactions between children and the environment.

References

Arez, A. and Neto, C. (2000) The study of independent mobility and perception of the physical environment in rural and urban children. In Neto, C., ed. XIV IPA World Conference, 1999 Lisboa: Edições CML.

Figueiredo, A., Portugal, G. and Neto, C. (2011) 'Emotional dimensions of affordances in childhood contexts', *EECERA*. Genève (unpublished).

Figueiredo, A., Portugal, G. and Neto, C. (2012a) 'Children's interaction with the outdoor environment during free play', *ICCP.* Tallinn, Estonia (unpublished).

Figueiredo, A., Portugal, G. and Neto, C. (2012b) 'Outdoor play in early childhood contexts', *Child in the City.* Zagreb, Croatia (unpublished).

Kittä, M. (2003) Children in Outdoor Contexts: Affordances and Independent Mobility in the Assessment of Environmental Child Friendliness. Unpublished doctoral thesis, Helsinki University of Technology.

Laevers, F. and Sanden, P.V. (1997) *Pour une approche experientielle au niveau pré-scolaire: Livre de base.* Bélgica: Col. Education et Enseignement Expérientiel.

Ministério Educação (1997a) *Orientações curriculares para a educação pré-escolar.* Lisbon: Ministério da Educação, Departamento de Educação Básica.

Ministério Educação (1997b) Despacho Conjunto no. 258/97, 21 August. Lisbon: DGIDC.

Ministério Educação (2009) Decreto-Lei no. 119/2009, 19 May. Lisbon: Diário da República, 1a série, No. 96.

Moser, T. and Martinsen, M. (2010) 'The outdoor environment in Norwegian kindergartens as pedagogical space for toddlers' play, learning and development', *European Early Childhood Education Research Journal*, 18 (4): 457–471.

Neto, C. (n.d.) *A criança e o jogo: Perspectivas de Investigação.* Lisbon: FMH.

Neto, C. (1980) *Jogo na infância e desenvolvimento motor.* Lisbon: FMH.

7

Building Sustainability through Consumption in Brazil

Edson Grandisoli

Chapter overview

The object of this chapter is to help elementary and high school teachers better explore the theme of sustainability, combining indoor and outdoor activities (through fieldwork, research and interviews). For that, I have created six class plans focusing on consumption and consumerism. Most of the activities have being tested in elementary and high schools in Brazil, and the results are promising regarding increasing comprehension of sustainability as well as offering incentives to embody daily actions to build a more sustainable society and, above all, more conscious and responsible citizens.

Sustainable development

The United Nations Decade of Education for Sustainable Development (2005–2014) seeks to integrate the principles, values and practices of sustainable development into all aspects of education and learning, in order to address the social, economic, cultural and environmental problems we face in the 21st century (UNESCO Education Sector, 2010). In consideration of this, the concept of sustainability must be taught in schools in order to build an integrated view of nature–society relationships. As pointed out by McKeown (2002):

> Education is an essential tool for achieving sustainability. People around the world recognize that current economic development trends are not sustainable and that public awareness, education, and training are the key to moving society toward sustainability. (Online: unpaginated)

Several different countries in Europe, North America and Oceania are already taking part in the concept of Eco-Schools, an international programme aimed at raising students' awareness of sustainable development issues through classroom study as well as school and community action (Eco-Schools International Programme, 2009). However, most of the experiences in Eco- and Green-Schools focus on the impact of human activities on the local and global environment and do not propose changes to the formal curriculum.

One of only a few examples of curriculum reorientation incorporating the concept of sustainability took place in Portugal in 2001–2002, when a new curriculum was proposed for students in the 7th to 9th grades. This new curriculum combined four different themes: *Earth and space, Earth in transformation, Sustainability on Earth* and *A better living on Earth*. These four themes are essentially interdisciplinary and use active learning (Freire, 2007). Despite some efforts, very little has been proposed regarding a reorientation of basic schools' curricula towards sustainability and this is especially true in South American countries. In Brazil, the *Escolas Sustentáveis* and *COM-VIDA* are initiatives that are basically following in the steps of international Eco- and Green-Schools by organizing different activities in public schools, in order to involve students and the community in looking for a better and more ecological way of life.

It seems imperative to go beyond the eco-efficiency paradigm and develop lesson plans that better support teachers interested in integrated working with the three classical sustainable development dimensions.

Setting the context

In Brazil, the Environmental Education National Policy of April 1999 (Law 9795) made environmental education compulsory in basic formal education. Of course, environmental education programs were already under way in different schools in Brazil before 1999, but countless governmental, private and also non-governmental initiatives arose thanks to this law.

The concept of sustainable development (or sustainability) was already part of national policy at that time. Article 4 (para II), related to the basic principles guiding environmental education initiatives in school, states that it is vital to understand 'the conception of environment as a whole, considering natural, socioeconomic and cultural interdependency, under a sustainability focus' (Article 4, paragraph 2, Brazilian Environmental Education National Policy, April 1999, Law 9795).

Despite the importance of the concept adopted during the United Nations Conference on Environment and Development, Rio-92, only very recently has the idea of working with sustainability gained more attention in some Brazilian public and private schools.

In 2010, a top private high school in São Paulo, Brazil asked me to start from scratch with an extra-curricular activity for high school students on sustainability. After three years of working on this, I am convinced of the importance of the Education for Sustainability Project for the teachers and volunteer students involved and, above all, for the school's community as a whole.

The first step in the Education for Sustainability Project was to invite teachers from different disciplines (such as Biology, Chemistry, Language, Geography and the Arts) to help design and carry out the project. It is not possible to create a project on sustainability without an interdisciplinary team. Our second step was to design a structured questionnaire to assess the knowledge of, attitudes and behaviour towards sustainability among elementary students (aged 11 to 16 years). It is very important to know and listen to your target audience. Only that way will you gather vital information that will help you create activities that really makes sense, and be able to build new values and change behaviour. Many projects on environmental education and education for sustainability fail because they simply skip that step.

The results of the diagnostic indicated that students from different grades have similar levels of knowledge, attitudes and behaviour regarding sustainability (Grandisoli et al., 2011). In short, the students clearly associated the word 'sustainability' with nature and natural resource preservation and had a positive attitude to that, and try to act in a sustainable way in their everyday lives, despite some gaps. One of these gaps particularly attracted our attention. Apparently, the older the respondent, the harder it is 'to always buy or consume only the essential'. These results seem to show an important turning point in consumption and indicate that the issue deserves attention and should be addressed by parents and schools, especially in a consumer-driven society such as ours.

The lost connection

Most of the Earth's population lives in cities where there is little or no contact with nature. Thus, over time, we have developed a utilitarian relationship with the environment from which we extract everything to ensure our comfort, staying unaware – and unconcerned – about the impacts of our lifestyle. The fact is that most of us only indirectly relate to nature via consumption of energy and natural resources like water, wood, energy, minerals, processed and transformed into goods. Fortunately, this reality has slowly changed over the past few decades, but we are still far from having a balanced and fair relationship with nature.

The demand for natural resources worldwide has increased in recent decades. The main drivers have been growth in population, wealth and consumption, with high population growth mainly in developing countries and the highest levels of wealth and consumption in developed countries (European Environmental Agency, 2010). The exploitation of resources to maintain levels of consumption has put increasing pressure on Earth's systems, and in the process has disrupted the ecological systems on which humanity and countless other species depend (Assadourian, 2010). The cause of all current crises is our disconnection with the place where we belong (Kumar, 2009).

One of the most important challenges today is trying to reconnect humans and nature, both in cognitive and in affective ways, and then engaging in a new era of common responsibility and concern for the collective, and school is a key institution for that. Schools are of fundamental importance in developing behaviour and views of the surrounding environment. Since it is crucial that the younger generation becomes more aware of the fundamental facts of sustainability, such subjects need to be integrated into their mandatory classes (Martins et al., 2006).

This chapter proposes a sequence of sessions to help teachers work effectively with sustainability in the classroom. These plans develop abilities such as observation, research, discussion, critical thinking, problem solving and an integrated analysis between environment, economy and society, using the theme of consumption as a guideline.

Sustainability through consumption

Consumption and consumerism prove to be excellent subjects to develop the ability to think systemically, giving learners of all ages the potential to maximize their diverse learning experiences and contribute to how we can better understand our complex interconnected world (Strachan, 2009: 84). The following plans would be suitable for secondary students, but can be easily adapted for younger students.

Each class will bring:

- a list of disciplines that can take part in activities and discussions

- a suggested activity duration

- brief indoor and outdoor activity descriptions

- a 'going further' item with subject extensions and deepening.

It is important to point out that the environmental, social and economic aspects of consumption are distinctly represented in each class. Valuing complexity is the key to developing more critical citizens, aware of their responsibilities, and, most importantly, empowered to act and collaborate to build a more sustainable society through a sustainable consumption.

Lesson 1: What is sustainability?

Unfortunately, sustainability is very difficult to define because of its scope.

According to John Huckle:

> Like liberty, justice and democracy, sustainability has no single and agreed meaning. It takes on meaning within different political ideologies and programmes underpinned by different kinds of knowledge, values and philosophy. Its meanings are contested and a key function to education for sustainability (EFS) is to help people reflect and act on these meanings and so realize alternative futures in more informed and democratic ways. (Huckle and Sterling, 2001: 3)

So, it is essential that students comprehend from the very beginning that sustainability is always related to processes involving, at least, three interrelated dimensions: ecological, social and economic. Even this classical approach is criticized by some authors such as Sachs (1993), who considers two additional dimensions: spatial and cultural.

Activity: Understanding the sustainability concept

Disciplines: all

Time: 100 minutes

Indoors:

Students must write on a small piece of paper (with five lines at most) a formal meaning or what they think when they hear the word 'sustainability'. The definitions must not be identified and during this step, students are not allowed to communicate with each other. All papers should then be collected, folded and shuffled over a table. Each student should then pick up one piece of paper from the table, while checking whether it contains his/her own definition.

If possible, organize the class in a circle and ask for all students to read aloud the definition chosen and then ask them to make any comment or observation regarding the definition just read. Try to ask questions that explore what students understand about key concepts such as development, environment, growth, nature and resources, among other things. Other students can also participate and discuss the definitions. In my experience, most of the definitions bring to the surface ideas of conservation or preservation of nature and natural resources, meaning that most of the students better comprehend that 'sustainability' is related to the ecological (or environmental) dimension. Only a few students relate 'sustainability' in a really integrated and complex way to social and economic dimensions.

This kind of scenario is similar in principle to a focus group, and can be very useful to clarify ideas regarding sustainability and sustainable development, allowing teachers to better identify mis-interpretations, conceptual gaps and students' prior knowledge as a whole.

Outdoors:

It is important that students understand that 'sustainability' is a concept still under construction and that it depends, among other factors, on the cultural and social reality of every individual. Encourage your students to ask others in the school community, as well as parents, relatives, neighbours, etc., what they understand about 'sustainability' and how they relate to it. Students can record or write down the answers and try to establish correlations between the concept itself and occupation, religion, social class, etc. The answers must be brought to the classroom and analysed together

(Continued)

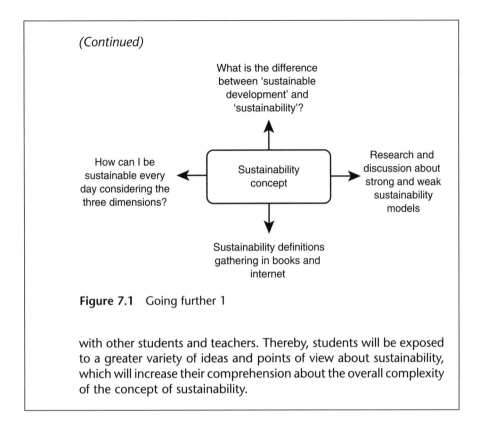

Figure 7.1   Going further 1

with other students and teachers. Thereby, students will be exposed to a greater variety of ideas and points of view about sustainability, which will increase their comprehension about the overall complexity of the concept of sustainability.

Lesson 2: What do I consume in a week?

From the moment we wake, we assume our role as consumers. We almost immediately start consuming energy, water, etc., and this is so customary and automatic that most of us are not aware of the connections between our lifestyle and natural resources. Everything has an origin, and the origin of everything depends – directly or indirectly – on natural resources. That connection seems to have been lost at some point in the past and because of that, we have also lost the idea of limits.

Nevertheless, levels of awareness have increased, especially since the 1960s, when the environmental movement started gaining force. Recycling and reusing, for instance, are already a part of many people's lives. But focusing on the end of the consumption course diverts us from its beginning, where most of the changes and technological improvements should be implemented. Today, our connections to nature and natural resource usage take place through consumer goods, and we will try to skip the intermediary by analysing our weekly consumption quantitatively.

Activity: My weekly consumption

Disciplines: all

Time: 5 days of data collection and 100 minutes in the classroom

Outdoors:

Despite being simple, this activity works as a major wake-up call for students once they realize what they consume over the working week (Monday to Friday). Everything they buy or consume (except meals) at home or elsewhere must be recorded in a table, such as the following suggestion (Figure 7.2). I think it would also be useful to record whenever consumption produces rubbish, and what was its destination (general rubbish bin, recycling bin, reuse, etc.). Feel free to add new enquiries depending on your needs and objectives.

What have you consumed?	Place of consumption	Rubbish produced	Rubbish destination	Weight of the rubbish produced
Chocolate bar	Home	Paper package	Common rubbish	0.1 oz
Glue pot	Stationery	No	–	–

Figure 7.2   Table suggestion

Indoors:

After the 5 days of data collection, students should bring their table to the class.

At first, organize the students into trios, and ask them to talk about their results and afterwards answer the following questions:

- What was your first impression when you saw your colleagues' tables?

- What most caught your attention in the tables presented?

- What would be the conclusions about *your* consumption?

Try to follow up the trios' discussions by sharing the answers of some volunteer students as a strategy to involve all into a bigger discussion. This closure ideally should focus on the amount of things consumed over the week. The important question is: Would it be possible for me to consume less?

(Continued)

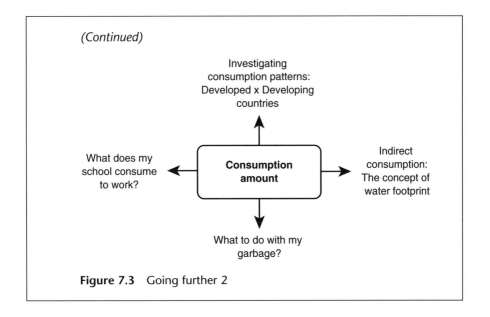

(Continued)

Figure 7.3   Going further 2

Lesson 3: Where do things come from?

The word 'resource' has its roots in the Latin verb *surgere*, which evokes the image of a spring that continually rises from the ground. A 're-source' rises again and again, even if it has been repeatedly used and consumed. With the advent of industrialism and colonialism, natural resources have turned into containers of raw materials waiting to be transformed into inputs to commodity production (Shiva, 1992: 206). The situation described by Shiva just escalates and today most people live in cities disconnected from nature and connected to natural resources only by consumption, remaining unaware of the impacts of their lifestyle.

Activity: Our daily resource consumption

Disciplines: especially Biology, Physics, Maths, Geography and History

Time: 100 minutes

Outdoors:

Students revisit the information recorded in the previous activity and pick one or two objects consumed during the 5 days. Each student

(Continued)

(Continued)

brings the chosen object(s) to class and, organized again in trios, examines in detail each object to determine the kinds of materials and resources that have been used to make them. Students help each other to be as accurate and detailed as possible. Their findings are written down and they research in books and/or on the internet, trying to find out:

- where the main reserves of each natural resource are listed

- whether each resource is renewable or non-renewable

- what the current availability of each resource is

- which other objects use the same resources.

Indoors:

The research is brought to class and shared, and one student lists on the blackboard a ranking of the 'most commonly used resources'. Afterwards, the results should be discussed. This activity complements, in a qualitative way, the results and discussions that took place during the second activity, and sets out a broad picture of intensive use of non-renewable resources like oil and minerals.

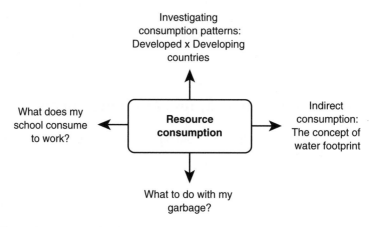

Figure 7.4   Going further 3

Lesson 4: Needs and wants

Desire is part of our everyday lives. We work desiring a better future for ourselves and our families, we practise sports desiring better fitness and health, we travel to learn about our own culture and that of others, and we buy things desiring … what really? We live in a market-driven world. Everything around us has been carefully designed to remind us to buy, to use, to consume.

According to Gardner et al. (2004), there are now more than 1.7 billion in 'the consumer class' – nearly half of these are in the developing world. Worldwide, private consumption expenditure – the amount spent at the household level – topped $20 trillion in 2000, a four-fold increase on 1960. That is a two-sided story, because increasing consumption has driven individuals to also increase their personal costs: their financial debt; the time (and stress) spent working to support high consumption; the time required to clean, upgrade, store or maintain possessions; and the ways in which consumption replaces time spent with family and friends. It is crucial that we stop, analyse and rethink our consumption, not only from a utilitarian point of view, but also from an affective one.

 Activity: Needs and wants – where is the true happiness?

Disciplines: all

Time: 100 minutes

Indoors:

One of the most basic concepts of economics is 'needs and wants'. A *need* is something that all of us must have for survival. For example, people need air, food, water and shelter. A *want* is something someone would like to have. For example, bikes, games and mobile (or cell) phones are wants because people can survive without them.

Without presenting these definitions of needs and wants, ask your students to make a list of everything they consider important in their lives. Explain that the list has no limit and that they must think

(Continued)

(Continued)

carefully about their everyday lives. Afterwards, the students must underline everything in the list they consider to be essential, in other words, the things they would never give up.

Answer the following questions:

- What percentage of the list has been underlined?

- Why are the underlined items so important to you?

Then present the basic definitions of needs and wants to the students and ask them to revisit their underlined words. Now, ask them to answer the following: Do I need more than I want or do I want more than I need? It is possible to develop the same activity proposed here by using the list produced in the second activity (my weekly consumption)?

Outdoors:

Encourage your students to go and ask other students, teachers, colleagues, neighbours, etc. what they consider to be important in their lives. With the responses in mind, ask them to make a personal reflection on materialism and the role that it plays in our society and how it can affect our decisions.

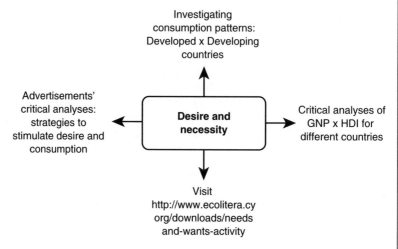

Figure 7.5 Going further 4

Lesson 5: Sustainable consumption

There are several different definitions and aims for sustainable consumption (SC):

> Sustainable Consumption is about finding workable solutions to imbalances – social and environmental – through more responsible behaviour from everyone. In particular, SC is linked to production and distribution, use and disposal of products and services and provides the means to rethink their lifecycle. (UNESCO-UNEP, 2008: unpaginated)

> Sustainable consumption and production is about achieving more with less. This means not only looking at how goods and services are produced, but also the impacts of products and materials across their whole lifecycle and building on people's awareness of social and environmental concerns. (HM Government, 2005: unpaginated)

> Education for Sustainable Consumption (ESC) aims at providing knowledge, values and skills to enable individuals and social groups to become actors of change towards more sustainable consumption behaviors. (UNESCO-UNEP, 2008: unpaginated)

The concept of sustainable consumption is vague and hard to pinpoint. Nevertheless, there are two important features associated with every act of consumption that must be observed: quantity and quality. Quantity is directly related, broadly speaking, to how much of a resource is actually used and discarded in the production, distribution and selling of any kind of goods. Quality, on the other hand, is directly related to how the resources are actually explored, used and discarded. It is also crucial to consider who is involved in the production and what their working conditions are. So, both quantity and quality are related to the idea of (eco)efficiency, human rights and social justice.

Consumption is not bad per se. Overconsumption, disinformation and indifference are the real villains in the quest for more sustainable societies. So, it is imperative to empower people to make wiser, more responsible choices every day.

 ## Activity: Fish and chips' foodprint

Disciplines: especially Biology, Chemistry, Maths and Geography

Time: 200 minutes

(Continued)

(Continued)

Indoors:

All consumer goods, including food, have their own ecological and social footprint. According to the World Wide Fund for Nature (WWF) (Audsley et al., 2009), around 30 percent of the UK's carbon footprint is related to food production (especially associated with supply chain emissions and land use) and consumption. Fish and chips is probably the most well-known UK dish, and, as with every other dish, it has its own *foodprint*. *Foodprint* is a term used to symbolize every natural resource used and all the people who worked to make the dish reach your table. So, *foodprint* should encompass not only environmental but also socially related impacts.

It is important for teachers involved in this activity to understand how long food can travel before reaching our plates and, of course, all the environmental and health consequences that arise from that. So, I suggest teachers read *Food and Farming* by Friends of the Earth (2004).

To better understand how to make more sustainable choices, let's take a close look at Jamie Oliver's (2012) fish and chips recipe.

Fish and chips

Ingredients
For the chips:

> 3 3/4 pints (2 litres) vegetable oil
> 2 pounds (950 grams) floury potatoes, like russets, peeled and cut into large chips

For the batter:

> 1 cup plain flour
> 1 cup beer
> 2 egg whites, whipped to soft peaks
> Salt
> 4 (9 ounce/250 grams) fillets of haddock or cod, skin on, and pin boned

Directions
Pour all the vegetable oil into a deep pan or deep fat fryer, and heat to 300 degrees F (160 degrees C.) Blanch the cut potatoes in the oil until soft, but not colored, about 4 minutes. Remove and drain.

Mix together the flour and the beer, then fold in the egg whites. Turn up the heat of the oil to 350 degrees F (180 degrees C). Dip the fish in the batter and fry for a few minutes with the chips until golden brown.

Drain on kitchen paper and serve with bread and butter, wally's (battered, deep fried pickles served with ranch dressing), and pickled eggs.

Figure 7.6   Fish and chips

(Continued)

(Continued)

Today, few of us are involved in growing our own food or raising animals, and we buy over 75 percent of our food from supermarkets (Friends of the Earth, 2004). Thus, the first step in the classroom is to make a list of every ingredient present in the recipe (including the ones hidden in the beer, for example). This part of the activity is important to connect students back to the Earth and re-establish or construct the concept of dependence on and respect for the environment and for those who produce our food. It is important to point out that students can also bring to school old family recipes typical of their cultural origins, and replicate the activity with those.

Outdoors:

After that, students should work in groups and research in books, on the internet and by contacting and/or visiting different food manufacturers and supermarkets to answer the following questions about a chosen food(s):

- Where are the ingredients produced?
- Are pesticides used in the production of the ingredients? Can pesticides be harmful to health?
- Are food additives present? Can they be harmful to health?
- Who is involved in production? Are there any registered cases of human rights violations?

Every group must make a short PowerPoint presentation of its research and, using a paper world map, pins and colored strings, trace the way the food had to travel to reach their plates. This provides a special opportunity to introduce and work with the concept of *carbon foodprint*. Finally, organize a plenary to discuss what would be better for us, the environment and the economy. Consider here the following questions:

- Are some of the ingredients used to prepare fish and chips produced locally?
- How is food transported to us from different countries? What are the consequences of that?
- How does the food stay fresh when it travels so far?
- Would it be better for us and the environment to get food from local places? Why?
- Why don't we eat more food from local sources? Why is it important for the environment, the producers and the economy?
- What can we do to improve the situation?

(Continued)

(Continued)

To summarize, the overriding challenges related to sustainable consumption are (as adapted from McKeown, 2002):

- to respect the Earth, life in all its diversity, natural processes and complexity
- to adopt patterns of consumption and production that safeguard human rights and community well-being
- to support low-impact local production
- to respect the regenerative capacities of the Earth and to ensure that economic activities at all levels promote human development in an equitable and sustainable manner.

It is important to point out that the global idea of this activity can be extrapolated to every good we consume.

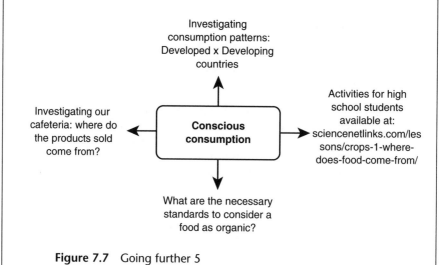

Figure 7.7   Going further 5

Lesson 6: Be the change

Mahatma Gandhi (1913: 241) once said: 'If we could change ourselves, the tendencies in the world would also change. As a man changes his own nature, so does the attitude of the world change towards him.'

Individual changes in values, attitudes and behaviour are the first steps to building a more sustainable society. Nevertheless, it is important that the task of creating a new model of civilization is not only based on personal efforts, but is also a collective project based on friendship, partnership and cooperation, and not on feelings of guilt or revolt. Only in that way are people able to keep doing what they think is right, both for themselves and others. We are a social species, and like ants, termites or honeybees, we should work together to reach our objectives. Can you imagine a honeybee living on her own?

That seems to be a very obvious train of thoughts and conclusions, but historically we are doing exactly the opposite. Our society is highly fragmented and people who should be working together – because they are pursuing the same goal – are separated. The excess of individualism associated with consumerist hedonism may be responsible for both the state of society and of the environment today. Thus, perhaps the most important social movement nowadays is to re-establish ourselves as a social and collaborative species, where 'one [is] for all, [and] all [is] for one'. Once reorganized, society will be able to act and democratically demand the necessary changes.

 Activity: *The Story of Change*

Disciplines: all

Time: 60 minutes

Indoors:

It is hard to keep doing the right things every day when you have the perception that you are the only one doing it. I think the film *The Story of Change* (available at http://www.youtube.com/watch?v=oIQdYXCKUv0) is at the same time informative and motivational. It praises and stimulates action through democratic, collective and organized participation, and, above all, it celebrates a passion for what is right and necessary for a more sustainable society.

Watch the film with your students and ask them to think about their neighbourhood, school and home and how they believe they could collectively and democratically make a difference, make a change. I believe this closing activity is not the end, but the start of a new

(Continued)

(Continued)

way to see the world around us and feel empowered to act. Here are a few questions that can help to spice up the final discussion:

- Who is responsible for building a more sustainable society?
- Based on the film's categories, what kind of change marker are you?
- How can we change the 'rules of the game'? Give practical examples.
- How can you make the difference today?

Outdoors:

As a closing activity, encourage your students to research and visit local non-governmental organisations (NGOs) and community associations that are trying to make a difference locally. Ask them to find out if these NGOs and associations have volunteer programs and how teachers, students and the school as a whole could collaborate on spreading the word. It is crucial that students learn that they have a key role as citizens in their community, and, above all, that they learn where, how and why to cooperate. Participation is the bottom line to build a more sustainable society.

Further reading

Clarke, P. (2012) *Education for Sustainability: Becoming Naturally Smart*. New York and London: Routledge.

Dauvergne, P. (2008) *The Shadows of Consumption: Consequences for the Global Environment*. Cambridge, MA: MIT Press.

Franklin, A. and Blyton, P. (eds) (2011) *Researching Sustainability: A Guide to Social Science Methods, Practice and Engagement*. New York: Earthscan.

Timpson, W.M., Dunbar, B., Kimmel, G., Bruyere, B., Newman, P. and Mizia, H. (2006) *147 Tips for Teaching Sustainability*. Madison, WI: Atwood Publishing.

Information for practice

It is well known that some teachers do not work well – or do not work at all – with the concept of sustainability because of its intrinsic complexity. At the same time, there is a huge lack of practical activities that support and encourage elementary and high school teachers to work with the concept of sustainability. I hope the six hands-on activities presented really encourage you to use consumption and consumerism as a guideline, in order to highlight all the complexity lying behind today's society, to stimulate your students' reflections and critical views, and to empower them to change unsustainable behaviours in the construction of a more sustainable world.

References

Assadourian, E. (2010) 'The rise and fall of consumer cultures', in L. Starke and L. Mastny (eds) A Worldwatch Institute Report on Progress Toward a Sustainable Society: State of the World – From Consumerism to Sustainability [online]. Available at: http://www.worldwatch.org/files/pdf/Chapter%201.pdf (accessed 24 October 2012).

Audsley, E., Brander, M., Chatterton, J., Murphy-Bokern, D., Webster, C. and Williams, A. (2009) How Low Can We Go? An Assessment of Greenhouse Gas Emissions from the UK Food System and the Scope to Reduce Them by 2050. WWF-UK [online]. Available at: http://assets.wwf.org.uk/downloads/how_low_can_we_go.pdf (accessed 24 October 2012).

Eco-Schools International Programme (2009) Eco-Schools Programme [online]. Available at: http://www.eco-schools.org/brochure_eco.pdf (accessed 24 October 2012).

European Environmental Agency (2010) Consumption and the Environment: Stand and Outlook 2010 [online]. Available at: http://www.ypeka.gr/LinkClick. aspx?fileticket=dc6v5xtmuBQ%3D&tabid=467&language=el-GR (accessed 24 October 2012).

Freire, A.M. (2007) 'Educação para a sustentabilidade: implicações para o currículo escolar e para a formação de professores', *Pesquisa em Educação Ambiental* 2(1): 141–154.

Friends of the Earth (2004) Food and Farming [online]. Available at: http://www.foe. co.uk/resource/factsheets/food_farming.pdf (accessed 24 October 2012).

Gandhi, M. (1913) *General Knowledge about Health*, 13(153): 241, in the *Indian Opinion*, 9 August 1913, from *The Collected Works of M. K. Gandhi*. New Delhi: The Publications Division.

Gardner, G., Assadourian, E. and Sarin, R. (2004) The State of Consumption Today, State of the World (The Consumer Society): Worldwatch Institute Report [online]. Available at: http://www-rohan.sdsu.edu/faculty/dunnweb/StateofWorld2004.dat. pdf (accessed 24 October 2012).

Grandisoli, E., Telles, R., Mattos Assumpção, C. and Curi, D. (2011) 'The concept of sustainability among elementary students in Brazil', *Literacy Information and Computer Education Journal (LICEJ)* 2(1): 310–316.

HM Government (2005) Securing the Future [online]. Available at: http://www.defra. gov.uk/publications/files/pb10589-securing-the-future-050307.pdf (accessed 24 October 2012).

Huckle, J. and Sterling, S. (2001) *Education for Sustainability*. London: Earthscan.

Kumar, S. (2009) 'Grounded economic awareness', in A. Stibbe (ed.) *The Handbook of Sustainable Literacy: Skills for a Changing World*. Dartington: Green Books.

Martins, A.A., Mata, T.M. and Costa, C.A.V. (2006) 'Education for sustainability: challenges and trends', *Clean Technology and Environmental Policy* 8: 31–37.

McKeown, R. (2002) Education for Sustainable Development Toolkit. UNESCO, version 2 [online]. Available at: http://www.esdtoolkit.org/esd_toolkit_v2.pdf (accessed 22 October 2012).

Oliver, J. (2012) Fish and Chips [online]. Available at: http://www.foodnetwork.com/ recipes/jamie-oliver/fish-and-chips-recipe/index.html (accessed 7 December 2012).

Sachs, I. (1993) *Estratégias de transição para o século XXI: desenvolvimento e meio ambiente*. São Paulo: Studio Nobel e FUNDAP.

Shiva, V. (1992) 'Resources', in W. Sachs (ed.) *The Development Dictionary: A Guide to Knowledge as Power*. London: Zed Books, pp. 206–218.

Strachan, G. (2009) 'Systems thinking: the ability to recognize and analyze the interconnections within and between systems', in A. Stibbe (ed.) *The Handbook of Sustainable Literacy: Skills for a Changing World.* Dartington: Green Books, pp. 84–88.

UNESCO Education Sector (2010) Education for Sustainable Development Lens: A Policy and Practice Review Tool. Education for Sustainable Development in Action. Learning and Training Tools No. 2 [online]. Available at: http://unesdoc.unesco.org/images/0019/001908/190898e.pdf (accessed 22 October 2012).

UNESCO-UNEP (2008) Youth X Change: Training Kit on Responsible Consumption – The Guide [online]. Available at: http://unesdoc.unesco.org/images/0015/001587/158700e.pdf (accessed 24 October 2012).

8

The 'Veggie Bag' and its Potential for 'Connected Knowing': An Experience from a South African Context

Theodora Papatheodorou

Chapter overview

In this chapter, I discuss the introduction of the 'veggie bag' in deep rural communities in South Africa and its potential for young children's learning. With reference to relevant literature, I illustrate in this chapter how the veggie bag can be utilised in order to: (i) offer children opportunities for academic outcomes by starting from their experiences and the resources available to them; (ii) foster intergenerational learning and the development of skills that are vital for their community; and (iii) enable them to gain understanding of their natural habitat and maintain a positive relationship and connectivity with it.

Whilst the veggie bag was introduced with the main aim to improve the nutrition of families, its potential for children's learning cannot be underestimated. Working alongside expert garden motivators and/or members of their families and communities, children can act on their environment and see the impact of such actions on their lives. They can learn how to tend for and care about the natural environment and, at the same time, learn how to acquire dispositions necessary for academic outcomes. Children can maintain continuity and connectivity between their own lived experiences and the new worlds opened up to them through their engagement with a real-life project.

Case study: Introduction of the 'veggie bag' in deep rural communities

In deep rural communities in KwaZulu Natal, a local early childhood Non-Governmental Organisation (NGO) (LETCEE) has initiated the 'veggie bag' (Figure 8.1) and introduced it to each family with which it works. Depending on its size, the 'veggie bag' may include up to 90 plants (e.g. spinach, onions, papers, butternut, chillies, etc.) planted on top and all around the side of the bag. The concept is simple; the veggie bag requires a used 25 kg bag (e.g. from flour, potatoes, etc.), a growing medium (soil/compost) and seedlings. The bag is filled up with soil step by step as a core pillar of stones is piled up in the middle, from bottom to top. On a hot day, the stones lock in the water and on a wet day drain it away; 1–2 litres of water is enough to water the veggie bag, every day, and 'grey' water (e.g. from dish washing) can also be used. A couple of marigold and chilli seedlings are planted to keep the bugs away. The veggie bag is supported by three or four durable wooden poles and it takes no more than a square metre; it is easy and considerably less expensive to fence it in (Figure 8.2). If the veggie bag is tended properly, it can provide vegetables to feed a family of four.

Questions for reflection

- What is the potential of the veggie bag for children's learning? Think of knowledge, skills, attitudes and behaviours.

- What are the benefits of the veggie bag to a family?

Supporting children's learning

In deep rural communities in South Africa, children can afford beautiful surroundings that enable them to roam relatively free and enjoy the pleasure of being in a natural habitat (Figure 8.3). However, the same surroundings also present enormous challenges, with life often being tough and harsh. Hamlets are scattered across vast mountainous areas (Figure 8.4), where basic facilities such as running water and electricity are often unavailable. Unemployment is high, with many adults leaving their families behind to seek employment elsewhere. Households are often led by grandparents and/or older children as young as the age of 8. Poverty is deep-rooted, accompanied by accumulated disadvantages of poor health and lack of opportunity for

Figure 8.1   The veggie bag

Figure 8.2   Building up the veggie bag

Figure 8.3   Concentration

Figure 8.4   Hamlets scattered across mountainous areas

organised educational and recreational activities. As a result, beautiful natural surroundings associated with such living conditions may not be appreciated for their potential and the opportunities they offer for experiential learning and for bettering life conditions. Even worse, such conditions may force young adults to seek opportunities for a better life elsewhere, usually in urban or industrialised areas.

It is in this context that LETCEE (see case study above) has introduced the veggie bag, as a feasible and viable way of improving the nutrition of families, while fostering intergenerational learning and supporting children's learning and their understanding of the world. The Director of LETCEE explains that the veggie bag requires little space and water, both of which are at a premium in deep rural communities. Despite the vastness of the rural areas, grounds that are easily cultivated are limited. Even if space is available, a large vegetable garden cannot be sustained, because water has to be fetched from long distances. A veggie bag however can be maintained by every family, as it requires less than a square metre and it can even be fed with 'grey' water. The Director of LETCEE points out that the same number of plants, in the ground, would require a space of approximately 1.60 x 2.50 m, requiring a lot of water and fencing in comparison with the veggie bag.

The organisation's intention is that each family will start with one veggie bag and gradually increase to two or more, depending on need, the availability of space and the capacity for maintaining them. A community gardening motivator supports the families in starting up and maintaining their veggie bag. The primary aim of the introduction of the veggie bag is to improve the nutrition of families, but its potential benefits for children's development and learning, intergenerational engagement, appreciation of and connectivity with the natural habitat, and a sense of contribution and belonging cannot be underestimated. These benefits will be discussed next with reference to the relevant literature, while linking their relevance to building up and maintaining a veggie bag.

Natural places: developmental perspectives

Over the past few decades, urbanisation and high-tech modern life, at least in 'developed' countries (such as those in Northern Europe, North America and Australia), have dramatically limited children's opportunities for being outdoors and for engaging with activities and play in the natural environment. Children spend most of their time indoors, playing with manufactured toys and games, and/or confined to the home garden (Papatheodorou, 2010a). Such experiences have gradually limited and narrowed children's physical development, and psychological and social growth (Louv, 2005).

These concerns led researchers and practitioners from many fields of study and practice (e.g. education, health, sustainable education) to raise awareness about the benefits of children's access to natural places and play in the outdoors. Some of the benefits include increased levels of enjoyment, physical activity and energy, learning and academic attainment, understanding of the world, health and psychological well-being (Johnston et al., 2005; Knight, 2009; White, 2004).

Such evidence has now been used to advocate for children's access to the outdoors and to influence national policies aiming at re-engaging children with natural places. For example, in England, the National Play Strategy advocates for increased opportunities for outdoor play (DCSF, 2008) and the Early Years Foundation Stage (EYFS) statutory framework mandates that young children have daily access to outdoor experiences (DCSF, 2007a, 2007b). Similarly, countries with emerging economies, characterised by increased urban migration (e.g. India, China, Indonesia), and less industrialised countries (e.g. Eastern Europe) have also started to acknowledge the importance of children's living conditions and the impact of limited access to safe outdoor and natural places (see Iltus, 2012; Knight, 2012).

As a result, systematic efforts are now being made so that children can experience natural places and the outdoors. In these environments, young children are encouraged to explore, investigate and take risks, and develop awareness of their senses and the environment. Miller (2007) and Chawla (2012) detail a range of key benefits of children's experience with natural environments. These include:

- developmental benefits, such as increased wonder and imagination, creativity, personal and social skills, self-efficacy, ability to deal with stress and adversity, self-understanding and increased engagement for children with behavioural problems or attention issues

- academic/scholastic benefits, that is concentration, observational skills, increased analytical, problem-solving and critical thinking skills, and the integration of maths, science, language, arts, social sciences and other subjects

- increased understanding and concern for the environment, such as knowledge and understanding of geographical, ecological or food production processes and more positive attitudes about environmental issues.

Miller (2007) reports similar themes emerging from her gardening project with young children, which in summary are that:

- children develop important skills and meaningful learning that enable them to be more successful in school and in navigating their world

- children communicate what they know about their world in much more sophisticated ways than they can verbalise and we realise. This however requires of adults close observation, attention and listening to gain an insight into their ways of knowing the world

- children 'feel' more connected to nature and are enabled to process their emotions, take risks, develop self-confidence and gain mastery over their fears.

Intergenerational learning, connectivity and interrelatedness with environment

Working alongside adults in outdoor settings and especially gardening projects, children communicate and re-engage with them on new terms as well as give new meaning to their experiences and acquire wider awareness of their environment (Knight, 2012). Intergenerational activities offer a social context where children, as legitimate peripheral participants (after Lave and Wenger, 1991), foster relationships and acquire environmental consciousness. Based on these ideas, Mayer-Smith and colleagues (2007) teamed children and adults together with the aim of growing food and increasing environmental consciousness. Their findings showed that children shifted from seeing their environment as an object of utilitarian use to a place of interconnectedness and relatedness with it. As their experience grew, so did the children's care for plants and their relationship with the environment.

Phenice and Griffore (2003) argue that children, who are not in contact with their natural worlds, see themselves as disconnected or not being part of it. As a result, their natural environment becomes an object of utilitarian usage rather than something to be appreciated, tended to, maintained and loved. The environment however is a living and changing system, which provides fluidity of intellectual, social and sensory experiences that transform and are transformed by the individual. It reflects and responds to individual and communal needs, ideas and values, and the culture of people who live within it

(Papatheodorou, 2010b). It is the canvas, where personal experiences and stories, images and memories unfold and are created to gain meaning and enable a sense of belonging and identity formation (Babacan, 2005; Greenman, 1988).

It is interesting to note here that early sensory (especially visual, spatial, tactile and olfactory) and emotional experiences afforded by natural environments are linked with adults' memory and recollection of information and early life events (Grawley and Eacott, 2006). Being outdoors or in the woods, running barefoot, making things such as mud pies or rose petal perfume and being full of surprise are often cited as adults' most memorable childhood experiences; their memories are made of being outdoors, making and feeling things (Papatheodorou, 2010a).

Adults' memories and recollections from childhood resonate; Heidegger (cited in Avriel-Avni et al., 2010) speaks of 'dwelling thinking' which results from 'dwelling activity', that is, people's authentic and intentional actions in the locations where they reside in order to create meaningful spaces. 'Dwelling thinking' reflects people's connectivity and relationship with natural places. It is a state of mind that they carry with them and it enables them to find connectivity with whichever place they may inhabit. In contrast, an absence of 'dwelling thinking' leaves people alienated from their place and any place they may seek to inhabit.

Considering the notion of 'dwelling thinking', Avriel-Avni and colleagues (2010) conducted their own study among young children. Using children's pictorial representation of the places where they lived, the researchers identified four emerging patterns that reflected children's different level of connectivity with place. These are:

- the Sitting Tenant's perception, which portrayed children's love of their place, their identification with landmarks of place and their participation in social life. It depicted a sense of belonging and confidence in being there; a place of ownership, contentment and peace

- the Lodger's perception, which showed a place of beauty and interest, but where there was a lack of environmental knowledge or participation in social life. It depicted a lack of permanence and identification with place

- the Tourist's perception, which illustrated a place of beauty and attraction, but gave the sense of a temporary/transient residence

- the Captive's perception, which demonstrated emptiness, a lack of plans and social life. It illustrated a place not suitable for modern living.

The four emergent patterns demonstrate different levels of children's being and belonging in place. The Sitting Tenant's perception shows connectivity with the physical environment and the social life taking place there; it reflects 'dwelling thinking'. The Captive's perception demonstrates young people's alienation from place, forcing them to move out and seek a better life elsewhere (Avriel-Anvi et al., 2010). Ideally, children's environment and their experience in the places where they live should foster and forge the Sitting Tenant's dwelling thinking, so that children are in harmony with place.

Environmental stimuli: sources for educative experiences

'Dwelling thinking' starts early in life by developing children's innate sense of relatedness to nature. Crowe (1984) argues that children's senses cry out for experiences that they will later need in order to connect with the world they inhabit. She argues that 'Children must feel the world, listen to it, see it, taste it, smell it, "know" it ... That takes time and a great deal of silent investigation in peace and privacy' (p. 39). Crowe's observations summarise the potential of the veggie bag, as an environmental stimulus that offers children opportunities for learning that cultivate life skills and skills for life.

The veggie bag is a small and manageable project which offers concrete experiences and a social context where children, working alongside knowledgeable adults and within their zone of proximal development (after Vygotsky, 1978), acquire knowledge and a range of skills and behaviours. It is both playful and serious business. It comprises both exploration and application of skill and fosters children's empathetic understanding of their context and circumstances. It is a real-life project with tangible outcomes that relate to children's lives and provide ample opportunities for learning.

The veggie bag is the environmental stimulus that facilitates and mediates individual and shared activity, forges interactions and inter-relationships, generates ideas and actions, encourages communication and co-operation and supports independence and interdependence. It enables an invisible pedagogy, where the construction of learning does not take place in a linear and progressive way, but in an evolving network of interwoven and interconnected elements. Perception, action and reflection are the fundamental, although not always explicitly recorded and articulated, learning strategies.

Consider, for instance, the knowledge and skills which children may acquire by:

- building up the veggie bag with a core of stones in the middle from bottom to top; deciding the kind of soil/compost that is required; choosing the size of stones to be used; deciding the thickness and length of, and the space between, the supporting posts

- making judgements of how to space the seedlings on the side of the bag, in order to plant as many as possible; deciding which seedlings should be planted at the top of the bag and which ones at the bottom and lower level (see Figure 8.5)

- choosing the right location of the veggie bag in order to maximise exposure to, or protection from, direct sun or wind; planting seedlings at the right side of the veggie bag, depending on their need for direct exposure to the sun; selecting plants that grow best under different weather conditions (e.g. winter, summer); protecting plants from frost or bad weather conditions

- planting chillies and marigolds to protect plants from bugs; thinking how often and when to water the veggie bag

- deciding when it is the right time to pick the vegetables; knowing which vegetables can be eaten raw or cooked; gaining knowledge about the nutritional value of vegetables and the ways of preserving them.

These are some indicative learning opportunities (and you may think of many more) that enable children to sharpen their observational skills and reasoning abilities, to link cause and effect and to see the impact of their actions on their everyday life. Children's engagement with this project fosters habitual learning and positive dispositions without being exposed to direct instruction. Children's efforts, endeavours and achievement need not always be tidily documented, for instance in portfolios or learning journeys. Instead, they should be invited and permitted to alter their environment through their actions and enjoy the fruits of their doings (e.g. see the vegetables growing, eat the vegetables), to realise their skills and potential, to work within as well as extend their potential, to enhance their knowledge and understanding of their own lived

Figure 8.5   Arranging and spacing plants on the veggie bag

world. Children need experiences which not only transform and condition them to what Ellsworth (2005: 16) calls 'learning compliance', but experiences that are responsive and transformable because of their action; experiences which require children's self-presence and reinforce concentration and absorption in what they do.

This reminds us of Dewey (1997: 25–27) who cautioned that:

> not all experiences are genuine or equally educative. Experience and education cannot be directly equated to each other. For some experiences are mis-educative. Any experience is mis-educative that has the effect of arresting or distorting the growth of further experience ... An experience may be immediately enjoyable and yet promote the formation of a slack and careless attitude; this attitude then operates to modify the quality of subsequent experiences as to prevent a person from getting out of them what they have to give ... Again, experience may be so disconnected from one another that, while each is agreeable or even exciting in itself, they are not linked cumulative to one another. Energy then is dissipated and a person becomes scatter brained.

Dewey's argument demonstrates the importance of having experiences that harmonise purpose, enjoyment and meaning in an environment that offers children the opportunity of seeing the impact of their actions and thus sustaining their interest and motivation, their efforts, perseverance and persistence. In this sense, children's environment becomes the canvas on which their experience and efforts are imprinted and through which their lived experience is narrated (Papatheodorou, 2010b). To recall Gardner (1991), children's engagement with projects and tasks that are pertinent and meaningful to their particular context and circumstances fosters 'connected knowing', meaning that their learning is part of, rather than separate from, life.

Conclusion

The case study above illustrates how some creative and simple ideas can be turned into projects that respond to the specific needs of communities and families. It shows the potential of natural resources for solving problems that are pertinent to communities, and, at the same time, reinforces the use and the furthering of certain skills and knowledge. It also demonstrates how awareness of learning takes place with hands-on activities, in a subtle way and through intergenerational apprenticeship rather than in a didactic way with a school-centred focus. By mobilising and supporting a viable intergenerational activity, aiming to raise community awareness of nutrition and its importance for health, one organisation (LETCEE) brought together health and education, in subtle and unquantified ways. The Director of LETCEE explains that for many young children, whose parents are absent from the immediate family scene, the veggie bag, being a long-term and all-year-round project, gives them a sense of continuity, an opportunity for making a contribution and fosters a sense of belonging and wellness.

Further reading

Global perspectives on children and nature from different theoretical stances are outlined in:

Kahn Jr., P. and Kellert, S. (eds) (2002) *Children and Nature*. London: MIT Press.

Additional case studies about children's sense of place, their 'dwelling thinking', can be found in:

Kraftl, P., Horton, J. and Tucker, F. (eds) (2012) *Critical Geographies of Childhood and Youth*. Bristol: Policy Press.

Ideas for growing with young children in the northern hemisphere are described in:

Watts, A. (2011) *Every Nursery needs a Garden*. London: Routledge.

Information for practice

The veggie bag is a small project that can be replicated in any early childhood setting and in as small a space as is available, either outdoors or indoors. Consider how to initiate and monitor it systematically to record and evaluate children's engagement and their learning, linked with:

- problem solving and mathematical thinking

- reasoning and language

- interactions and communication

- observational and explorational skills

- application of skills

- empathetic understanding of their environment.

References

Avriel-Avni, N., Spektor-Levy, O., Zion, M. and Levi, N.R. (2010) 'Children's sense of place in desert towns: a phenomenographic enquiry', *International Research in Geographical and Environmental Education* 19(3): 241–259.

Babacan, H. (2005) Locating Identity: Sense of Space, Place and Belonging. Paper presented at the Diversity Conference, Beijing, China, 30 June – 3 July.

Chawla, L. (2012) 'The importance of access to nature for young children', *Early Childhood Matters: Living Conditions on Young Children's Health*, 118. The Hague: Bernard van Leer Foundation.

Crowe, B. (1984) *Play is a Feeling*. London: Unwin.

Department of Children, Schools and Families (DCSF) (2007a) *EYFS Statutory Framework*. Nottingham: DCSF.

Department of Children, Schools and Families (DCSF) (2007b) *The Early Years Foundation Stage – Effective Practice: Outdoor Learning*. Nottingham: DCSF.

Department of Children, Schools and Families (DCSF) (2008) *The National Play Strategy*. Nottingham: DCSF.

Dewey, J. (1997) *Experience and Education*. New York: Touchstone.

Ellsworth, E. (2005) *Places of Learning: Media Architecture Pedagogy*. New York: RoutledgeFalmer.

Gardner, H. (1991) 'The tensions between education and development', *Journal of Moral Development* 20(2): 113–125.

Grawley, R.A. and Eacott, M.J. (2006) 'Memories of early childhood: qualities of the experience of recollection', *Memory and Cognition* 34(2): 287–294.

Greenman, J. (1988) *Caring Spaces, Learning Spaces: Children's Environments that Work*. Redmond, WA: Exchange Press.

Iltus, S. (2012) 'Recognising the importance of the living conditions children grow up in', *Early Childhood Matters: Living Conditions on Young Children's Health*, 118. The Hague: Bernard van Leer Foundation.

Johnston, J.E., Christie, J.F. and Wardle, F. (2005) *Play, Development and Early Education*. New York: Alyn & Bacon.

Knight, S. (2009) *Forest Schools and Outdoor Learning in the Early Years*. London: Sage.

Knight, S. (2012) 'Valuing outdoor spaces: different models of outdoor learning in the early years', in T. Papatheodorou and J. Moyles (eds) *Cross-Cultural Perspectives on Early Childhood*. London: Sage, pp. 33.

Lave, J. and Wenger, E. (1991) *Situated Learning: Legitimate Peripheral Participation*. Cambridge: Cambridge University Press.

Louv, R. (2005) *Last Child in the Woods: Saving our Children from Nature-deficit Disorder*. Chapel Hill, NC: Algonquin Books.

Mayer-Smith, J., Bartosh, O. and Peterat, L. (2007) 'Teaming children and elders to grow food and environmental consciousness', *Applied Environmental Education & Communication* 6: 77–85.

Miller, D. (2007) 'The seeds of learning: young children develop important skills through their gardening activities at a Midwestern early education program', *Applied Environmental Education and Communication* 6: 49–66.

Papatheodorou, T. (2010a) Sensory Play, report submitted to *Play to Z*. Chelmsford: Anglia Ruskin University. [Funded by an EEDA innovation voucher: 09/062.]

Papatheodorou, T. (2010b) 'The pedagogy of play(ful) learning environments: turning spaces into places', in J. Moyles (ed.) *Thinking About Play: Developing a Reflective Approach*. Maidenhead: Open University Press & McGraw-Hill.

Phenice, L. and Griffore, R. (2003) 'Young children and the natural world', *Contemporary Issues in Early Childhood* 4(2): 167–178.

Vygotsky, L.S. (1978) *Mind in Society: The Development of Higher Psychological Processes*. Cambridge, MA: Harvard University Press (eds M. Cole, V. John-Steiner, S. Schriber and E. Souberman).

White, R. (2004) Young Children's Relationship with Nature: Its Importance to Children's Development and the Earth's Future [online]. Available at: http://www.childrennatureandyou.org/Young%20Children's%20Relationship%20with%20Nature-%20White.pdf (accessed 1 September 2012).

9

Play in Nature: Bush Kinder in Australia

Sue Elliott

Chapter overview

This chapter initially outlines current elements and issues related to play in nature in the Australian early childhood education context. The early childhood field is experiencing a raft of changes driven by the Australian federal government quality agenda (COAG, 2008). Key government publications (ACECQA, 2011; Commonwealth DEEWR, 2009) now offer systemic support for the provision of opportunities for play in nature in the early childhood years. Also, a number of broader social and health issues underscore these contextual elements in Australia. Like many western countries, Australia is witnessing the negative impacts of urban living, risk aversion, sedentary technology and limited outdoor play on children's health, well-being and development.

The current contextual elements and issues have provided a fertile backdrop for the emergence of initiatives to explicitly promote play in nature. A number of such initiatives are cited in this chapter, but of particular focus here is the Westgarth Kindergarten Bush Kinder. The Bush Kinder is a uniquely Australian interpretation of the forest preschools or nature kindergartens of Scandinavia and the UK and offers a different way of viewing and implementing preschool provision in

(Continued)

(Continued)

Australia. Elliott and Chancellor (2012) recently evaluated the establishment and operation of the Bush Kinder pilot and their insights into how the Bush Kinder programme impacted on all participants are outlined. The overall intent of this chapter is to demonstrate that play in nature is a well-supported emerging theme in the Australian early childhood education field (Bundy et al., 2009; Elliott, 2008; Moore, 2010).

The early childhood education landscape in Australia is undergoing significant change at many levels prompted by a federal government quality improvement agenda (COAG, 2008). The documents driving this agenda include the first ever national curriculum framework *Belonging, Being and Becoming: The Early Years Learning Framework for Australia* (Commonwealth DEEWR, 2009) and the *National Quality Standards* (ACECQA, 2011). Both offer significant support for children's engagement with natural elements and risk taking in outdoor play (ACECQA, 2011; Commonwealth DEEWR, 2009). Simultaneously, there are increasing concerns about children's health, well-being and development that have been linked to urbanisation, adult aversion to risky play, sedentary screen-based experiences and limited opportunities to access outdoor playspaces. According to a number of international publications (England Marketing, 2009; Lester and Maudsley, 2006; Moore and Cooper-Marcus, 2008; Munoz, 2009), outdoor play in nature is the antidote to these concerns. The current dynamic landscape in Australian early childhood education has inspired creativity in preschool provision and the Westgarth Kindergarten community has responded by establishing a pilot Bush Kinder programme. The evaluation of this Australian interpretation of forest preschools by Elliott and Chancellor (2012) has identified a range of positive impacts for all concerned. Play in nature is becoming a strong theme in Australian early childhood education, as illustrated by this chapter.

Australian contextual elements and issues

In 2008, the Council of Australian Governments (COAG) prepared a discussion paper outlining a national quality improvement agenda for early childhood education in Australia (COAG, 2008). The agenda highlighted the need for more tertiary-qualified early childhood professionals, a national early childhood curriculum framework and nationally agreed regulations integrated with a quality accreditation process for all early childhood service types. Furthermore, a universal access initiative that ensured all children attended 15 hours of preschool provision per week in the year before commencing school was instigated. The ongoing implementation of these government priorities has brought early childhood education to prominence in the Australian socio-political landscape generally, and prompted much critical reflection and discussion among early childhood professionals.

Two key documents, the first ever Australian early childhood curriculum statement *Belonging, Being and Becoming: The Early Years Learning Framework for Australia* (EYLF) (Commonwealth DEEWR, 2009) and the *National Quality Standards* (NQS) (ACECQA, 2011) offer both guidance and provocation essential to national quality improvement processes. In particular, a number of points within these documents explicitly alert educators to the importance of outdoor play in nature, and less explicitly, the potential links to be explored.

First, the EYLF (Commonwealth DEEWR, 2009) is informed by the overarching themes of *Belonging, Being and Becoming* and five broad principles namely: secure, respectful and reciprocal relationships; partnerships; high expectations and equity; respect for diversity; and ongoing learning and reflective practice. Further, eight pedagogical practices and five learning outcomes for children that guide practice are listed below.

Pedagogical practices:

- holistic approaches

- responsiveness to children

- learning through play

- intentional teaching

- learning environments

- cultural competence

- continuity of learning and transitions

- assessment for learning.

Learning outcomes for children:

- Children have a strong sense of identity.

- Children are connected with and contribute to their world.

- Children have a strong sense of well-being.

- Children are confident and involved learners.

- Children are effective communicators.

This multi-layered framework invites interpretation and critical reflection by practitioners and offers many potential links with outdoor play in natural settings. Some illustrative links are highlighted below:

- *Belonging, Being and Becoming* is most commonly interpreted from the perspective of people and their sociocultural contexts, but it can be extended to natural environments and how these impact on young children's belongings, beings and becomings (Elliott, 2010a). In natural playspaces, there are opportunities for children to experience relationships of *belonging* with nature and to capture moments of *being* in nature. Natural outdoor playspaces also offer agency, essential to *becoming* socially active and empowered participants in a rapidly changing global environment (Elliott, 2010b). Such experiences are critical to shifting ways of thinking and acting for a sustainable future.

- A natural outdoor playspace offers a unique and dynamic context for embedding the principles of the EYLF. For example, *partnerships* between families and educators can be promoted by working together to develop and maintain natural outdoor playspaces, and *respect for diversity* can be demonstrated with culturally relevant planting or nature-inspired artistic elements. Also, children's play in natural environments invites *reflective practice*. Educators might question how children are engaging with the dynamics of a natural playspace, what play affordances the space communicates and how we understand, interpret and document children's play and learning in this different space.

- Pedagogical practices offer another layer of possibility and natural learning environments are explicitly supported in the framework. It states: 'these spaces invite open-ended interactions, spontaneity, risk-taking, exploration, discovery and connection with nature' (Commonwealth DEEWR, 2009: 16). There is no shortage of opportunities for *learning through play* in natural playspaces from the negotiation of play scenarios with open-ended materials to the collaboration and physical skill required for moving a log or boulder. *Holistic approaches* are fundamental to understanding the interdependencies of humans and nature; playing in nature offers direct experience of these interdependencies and also opportunities for *intentional teaching* about nature.

- The potential for promoting the five outcomes for children can be readily interpreted in natural playspaces. Children's sense of identity

(1) is supported by opportunities to manipulate and explore natural elements; agency, resilience, risk management and interdependence may all contribute to identity. Opportunities to contribute to the world (2) are feasible when natural elements invite shared direct experiences such as gardening, composting and caring for animals. Well-being, both physical and mental (3), is positively impacted by play in nature and there is no shortage of research to substantiate this claim. Children must become confident and involved learners (4) in natural spaces. There is much to discover, investigate and wonder about as each day brings new possibilities inspired by the dynamics of nature. There is also much to communicate (5) about with peers and adults in natural spaces. Feelings about nature can be expressed, new language can be practised and nature offers evocative sensory experiences for interpretation and description.

Second, the NQS (ACECQA, 2011), as the first document to nationally align quality accreditation and regulations, offers direct guidance regarding natural elements, risk taking and outdoor play. For example, Quality Area 3: Physical Environments, explicitly states: 'children need opportunities to be outdoors as much as indoors' (ACECQA, 2011: 86) and the assessors' guide suggests that 'outdoor spaces that include plants, trees, edible gardens, rocks, mud, water and other elements from nature' (ACECQA, 2011: 89) may be observed. Also, embedded in Quality Area 3 are appropriate challenge and risk taking which are seen as integral to children's outdoor play opportunities (ACECQA, 2011: 102). The relevant regulations specify that a minimum of 7 square metres per child is required outdoors and that natural elements must be evident in the outdoor playspace.

When combined, the EYLF (Commonwealth DEEWR, 2009) and NQS (ACECQA, 2011) offer compelling provocation for early childhood educators to create natural playspaces and ensure that children have an abundance of opportunities to play outdoors and practise risk taking. Further provocation is also derived from the issues now arising related to children's health, well-being and development. While the iconic notion of all Australians being outdoors and active among the natural elements of bush, sand and surf is capitalised on in the media, in reality this is not so for many Australians and is increasingly not the case for young children. Opportunities to be active outdoors are declining for children in Australia (Planet Ark, 2011), reflecting internationally reported trends (England Marketing, 2009; Munoz, 2009; Skar and Krogh, 2009). The levels of obese or overweight children in Australia have reached 25 percent, and if such trends continue, this will reach 50 percent by 2020 (Magarey et al., 2001). This concern has in part led to the development of *National Physical Activity Recommendations for Children 0–5 Years* (Commonwealth DHA, 2010).

The recommendations state that screen-based activities for children under 2 years of age are unacceptable and only up to one hour per day is recommended for children aged 3–5. Access to outdoor play is another well-documented issue as increasingly children live in large houses on small allotments with limited outdoor spaces or in high-density inner-city apartments or townhouses (Hall, 2010).

As Moore and Cooper-Marcus (2008: 160) state: 'the cure for the lifestyle maladies of contemporary childhood seems glaringly obvious and simple: outdoor play in nature'. This response is well supported internationally by organisations such as the Early Childhood World Forum Nature Action Collaborative and the Children and Nature Network, and authors including Kahn and Kellert (2002), Lester and Maudsley (2006) and Munoz (2009). In Australia, advocacy for play in nature has emerged over the past decade through networks and organisations including Play Australia, Kidsafe New South Wales, Environmental Education in Early Childhood Victoria, the Western Australian Department of Sport and Recreation Nature Play (http://www.natureplaywa.org.au) and the Victorian Child and Nature Connection. Further, the media now regularly turn community attention to the perils of a childhood without nature, employing headlines such as 'Go back to the great outdoors' (Jean, 2010), 'Bush therapy' (Alexander, 2012) and 'Suffering an unnatural deficit: essential greens' (O'Connor, 2010). One response to these calls internationally has been the emergence of forest preschools and schools in the UK, Japan, Canada and New Zealand, and now this international movement has reached Australia. The current Australian contextual elements and issues have provided a fertile backdrop for the development of initiatives to explicitly promote play in nature for young children. The Westgarth Kindergarten Bush Kinder established in May 2011 offers an example of one such initiative, yet, somewhat rapidly, further bush and beach playgroups, preschool and school programmes are being established.

Box 9.1   Play, play theories and natural playspaces: play units, loose parts, affordances and risk

Links between nature and play have been identified in this chapter from the perspective of the Australian contexts and issues that have provoked Bush Kinder programmes. Nature can also be viewed as a dynamic and inviting canvas for play from play theory and research perspectives. Here, I highlight key elements

(Continued)

(Continued)

of play theory and research that support this view and lend weight to the argument for bush or beach kinder programmes.

Play is the fundamental way that children engage with the real world and is often described as a vehicle for learning in the early years. Theories about children's play have evolved over centuries from Plato (Jenkinson, 2001) to Parten (1932), Piaget (1962), Smilansky (1968), Vygotsky (1978) and Sutton-Smith (1997), and play-based programmes are widely advocated in early childhood education (Arthur et al., 2008; Commonwealth DEEWR, 2009; Victorian DEECD and VCAA, 2009). Opportunities for outdoor play, in particular, are to be valued and promoted (Frost, 1992; Greenman, 1988; Hart, 1979; Moore, 1986; Nabhan and Trimble, 1994; Rivkin, 1995; Weinstein and David, 1987), yet, in practice, such opportunities are often limited (Herrington, 2008; Maynard and Waters, 2007). Support for children's outdoor play, particularly in natural playspaces, is garnered here from four areas of play theory and research: play units, loose parts, affordances and risk.

- The classic work of Kritchevsky and Prescott (1977) describes the notion of simple, complex and super play units to inform outdoor play. It is the latter two types of play unit that juxtapose manipulable materials and offer a diversity of play possibilities to actively engage and sustain children's interests. Elliott (2008), Greenfield (2007), Greenman (1988), Moore (1986), Prescott (1987) and Veitch et al. (2005) have raised concerns about simple play units, typified by commercial fixed equipment installed on a patch of synthetic softfall, that pervade many early childhood, school and public play-spaces. Such play units lack the 'real life' (Nimmo, 2008) complexity, dynamism and manipulability of natural play-spaces that children crave and deserve in play.

- Nicholson's (1971) theory of loose parts described the promotion of play through manipulation of loose parts, such as open-ended play equipment and natural or reusable materials, but according to Fjortoft (2004) the best loose parts are natural ones. 'Children immersed in a treasury of loose parts that they can use for experimentation and construction' (Chawla, 2006: 68) suggests children's agency in play with loose parts. Such experiences also foster dramatic play and social skills (Maxwell et al., 2008). Natural loose parts are engaging and inspiring play elements in natural outdoor playspaces.

(Continued)

(Continued)

- Affordances theory describes the unique relationship between an individual and his or her environment; that relationship is not only about awareness, but also about perceiving the potential for function (Gibson, 1986). For example, a tree might convey a climbing affordance. Hefts (1988) and later Kytta (2002) created a taxonomy of affordances that categorised the environmental qualities evident within the play affordances observed. Fjortoft and Sageie (2000) confirmed that natural playspaces with green elements, loose parts and varied topography communicate high affordances to children.

- Risk is an inherent aspect of children's play, yet until recently risk has been viewed through a negative safety lens. A number of researchers have examined the benefits of risky play and tensions around risk for early childhood educators (Fenech et al., 2006; Little and Wyver, 2008; New et al., 2005; Sandseter, 2007; Stephenson, 2003). Risk is an individual and contextual matter – each playspace is different and each child is different (Stine, 1997) – and early childhood educators must make ongoing professional decisions about risk (Elliot and Blanchet-Cohen, 2009; Maynard and Waters, 2007). Natural playspaces in particular are rich contexts for experiencing risk and practising risk-management skills (Fjortoft and Sageie, 2000; Waters and Begley, 2007).

Figure 9.1   Child and leaf. Just as this child views the world differently through a leaf skeleton, Bush Kinder programmes offer a different way of viewing preschool provision

Case study: Westgarth Kindergarten Bush Kinder

Westgarth Kindergarten is located in Melbourne, a capital city of four million inhabitants in the state of Victoria, Australia. The kindergarten is sited approximately 6 km north-east of the city centre and is best described as a typical community-owned and managed early childhood service for children aged 3 to 5. The kindergarten regularly offers sessional early childhood programmes for two 4-year-old groups of about 25 children each (12 hours per week) and one 3-year-old group of about 20 children (4 hours per week). The centre is managed by a parent committee and employs a small team of teachers and assistants to implement the programme and a teaching director to manage the service. The kindergarten has a reputation for promoting children's outdoor play in their natural playspace, and the local parent community has responded positively to the predominately outdoor programme over many years. In 2010, the Australian government announced a universal access initiative that would require all 4-year-olds to attend 15 hours of preschool per week (an increase of 3 hours per week) to be implemented from January 2013. Like many other similar services, the Westgarth Kindergarten community's response was that such an increase in hours would lead to loss of the centre's much-valued 3-year-old group, due to space and time constraints. The Westgarth Kindergarten Committee and educators proactively responded to this concern by developing a pilot Bush Kinder programme in 2011. This new programme would align with the kindergarten's outdoor play ethos and permit the additional 3 hours of preschool to be undertaken in a local bushland setting as a regular excursion to augment the 12 hours undertaken at the kindergarten.

Establishment and operation

To develop and manage the new pilot programme, the Westgarth Kindergarten Committee, in close collaboration with the director, established a Bush Kinder Sub-Committee. An initial step was the drafting of a Bush Kinder vision to guide the pilot programme's development. The vision, documented below, well encapsulates concerns about children and their families as participants in the local community, particularly in relation to their connections with nature, health and well-being.

Bush Kinder vision for the Westgarth community and beyond:

- a community with a closer connection with nature

- a community that values and participates in nature-based activities more regularly

(Continued)

(Continued)

- a healthier and more environmentally aware community
- a well connected and cohesive community
- creative, independent and resilient children (Westgarth Kindergarten, 2011).

The establishment of the pilot also involved negotiation with the Department of Education and Early Childhood Development (DEECD) to determine how to proceed within regulations and to ensure risk-management policies addressed aspects including weather alerts, snakes, stray dogs and bushfire. Site selection in the local geographic area and subsequently within the Darebin Parklands was carefully considered from the perspectives of proximity, supervision, risk management, play affordances and accessibility. Also, consultation with relevant stakeholders occurred including: the local Darebin Council; the Darebin Parklands Association Committee of Management; current and prospective parents; and professionals with expertise in outdoor nature play research. As with many new community-based ventures, funding was a factor and sponsorship was sought and provided by some local businesses.

The Westgarth Kindergarten Bush Kinder pilot programme began in May 2011 with one of the kindergarten's 4-year-old groups. The participating children attended the home kindergarten for two 6-hour

Figure 9.2   Mud play. Mud, the quintessential Bush Kinder experience, in appropriate wet weather clothing, of course!

(Continued)

(Continued)

sessions and the Bush Kinder for one 3-hour session per week, making a total of 15 hours per week. The Bush Kinder operated on Wednesdays for two sub-groups of the 4-year-old group, one sub-group in the morning (9.15 a.m. to 12.15 p.m.) and the other in the afternoon (1.15 p.m. to 4.15 p.m.). Two teachers and often additional parent volunteers worked with each group of 12–14 children during the 3-hour Bush Kinder session. The Bush Kinder venue was located approximately 2.5 km from Westgarth Kindergarten in the Darebin Parklands, Alphington. Beyond these operational aspects, in establishing the programme the teachers drew on their early childhood philosophical and pedagogical understandings and also on their interpretations of the national early childhood curriculum framework (Commonwealth DEEWR, 2009).

Evaluation

The purpose of the Bush Kinder evaluative study undertaken by Elliott and Chancellor (2012) was to inform further development of the pilot programme as part of Westgarth Kindergarten's ongoing operation, but also to inform other early childhood services that may wish to establish similar programmes. The study focused on the impacts of the Bush Kinder pilot programme for teachers, children, their families and the local community, the challenges experienced and factors perceived as critical to the ongoing success of the Bush Kinder programme. The evaluative study was conducted during November and December 2011 towards the conclusion of the first year of the pilot.

An outcomes-based evaluation model as described by Wadsworth (1997: 98) was employed to examine the effectiveness of the Bush Kinder pilot programme. This model focuses on the long-term effects of services or programmes by attempting to check against broader goals or philosophical mission statements and importantly is open-ended, inviting the emergence of unexpected findings. The evaluative study methods included audio-recorded interviews with teachers, questionnaires completed by parents and an audio-recorded teacher–parent focus group discussion. Elliott and Chancellor (2012) employed interpretive analysis (Denzin and Lincoln, 2003) to identify impacts of the pilot programme on participants from the collated data.

Overall, the collated responses offered a clear and highly positive consensus about the value of the Westgarth programme for all participants. The following paragraphs highlight the positive impacts described for parents, children, teachers and the community.

(Continued)

(Continued)

Parents: Parents described learning more about their children and some, how relationships with their children had been enhanced. 'I love mud cakes and the glee of jumping in puddles. I saw how much fun it is to be a kid and how much as a parent we can learn from them. I learnt to trust, give space and time to her and myself' (Parent). Relationships appeared to be fostered by parents and grandparents sharing their childhood stories about play in response to the children's Bush Kinder experiences. Parents appreciated opportunities to slow down at Bush Kinder, be involved in different ways in the kindergarten programme and share specific knowledge or skills. They also became keen observers of their children's play at Bush Kinder and more readily identified the 'value of unrestricted outdoor play' and the potential of visits to parks and camping holidays with their children. At the inaugural Bush Kinder parent group, a strong sense of trailblazing and ownership of the new initiative was conveyed when parents described conversations with friends, relatives and community members.

Teachers: For both teachers, the Bush Kinder experience promoted professional growth offering 'an opportunity to push myself' or 'new life in my teaching'. There were multiple professional growth aspects, including the use of new technologies for online in-situ research with

Figure 9.3 Tree climbing. Risk management, care and respect for others, social interaction, constructing understandings about insect damage and opportunities to practice physical skills were all integral to climbing this dead tree at Bush Kinder

(Continued)

(Continued)

children, professional responses to print and electronic media requests and participation with the children in snake and dog risk management training. Confidence in one's abilities as a teacher was considered vital as Bush Kinder was described as a 'deeper experience that challenges all your teaching'. The impact of a natural bushland setting that lacked the typical equipment of built kindergartens was keenly felt and promoted an intensity of relationships. As one teacher stated: 'It's all about relationships, belonging and community … the difference is there is no stuff, so the relationships are intensified; your role as a teacher is freed and you become stronger without clutter; it is really quite empowering.' Bush Kinder continues to be an empowering professional process for the teachers involved.

Children: The teachers commented on the impacts of the programme on children's play, particularly the changing types of play, group dynamics and relationships, physical skills and observation skills. For example, less gendered play was observed in the Bush Kinder programme and the play evolved from predictable physical games such as chasing and hiding to more dramatic and imaginative play scenarios as children became more familiar with the bushland setting. Children were often observed caring for and supporting each other with challenges such as moving a log or rock, and children's attitudes towards nature and knowledge about nature appeared enhanced. It was acknowledged in the evaluative study that children were not direct participants, but there is much potential for research with children in the Bush Kinder programme.

Community: The impacts on the community were both positive and varied. Collaborative relationships were established between the Bush Kinder participants and the Darebin Parklands park rangers. For example, the teachers, children and rangers worked together on a native revegetation project. Children became visible in the community as regular park visitors became aware of their playful presence each week. Families described accessing Darebin Parklands more often, particularly revisiting to show other family members or friends where the children played at Bush Kinder. Also, the Bush Kinder supported various professional, government and media visits that raised the profile of the programme well beyond the local area.

Future directions

The evaluative study highlighted a number of areas for action to promote the ongoing development of the Bush Kinder programme.

- Policy review: a review of policies was considered relevant to determine their usefulness and appropriateness in the light of

(Continued)

(Continued)

the initial pilot experience. In particular, the drafting of a com-
munications/media policy was identified as essential to ensure a
clear and consistent message about the Bush Kinder vision and
its implementation was publicly conveyed.

- The teacher's role: the significance of the teacher's professional
  journey was acknowledged in the study. Their role in observing,
  interpreting and documenting children's learning in the different
  bushland setting was paramount to the success of the programme, and a need was identified to create opportunities for
  the teachers to critically reflect about pedagogy and philosophy.

- Parent engagement: while parents were engaged in the Bush
  Kinder programme, both on-site and via web-based media, they
  indicated that further strategies for engagement could be implemented, such as involvement in parklands projects.

- Government role: as a new initiative in response to the universal
  access directive, some regulatory negotiations were required, but
  ongoing advocacy and representation to government was identified
  as critical to better facilitate regulatory provision for programmes.

- Location: drawing on the site selection experience of the Bush
  Kinder Sub-Committee, the creation of a site selection criteria list
  was considered a proactive step in supporting others establishing similar programmes.

- Funding: while the programme was established and principally
  funded within the kindergarten's budget, with some external sponsorship, its long-term economic viability required a full assessment.

- Research: participants in the evaluative study recognised that the
  research conducted was the first about an Australian Bush Kinder
  programme and that there was much potential for further
  research. Possibilities identified included investigation of children's perspectives about Bush Kinder and exploration of the
  pedagogical role of teachers in such settings.

It is anticipated that the above actions will not only assure the future
of the Westgarth Kindergarten Bush Kinder, but also inform others
exploring this new approach to preschool provision in Australia. The
following statement from a Bush Kinder parent confirms why an
ongoing commitment to such programmes is essential from her
child's perspective:

> She would wake up and ask if it was going to be a Bush Kinder day,
> every day for the first 10 weeks! She loved the mud and the freedom.
> She loved learning to climb trees. Discovering bugs and fairies.
> Excavating and hanging out with friends. She loved the space and the
> softness. The open air, the weather, the rainbows, nests and especially
> the rocks and jumping. (Parent participant at a focus group)

Conclusion

A small, but growing number of early childhood services and schools are now establishing bush or beach programmes in Australia, and a new professional network is emerging to proactively share experiences and challenges. There are questions around many aspects of such programmes, from the practicalities of toileting to alignment with the relevant government documents (ACECQA, 2011; Commonwealth DEEWR, 2009), the potential for Australian Bush Kinder training and the incorporation of Indigenous perspectives. However, the current contextual elements and issues initially described here are both supportive and dynamic, and the time is right for creative responses to preschool provision in natural settings.

Further reading

The first two books listed here expand on the work being done in Australia to reconnect children with their environment:

Elliott, S. (2010) 'Children in the natural world', in J. Davis (ed.) *Young Children and the Environment: Early Education for Sustainability*. Melbourne: Cambridge Press, pp. 43–75.

Planet Ark (2011) *Climbing Trees: Getting Aussie Kids Back Outdoors*. Sydney: Planet Ark.

This third book examines one of the traditions that has informed the Australian Bush Kinder initiative:

Williams-Siegfredsen, J. (2012) *Understanding the Danish Forest School Approach*. Oxon: Routledge.

Information for practice

Practitioners can reflect on how a collaborative approach between parents, the community and academics on a small scale can influence practice on a much wider platform. What might prevent you from doing the same in your setting?

References

Alexander, L. (2012) 'Bush therapy', *Melbourne's Child*, September, pp. 16–18.

Arthur, L., Beecher, B., Death, E., Dockett, S. and Farmer, S. (2008) *Programming and Planning in Early Childhood Settings*, 4th edn. Sydney: Nelson.

Australian Children's Education and Care Quality Authority (ACECQA) (2011) *Guide to the National Quality Standard*. Available at: http://acecqa.gov.au/storage/3%20-%20 Guide%20to%20the%20National%20Quality%20Standard%20FINAL.pdf (accessed 8 November 2012).

Bundy, A.C., Luckett, O., Tranter, P., Naughton, G., Wyver, S., Ragen, J.L. and Spies, G. (2009) 'The risk is that there is "no risk": a simple, innovative intervention to increase children's activity levels', *International Journal of Early Years Education* 17(1): 33–45.

Chawla, L. (2006) 'Learning to love the natural world enough to protect it', *Barn* 2: 57–78.

Commonwealth of Australia Department of Education, Employment and Workplace Relations (Commonwealth DEEWR) (2009) *Belonging, Being and Becoming: Early Years Learning Framework for Australia.* Canberra: Commonwealth DEEWR.

Commonwealth of Australia Department of Health and Ageing (Commonwealth DHA) (2010) National Physical Activity Recommendations for Children 0–5 Years [online]. Available at: http://www.health.gov.au/internet/main/publishing.nsf/Content/npra-0-5yrs-brochure (accessed 8 November 2012).

Council of Australian Governments (COAG) (2008) *A National Quality Framework for Early Childhood Education and Care: A Discussion Paper.* Canberra: COAG.

Denzin, N.K. and Lincoln, Y.S. (2003) 'Introduction: the discipline and practice of qualitative research', in N.K. Denzin and Y.S. Lincoln (eds) *Strategies of Qualitative Inquiry,* 2nd edn. Thousand Oaks, CA: Sage, pp. 1–32.

Elliot, E. and Blanchet-Cohen, N. (2009) 'The possibilities and tensions of creating outdoor space with young children', in N.J. Harper (ed.) *Proceedings of Get Outside! It's in Our Nature Forum.* Available at: http://www.childnature.ca/wp-content/uploads/2009/02/get-outside-research-session-1.pdf (accessed 30 September 2009).

Elliott, S. and Chancellor, B. (2012) *Westgarth Kindergarten Bush Kinder Evaluation Report.* Westgarth, Melbourne: Westgarth Kindergarten and RMIT University.

Elliott, S. (ed.) (2008) *The Outdoor Playspace: Naturally.* Sydney: Pademelon Press.

Elliott, S. (2010a) 'Natural playspaces', *Community Child Care Victoria Early Years,* Term 1, pp. 11–14.

Elliott, S. (2010b) 'Children in the natural world', in J. Davis (ed.) *Young Children and the Environment: Early Education for Sustainability.* Melbourne: Cambridge Press, pp. 43–75.

England Marketing (2009) Report to Natural England on Childhood and Nature: A Survey on Changing Relationships with Nature across Generations [online]. Available at: http://www.englandmarketing.co.uk (accessed 20 December 2010).

Fenech, M., Sumsion, J. and Goodfellow, J. (2006) 'The regulatory environment in long day care: a "double edged sword" for early childhood professional practice', *Australian Journal of Early Childhood* 31(3): 49–59.

Fjortoft, I. (2004) 'Landscape as playscape: the effects of natural environments on children's play and motor development', *Children, Youth and Environments* 14(2): 21–44.

Fjortoft, I. and Sageie, J. (2000) 'The natural environment as a playground for children: landscape description and analyses of a natural playscape', *Landscape and Urban Planning* 48: 83–97.

Frost, J. (1992) *Play and Playscapes.* Albany, NY: Delmar.

Gibson, J. (1986) *The Ecological Approach to Visual Perception.* Mahwah, NJ: Lawrence Erlbaum.

Greenfield, C. (2007) Outside is Where we Need to Be [online]. Available at: http://www.manukau.ac.nz (accessed 22 May 2008).

Greenman, J. (1988) *Caring Spaces, Learning Spaces: Children's Environments that Work.* Redmond, WA: Exchange Press.

Hall, T. (2010) *The Life and Death of the Australian Backyard,* CSIRO. Melbourne: Collingwood.

Hart, R. (1979) *Children's Experience of Place.* New York: Irvington.

Hefts, H. (1988) 'Affordances of children's environments: a functional approach to environmental description', *Children's Environments Quarterly* 5(3): 29–37.

Herrington, S. (2008) 'Perspectives from the ground: early childhood educators' perceptions of outdoor playspaces at childcare centres', *Children, Youth & Environments* 18(2): 64–87.

Jean, D. (2010) 'Go back to the great outdoors', *The Adelaide Advertiser* [online]. Available at: http://www.adelaidenow.com.au (accessed 1 October 2010).

Jenkinson, S. (2001) *The Genius of Play.* Melbourne: Hawthorn Press.

Kahn, P.H. and Kellert, S.R. (eds) (2002) *Children and Nature.* Cambridge, MA: MIT Press.

Kritchevsky, S. and Prescott, E. with Walling, E. (1977) *Planning Environments for Young Children: Physical Space*, 2nd edn. Washington, DC: NAEYC.

Kytta, M. (2002) 'Affordances of children's environments in the context of cities, small towns, suburbs and rural villages in Finland and Belarus', *Journal of Environmental Psychology* 22: 109–123.

Lester, S. and Maudsley, M. (2006) *Play, Naturally: A Review of Children's Natural Play.* London: Children's Play Council.

Little, H. and Wyver, S. (2008) 'Outdoor play: does avoiding the risks reduce the benefits?', *Australian Journal of Early Childhood* 33(2): 33–40.

Magarey, A., Daniels, L.A. and Boulton, J.C. (2001) 'Prevalence of overweight and obesity in Australian children and adolescents: assessment of 1985 and 1995 data against new standard international definitions', *Medical Journal of Australia* 174: 561–564.

Maxwell, L.E., Mitchell, M.R. and Evans, G.W. (2008) 'Effects of play equipment and loose parts on preschool children's outdoor play behaviour: an observational study and design intervention', *Children, Youth and Environments* 18(2): 37–63.

Maynard, T. and Waters, J. (2007) 'Learning in the outdoor environment: a missed opportunity', *Early Years* 27(3): 255–265.

Moore, D. (2010) 'Only children can make secret places: children's secret places in early childhood settings', *Everychild* 15(3): 6–7.

Moore, R.C. (1986) *Childhood's Domain.* London: Croom Helm.

Moore, R.C. and Cooper-Marcus, C. (2008) 'Healthy planet, healthy children: designing nature into the daily spaces of childhood', in S.R. Kellert, J. Heerwagen and M. Mador (eds) *Biophilic Design: The Theory, Science and Practice of Bringing Buildings to Life.* Hoboken, NJ: Wiley, pp. 153–203.

Munoz, S. (2009) Children in the Outdoors: A Literature Review [online]. Available at: http://www.countrysiderecreation.org.uk/Children%20Outdoors.pdf (accessed 20 December 2010).

Nabhan, G. and Trimble, S. (1994) *The Geography of Childhood.* Boston, MA: Beacon Press.

New, R.S., Mardell, B. and Robinson, D. (2005) 'Early childhood education as risky business: going beyond what's safe to discovering what's possible', *Early Childhood Research and Practice* 7(2): 1–18.

Nicholson, S. (1971) 'How not to cheat children: the theory of loose parts', *Landscape Architecture* 62(1): 30–35.

Nimmo, J. (2008) 'Young children's access to *real life*: an examination of the growing boundaries between children in childcare and adults in the community', *Contemporary Issues in Early Childhood* 9(1): 3–13.

O'Connor, T. (2010) 'Suffering an unnatural deficit: essential greens', *The Australian* [online]. Available at: http://www.theaustralian.com.au/news/health-science/suffering-an-unnatural-deficit-essential-greens/story-e6frg8y6-1225866383176 (accessed 14 May 2010).

Parten, M.B. (1932) 'Social participation among preschool children', *Journal of Abnormal & Social Psychology* 27: 243–269.

Piaget, J. (1962) *Play, Dreams and Imitation in Childhood.* New York: Norton.

Planet Ark (2011) *Climbing Trees: Getting Aussie Kids Back Outdoors.* Sydney: Planet Ark.

Prescott, E. (1987) 'The environment as the organiser of intent childcare settings', in C. Weinstein and T. David (eds) *Spaces for Children.* New York: Plenum Press, pp. 73–88.

Rivkin, M. (1995) *The Great Outdoors: Restoring Children's Rights to Play Outside.* Washington, DC: NAEYC.

Sandseter, E.B.H. (2007) 'Categorising risky play: how can we identify risk-taking in children's play?', *European Early Childhood Education Research Journal* 15(2): 237–252.

Skar, M. and Krogh, E. (2009) 'Changes in children's nature based experiences near home: from spontaneous play to adult controlled, planned and organised activities', *Children's Geographies* 7(3): 339–354.

Smilansky, S. (1968) *The Effects of Socio-dramatic Play on Disadvantaged Preschool Children.* New York: Wiley.

Stephenson, A. (2003) 'Physical risk-taking: dangerous or endangered?', *Early Years* 3(1): 35–43.

Stine, L. (1997) *Landscapes for Learning: Creating Outdoor Environments for Children and Youth.* New York: Wiley.

Sutton-Smith, B. (1997) *The Ambiguity of Play.* Cambridge, MA: Harvard University Press.

Veitch, J., Bagley, S., Ball, K. and Salmon, J. (2005) 'Where do children play? A qualitative study of parents' perceptions of influences on children's active free-play', *Health & Place* 12(4): 383–393.

Victorian Department of Education and Early Childhood Development (DEECD) and Victorian Curriculum Assessment Authority (VCAA) (2009) *The Victorian Early Years Learning and Development Framework.* Melbourne: DEECD & VCAA.

Vygotsky, L. (1978) 'The role of play in development', in *Mind in Society* (trans. M. Cole). Cambridge, MA: Harvard University Press, pp. 92–104.

Wadsworth, Y. (1997) *Everyday Evaluation on the Run,* 2nd edn. St Leonards, NSW: Allen & Unwin.

Waters, J. and Begley, S. (2007) 'Supporting the development of risk taking behaviours in the early years: an exploratory study', *Education 3–13* 35(4): 365–377.

Weinstein, C. and David, T. (1987) *Spaces for Children.* New York: Plenum Press.

Westgarth Kindergarten (2011) Bush Kinder Vision [online]. Available at: http://www.wgkg.vic.edu.au/bush-kinder (accessed 10 February 2012).

10

Aboriginal Children's Participation and Engagement in Bush School

Libby Lee-Hammond and Elizabeth Jackson-Barrett

Chapter overview

In this chapter, we will discuss an outdoor learning project with young Aboriginal children (4–8 years), their teachers and their community in Perth, Western Australia. Due to the location of this project in the Perth region, there are no forests nearby; wild spaces within a short drive from the school are native bush areas and hence we refer to our outdoor learning project as 'Bush School' rather than 'Forest School'.

The reader will learn how a local community worked together to provide experiences for young children in an outdoor setting that enabled them to learn and experience the outdoors in a culturally appropriate way. This chapter will provide an important voice in the literature regarding outdoor learning, since it specifically works within an Aboriginal community context and emphasises traditional cultural knowledge about relationships with nature and a sense of belonging in the natural world. Teachers in a range of settings could adapt the experiences described in this chapter to local situations. More importantly, teachers involved in this (or other) outdoor learning experiences are provided with the opportunity to learn first-hand about traditional ways of 'knowing, being and doing' (Martin, 2005), and

(Continued)

(Continued)

this has enormous potential for programming when back in the brick-and-mortar classroom.

An important feature of this chapter is the incorporation of traditional cultural knowledge and spiritual connection to place that is highly significant for Aboriginal students and the communities to which they belong. The cultural perspectives discussed in this chapter may also be relevant for educators working with other First Nations communities such as the Pacific Islands, Australia, New Zealand, Scandinavia, Asia, Canada and North and South America.

Setting the scene

As a matter of respect and following the protocol of *'country'* it is important as the authors that we inform you, the reader, of some of the elements of *Noongar boodjar* (country) as a way of connecting. For those of you who are unfamiliar with this, *Noongar boodjar* (country) is located in the south-west corridor of Western Australia and extends from the south of Geraldton along the coast to Cape Leeuwin, continuing south to Esperance and then straight north-west to re-join the coast at Geraldton. It is an area of almost 3,000,000 hectares with 1,600 km of coastline; and it is a region that occupies 14 regional language groups (Green, 1984: 1). Our Bush School operates within the traditional *Whadjuck* area.

The outdoor setting in which the Bush School takes place is a wetlands area called *Walliabup* (this is the lake's traditional name according to the *Noongar* people of the region). The *Beeliar* wetlands are made up of a chain of lakes and *Walliabup* is an important aspect in this chain. *Walliabup* provides one of the last habitats for the endangered *karrak* (Carnaby Cockatoos) as well as the *Maarli* (Black Swan) and is host to numerous migrating birds. There are also *koya* (frogs), *booyi* (tortoises) and *nornt* (tiger snakes) living in the wetlands. Traditionally, the wetlands have great spiritual significance to the *Noongars* and hosted semi-permanent campsites for the *Beeliar Noongars* of the area and provided them with an abundantly rich source of food. This area is also where social and cultural obligations were fulfilled through traditional ceremonies, for *marman, yok and koolungar* (men, women and children). The *moyootj* (swamp area) is the source of an important story about how fire was stolen from the moon and brought to the *Beeliar Noongars* (see http://www.savenorthlake.com.au/documents/other/Firestick.pdf). The project was a collaboration between Aboriginal families in the local community, a local primary school, Murdoch University, and the local shire, which funded the project.

Twenty *Noongar Koolunger* (children), aged 4–7, took part one day a week in a term-long Bush School. The children were enrolled from Kindergarten to Year 3, and some of the children were siblings. The children were transported to the site by bus and were accompanied by a *Noongar* Elder, respectfully referred to as *Uncle*, as well as the school's Aboriginal Education Assistant, one classroom teacher, two members of the Murdoch research team and a project officer (who was also a parent).

Background

Aboriginal children's sense of cultural identity is known to have a clear impact on their school-based achievement and is jeopardised by the mainstream curriculum and poor integration of Indigenous knowledge in the classroom (Kickett-Tucker, 2008). In addition, psychological well-being is promoted when cultural identity is clarified and strengthened (Taylor and Usborne, 2010). Hence, this project sought to strengthen the cultural identity of Aboriginal children in order to improve their well-being and their academic success.

The gap in educational and social outcomes for Aboriginal students in Australia, compared to non-Aboriginal students, mirrors similar trends in other nations with Indigenous populations (Harrison, 2011; Taylor and Usborne, 2010). Numerous costly government initiatives have been trialled with limited success while other Aboriginal-led initiatives have been more successful; these were characterised by school leaders engaging local Elders to be their mentors, and this approach has brought enormous benefits to student learning and community participation in education (Commonwealth of Australia, 2012).

Traditionally, Elders had the responsibility for passing on important learning to *koolunger* (children). This learning was almost inevitably in the outdoors and was based around respect for and care for *country*, and the lessons needed to survive and thrive in a harsh climate. Language, kinship systems and The Law, Dreaming stories, weaving, tool making, hunting and gathering skills were passed on by Elders to the next generation orally and by modelling and demonstration. These practices were documented thoroughly by Coombs, Brandl and Snowdon (1984) who noted an exemplary instance where mothers taught young children how to find and dig for bush yams: 'they did not discuss the procedures; they just went and found the yams ... the children watched' (p. 97). Since the early days of colonisation when Aboriginal people were forbidden by white settlers to speak their own language or practise many of their traditional ceremonies, much of the rich culture and language has disappeared. In particular, several hundred Aboriginal languages have been lost (Bonython, 2003). There are some aspects of culture that can only be understood in the mother tongue and hence the practices and beliefs of some language groups have been marred forever by colonisation (Bonython, 2003). Many Aboriginal people now live in large cities and towns, adding to the complexity of maintaining a connection to natural places. What was previously a life completely in tune with nature, the seasons, the animals, the plants and a sustainable human inhabitation of the Earth, has been replaced by educational, social, emotional and economic disadvantage (Beresford et al., 2012). However, Aboriginal people the authors have *yarned with* (spoken to) do express an innate sense of connection to *country* and it is clear that despite the losses, that importance of place and identity has not been diluted in the hearts and minds of Aboriginal people in 21st-century Australia. Inevitably, when Aboriginal people meet all over Australia, the first words spoken are 'where you from?' The answer creates a discourse of either connecting to each other by way of *country* or by means of an already established relationship with someone from that *'country'* — connection to *country* establishes relationships through belonging, identity and well-being. This is consistent with Moreton-Robinson's (2003) thoughtful consideration of place and identity in Aboriginal consciousness in the current century.

One major issue contributing to the significantly lower educational outcomes for Aboriginal students is poor school attendance rates. The thinking behind addressing educational disadvantage has tended to be focused on improving attendance, which presumes that better attendance will improve outcomes and that the school classroom provides the most appropriate curriculum. However, the authors have often pondered the quality of school learning environments and their appropriateness for Aboriginal students. In light of the oral tradition of the Aboriginal cultures and the historic use of natural environments to share knowledge, it seemed a worthwhile endeavour to explore the possibility that an outdoor learning programme with a cultural emphasis might well go some way to bridging the gap in Aboriginal learning outcomes.

In order to undertake this work within an Aboriginal community, it was vital to develop a respectful relationship with the Elders and families who were part of the community. In the case of the Bush School described in this chapter, the authors worked closely with local Elders to receive initial support for the idea of Bush School and to refine the detail of its delivery. Approval and support from Elders in the initial stages of approaching the Bush School concept for Aboriginal students was a vital step in its development. This approach may be understood from an ecological perspective using Bronfenbrenner's

Ecological Systems Theory (1992), since it acknowledges and draws on the child's home, community and culture as the basis for developing an appropriate programme.

Box 10.1   Bronfenbrenner's Ecological Systems Theory

This theory provides insights into the significance of culture and community in shaping the child's experiences and hence their learning and growth. Bronfenbrenner (1992) saw the child's learning and development as being in relationship with multiple 'systems' such as family, school, culture, socio-economic status and the broader historical context in which the child is growing up. His work has had a lasting impact on the education of disadvantaged and marginalised students.

What is 'country'?

In a discussion of Aboriginal children's participation in a Bush School, it is very important to understand a significant spiritual concept about connection to the land. As a non-Aboriginal participant in this project, the author has endeavoured to faithfully represent this relationship with the land that is known as *'country'*. Rose (1996) provides a very comprehensive account of what *country* means to Aboriginal people:

> Country is a place that gives and receives life. Not just imagined or represented, it is lived in and lived with. Country in Aboriginal English is not only a common noun but also a proper noun. People talk about country in the same way that they would talk about a person: they speak to country, sing to country, visit country, worry about country, feel sorry for country, and long for country. People say that country knows, hears, smells, takes notice, takes care, is sorry or happy … country is a living entity with a yesterday, today and tomorrow, with a consciousness, and a will toward life. Because of this richness, country is home, and peace; nourishment for body, mind, and spirit; heart's ease. (1996: 7)

With this in mind, the Bush School has a unique emphasis on Aboriginal perspectives about *country* and this is drawn upon throughout the children's experiences in the outdoors. Further, having the focus on *country* exemplifies Martin's (2005) concept of 'relatedness', as *'country'* is an Aboriginal world view that Aboriginal students can connect and relate to; it is something they know and this in turn gives a sense of well-being when engaging in Bush School.

Forest School research and theory

The existing research and theory behind European and UK forest schools inform the Bush School concept. The earlier work of Knight (2009, 2011), Milchem (2011), O'Brien and Murray (2006) and Waller (2007) has provided a theoretical and practical framework for the conduct of a forest/bush school. In addition, the work of Sobel (2008) highlights the importance of children's relationship to place and connection to nature. Sobel's seven play motifs for children in nature are based on extensive observations of children spending time in the outdoors. The motifs, or principles, are:

Adventure – activities with a physical challenge

Fantasy and Imagination – stories, plays, dramatic play

Animal Allies – children's inherent empathy with wild and domestic animals

Maps and Paths – exploring local geographies

Special Places – forts, cubbies, hiding places

Small Worlds – miniature worlds that represent aspects of the 'big' world

Hunting and Gathering – treasure hunts, collecting things

(Sobel, 2008: 19–57)

Following Waller's (2007) work in the UK, the Bush School utilised the Leuven Involvement Scale (Laevers, 1994) to measure children's levels of involvement in experiences in the outdoors. Ratings of children's involvement levels were taken in both the outdoor setting and the classroom. Children's scores on involvement were unilaterally higher in the outdoor setting compared to those in the classroom; the overall rating for the outdoor setting was high with children 'continuously engaged in the activity and absorbed in it' (Laevers, 2005), while in the classroom the rating was medium whereby children were busy the whole time, but showed none of the energy and imagination captured in the outdoor setting. Some indicators in the original scale needed to be modified with regard to non-verbal signals since these have particular cultural interpretations. For example, eye contact is not necessarily an indication that a child is listening to what is being said. In some communities, eye contact with an adult is seen as disrespectful and hence there are *some* Aboriginal children whose eyes will wander when they are listening, as this is a culturally determined expectation. Laevers' scale describes an indicator of high-level involvement as 'without eyes wandering around space' but in the case of this research, it was deemed not to be an appropriate indicator because of the influence of culture on behavioural 'norms'.

Box 10.2   Laevers on child well-being and involvement

When we want to know how each of the children is doing in a setting, we first have to explore the degree to which children feel at ease, act spontaneously, and show vitality and self-confidence. All this indicates that their emotional **well-being** is OK and that their physical needs, the need for tenderness and affection, the need for safety and clarity, the need for social recognition, the need to feel competent and the need for meaning in life and moral value, are satisfied.

Involvement goes along with strong motivation, fascination and total implication: there is no distance between person and activity, no calculation of the possible benefits. Because of that, time perception is distorted (time passes by rapidly). Furthermore there is an openness to (relevant) stimuli and the perceptual and cognitive functioning has an intensity, lacking in activities of another kind. The meanings of words and ideas are felt more strongly and deeply. (Laevers, 2003: 15)

Bush School experiences

In this section, we explore the synergies between Aboriginal perspectives of learning and some of the key experiences of the Bush School and make connections to children's learning.

 Case study 1: Bush medicine

This is a brief case study about one boy who was intently listening to Uncle's stories of bush food and bush medicine. Uncle was explaining how to extract the nut from a seed to use for making flour. In extracting the seed from the sharp seed pod, the boy managed to cut the palm of his hand slightly and it bled. He immediately sought advice from the Elder as to what was a traditional treatment for bleeding, asking: 'What do Noongars do when they bleed?' On being asked this question, Uncle escorted the boy to a nearby tree and showed him a leaf that could be

(Continued)

(Continued)

wrapped around the cut to prevent infection. Several weeks after this event, the boy was able to recall every detail of what Uncle had told him. His first-hand experience of bush medicine had a lasting impact on his learning.

Figure 10.1 What to do when you bleed

Hunting and gathering

As Sobel (2008) notes, hunting and gathering are important and time-less themes in children's play. Experiences for young children to hunt and gather in the 21st century are few and far between. The odd bit of fishing or collecting berries is about the limit of our modern ver-sion of this in countries like Australia, particularly in large cities. However, a tradition of hunting native animals for food has existed in Aboriginal culture for thousands of years and is still practised today. Most often, this involves the use of spears, traps and boomerangs. In the Bush School, the Elder (Uncle) was well prepared to demonstrate to the children how to hunt and gather. The children were given pieces of dowel about 1.5 metres long with blunt edges and taught to hunt and gather. The dowel was used both as a spear and as a digging stick. The children enjoyed digging for bush onions, turtle eggs (large river stones hidden under the sand) and hunting kangaroos. Case study 2 below explains one of these experiences in detail.

Curriculum connections

The notion that the outdoors is a curriculum in itself is one that is gaining more and more recognition in Australian early childhood settings. The Australian Early Years Learning Framework specifically identifies children's connection with the world as an important outcome of early education, noting that educators promote this learning when they 'consider the nature of children's connectedness to the land' (Australian Government, 2009: 29). The framework also enshrines the notion that there is a spiritual dimension to this connection and that children should experience a sense of awe and wonder that promotes a sense of being and belonging. In providing experiences that were culturally relevant and engaging for young children, we also made very explicit links to the standard school curriculum areas in order to demonstrate to educators and school leaders that the outdoors is at least as significant for learning as a standard classroom.

 ## Case study 2: Spear throwing

One of the memorable tasks undertaken at the Bush School was an experience of hunting. In the context of understanding that the ancestors took only what they needed and ensured the species survived by taking, for example, half the eggs from a nest so the next generation could survive, the Elder in our Bush School introduced the children to hunting and gathering. Each child was issued with a piece of dowel and shown how to walk with it safely (adjacent to the body). The children were also taught the value of silence for stalking, as well as walking softly so as not to create vibrations that animals might feel. The children proceeded into the bush in single file; the last child in the line had responsibility for covering tracks. This created an atmosphere of excitement and intrigue as the children proceeded into the bush. Uncle had prepared and spread a kangaroo skin over a shrub and this was the 'prey'. The children were shown how to hold their spear on their shoulders and use a rocking motion to prepare their throw. They had turns at spearing the kangaroo and received immediate feedback about their throwing techniques.

After this experience, the children walked to a large clearing and lined up side by side to throw their spears as far as they could. We used this experience as an opportunity to make important connections to the school curriculum. We decided to measure the distances the spears were thrown and make comparisons. We used the spears

(Continued)

(Continued)

themselves to measure the distance, so, for example, Layla threw her spear 10 lengths, compared to Graham who threw his 14 spear lengths; we were able to consider the difference and decided to try again and compare the first throw to the second, and so on. Opportunities like this to link hands-on, real-life experiences to mathematical concepts are vital for children's development of concept.

Other curriculum links included history (the original use of spears), culture (the stories Uncle told of the 'old people' and how they hunted), geography (which parts of the landscape were likely hiding spots for different types of animals), physical education (walking softly, throwing technique) and science (the physics of throwing the spears, the life cycles of animals). In addition, Sobel's (2008) principles of *adventure* and *hunting and gathering* are both evident in this experience.

Figure 10.2 Young hunters

 Case study 3: Fishing traps

In this experience, children were invited to learn how to make a traditional fishing trap. Uncle showed them how to tie the lashings on the joins to make a frame and provided wooden fish with single

(Continued)

(Continued)

holes drilled in them. The fish were trapped at the end of the wading pool and spears were used to catch the fish. There were different roles for boys and girls in this game as per traditional practices. The boys built the traps and waded through the water to trap the fish, while the girls learned and danced the 'fishing dance', and were responsible for spearing and collecting the fish. Similar to the kangaroo hunting, this experience provided many curriculum links and additional opportunities for children to practise their fine and gross motor skills (tying the trap, wading through the water, guiding the trap, spearing the fish, dancing), and the inclusion of dance in this experience provided seamless integration of the performing arts. When the children revisited this game the next week, they introduced 'clapping sticks' and kept the rhythm while the dance took place.

Figure 10.3   Creating traps and playing the fishing game

 ## Case study 4: Cultural identity

Specific activities in this project were provided to strengthen and support Aboriginal children's cultural identity. Uncle used various resources to enable this. One experience was a particular highlight for the children and I use it to illustrate the significance of involving

(Continued)

(Continued)

knowledgeable Elders in Bush Schools for Aboriginal children. Uncle used paint to mark the children's faces with the *mopoke* (owl) totem he had been given permission to use from his Elders. The children waited silently as he carefully painted each one; the boys were painted in one way, the girls in another. Sharing the experience of the mopoke totem story creates the space where messages and meanings about the diversity of identity can be explored. The sharing of stories has been a way of communication across cultures for generations, and as such it creates a scaffold for understanding and sharing knowledge. It is through the experience of listening to stories that children are encouraged and involved in a naturalistic way that builds the confidence in them to explore diversity and difference, which, in turn, light the spirit of identity.

Box 10.3   Martin on identity

To know who you are in relatedness is the ultimate premise of Aboriginal worldview because this is the formation of identity. This is acquired through being immersed in situations, contexts, and elements through change and past, present and future. A child is guided through lifehood stages [...] from womb to tomb. Based on the theory, relatedness is to give function and service to the spirit of the child so that it emerges as the child grows and fulfils tasks of lifehood [...] it is not only physical, biological, emotional or cognitive but also spiritual and psychological. (Martin, 2005)

Figure 10.4   Mopoke Totem

On interviewing the Aboriginal Education Officer at the conclusion of the project, it was clear that these *Noongar koolungar* had not always experienced their cultural identity positively in the wider community. The Officer was very encouraged by the fact that, as a result of this project, the children grew to appreciate the beauty and wisdom of their culture and to see their cultural identity as something to treasure and be proud of.

Risk management

In the Australian bush, there are numerous animals whose bites are potentially fatal. Deadly snakes and spiders inhabit the general area where we conduct the Bush School. Children are taught about habitats for these creatures and encouraged to show great respect for animals in the wild. They are taught to identify and avoid likely homes for snakes and spiders (in thick scrub, under rocks and logs and near water). In addition, children are taught how to respond if they do stumble upon such a creature. When walking in grassy areas, they are encouraged to clap their hands and stamp their feet to ward off any snakes, and teachers are equipped with mobile phones and first aid kits in case of an emergency.

Further reading

To find out more about the early years curriculum in Australia, see:

Australian Government Department of Education, Employment and Workplace Relations (DEEWR) (2009) *Belonging, Being and Becoming: The Early Years Learning Framework for Australia.* Canberra: Commonwealth of Australia.

To better understand the research methodology used, access:

Laevers, F. (2003) 'Making care and education more effective through well being and involvement', in F. Laevers and L. Heylen (eds) *Involvement of Children and Teacher Style: Insights from an International Study on Experiential Education.* Leuven: Leuven University Press.

To learn more about Aboriginal culture and how it relates to young children's experiences of education, look at:

Martin, K. (2005) *Childhood, Lifehood and Relatedness: Aboriginal Ways of Being, Knowing and Doing,* in J. Phillips and J. Lampert (eds) *Introductory Indigenous Studies in Education.* Frenchs Forest, NSW: Pearson Education Australia.

Information for practice

We encourage you, in this chapter, to work collaboratively with local communities, embracing all stakeholders and inviting them to a shared experience that sustains practitioners, communities and children. We see possibilities for student teachers, who will work in contexts with Indigenous

(Continued)

(Continued)

students to enrich the teaching and learning of all curriculum areas and invite a further dimension of children's experiences to bring life to what it means to live sustainably, to appreciate and value cultural knowledge and experiences with a profound spiritual connection to place. Experiences such as Bush School provide rich opportunities for all *koolungar* (children) to engage and connect culturally with environments that are in their community's 'backyard'. It is these healthy environments which connect children to a strong spirit of well-being and light the spirit of identity.

Acknowledgement

The authors wish to acknowledge the support for this project offered by the Noongar Elders and their families in enabling the involvement of the children in this project. Thanks also to the staff at the school, who were open to new possibilities.

References

Australian Government Department of Education, Employment and Workplace Relations (DEEWR) (2009) *Belonging, Being and Becoming: The Early Years Learning Framework for Australia.* Canberra: Commonwealth of Australia.

Beresford, Q., Partington, G. and Gower, G. (eds) (2012) *Reform and Resistance in Aboriginal Education.* Perth: UWA Publishers.

Bonython, L. (2003) 'Aboriginal languages: too little, too late', *Second Language Learning and Teaching* 3 [online]. Available at: http://www.usq.edu.au/users/sonjb/sllt/ (accessed 20 September 2012).

Bronfenbrenner, U. (1992) 'Ecological systems theory', in R. Vasta (ed.) *Six Theories of Child Development: Revised Formulations and Current Issues.* London: Jessica Kingsley, pp. 187–249.

Commonwealth of Australia (2012) What Works Report: Success in Remote Schools [online]. Available at: http://www.whatworks.edu.au/upload/1341805220784_file_SuccessinRemoteSchools2012.pdf (accessed 7 September 2012).

Coombs, H.C., Brandl, M.M. and Snowdon, W.E. (1984) *A Certain Heritage: Programs for and by Aboriginal Families in Australia.* Centre for Resource and Environmental Studies, Monograph 9. Canberra: Australian National University.

Green, N. (1984) *Broken Spears: Aboriginals and Europeans in the Southwest of Australia.* Cottesloe, WA: Focus Education Services.

Harrison, N. (2011) *Teaching and Learning in Aboriginal Education,* 2nd edn. Melbourne: Oxford.

Kickett-Tucker, C. (2008) *Koordoormitj Culture, Identity and Self-esteem.* ARACY Grid Access, August [online]. Available at: http://www.aracy.org.au/index.cfm?pageName=publications_library&theme=A16D8A05-1EC9-79F9-594530ECF1FF2620 (accessed 30 October 2012).

Knight, S. (2009) *Forest Schools and Outdoor Learning in the Early Years.* London: Sage.

Knight, S. (2011) *Risk and Adventure in Early Years Outdoor Play: Learning from Forest Schools.* London: Sage.

Laevers, F. (ed.) (1994) *The Leuven Involvement Scale for Young Children*. Manual and video. Experiential Education Series, No. 1. Leuven: Centre for Experiential Education.

Laevers, F. (2003) 'Making care and education more effective through well being and involvement', in F. Laevers and L. Heylen (eds) *Involvement of Children and Teacher Style: Insights from an International Study on Experiential Education*. Leuven: Leuven University Press, pp. 13–24.

Laevers, F. (2005) 'The curriculum as means to raise the quality of ECE: implications for policy', *European Early Childhood Education Research Journal*, 13 (1): 17–30.

Martin, K. (2005) *Childhood, Lifehood and Relatedness: Aboriginal Ways of Being, Knowing and Doing*, in J. Phillips and J. Lampert (eds) *Introductory Indigenous Studies in Education*. Frenchs Forest, NSW: Pearson Education Australia.

Milchem, K. (2011) 'Breaking through concrete: the emergence of forest school in London', in S. Knight (ed.) *Forest School for All*. London: Sage, pp. 13–27.

Moreton-Robinson, A.M. (2003) 'I still call Australia home: Indigenous belonging and place in a white post colonising society', in S. Ahmed (ed.) *Uprootings/Regroundings: Questions of Home and Migration*. Oxford: Berg, pp. 23–40.

O'Brien, L. and Murray, R. (2006) *A Marvellous Opportunity for Children to Learn: A Participatory Evaluation of Forest School in England and Wales*. Forest Research, Farnham [online]. Available at: http://www.forestresearch.gov.uk/fr/INFD-5Z3JVZ (accessed 28 October 2012).

Rose, D. (1996) *Nourishing Terrains: Australian Aboriginal Views of Landscape and Wilderness*. Canberra: Australian Heritage Commission.

Sobel, D. (2008) *Childhood and Nature: Design Principles for Educators*. Portland, ME: Stenhouse.

Taylor, D.M. and Usborne, E. (2010) 'When I know who "we" are, I can be "me": the primary role of cultural identity clarity for psychological well-being', *Transcultural Psychiatry* 47(1): 93–111.

Waller, T. (2007) '"The trampoline tree and the swamp monster with 18 heads": outdoor play in the foundation stage and foundation phase', *Education 3–13* 35(4): 393–407.

11

Teaching Teachers to Use the Outdoor Environment in the USA

Christian Winterbottom and Vickie E. Lake

Chapter overview

The USA and Europe are contrasting examples when it comes to using outdoor learning environments. The USA has moved away from outdoor learning environments and towards lessons that are more didactic, while Europe has seen an increase in adventure playgrounds and forest schools. It has been argued that the outdoor play environment should be utilized as an extension of indoor classroom learning (Hart and Sheehan, 1986). Recent research (Olsen et al., 2011) has focused on informal outdoor learning spaces for children that include natural play areas; objects for the children to manipulate; and areas for gross motor activities such as swings, climbing units, open grass, and digging sites. Additionally, the outdoor environment offers types of service-learning opportunities that are different from those found indoors.

Imagine students planning and planting a garden in their school or collecting specimens and samples of flora at their local nature center. These are activities related to service-learning that integrate curriculum standards and outdoor learning. Using experiential learning, service-learning aids students in connecting their school curriculum with their community, at the same time increasing students' academic ability. This chapter (i) describes the need to integrate outdoor learning environment content area standards with service-learning standards; (ii) describes service-learning projects that have utilized the outdoor environment; and (iii) examines whether the outdoor service-learning projects significantly impacted on students socially.

Outdoor learning environments

The USA

In a time of competing play and leisure opportunities, outdoor play and learning experiences among children and youth seem to increasingly lose out against fast-paced, easily accessible, and often highly interactive electronic video games and other mainstream media. For adolescents, a 50 percent decrease in outdoor activities, such as camping, hiking, and walking, has been noted. At the same time, structured sports have doubled and passive, spectator-based leisure activities have increased sixfold (Doherty, 2004). Historically, children experienced most of their outdoor activities/learning during school. Unfortunately, in many schools across the USA, recess (break time) or developmental outside play has been dramatically cut. During elementary and middle grades, students have recess only three times a week, a number that drops to a level of 3 percent in high school (Lee et al., 2007).

In the USA, children are not going outside for play or learning. Using a national data set of 11,000 children, it was found that 30 percent of 3rd-graders had fewer than 15 minutes of recess a day (Barros et al., 2009). Recess or developmental play is often cut because of academic pressures or as punishment. A nationwide study on how 1st- through 5th-grade children spend their time in school established that on a randomly selected day, 21 percent of children did not have any recess and 39 percent of African American students versus 15 percent of Caucasian students did not have recess at all (Roth et al., 2003). Moreover, the same study suggests that 44 percent of children living below the poverty line are deprived of recess versus 17 percent of children living above the poverty line.

Fortunately, some US communities are utilizing outdoor service-learning by embracing beautification projects, nature centers, local parks and recreation centers, and growing food for pantries. In Boston, these types of initiative have spread with the introduction of the Boston Schoolyard program, which has seen a shift from using the outdoor environment as a place for special projects to becoming an instructional asset for everyday use (Manzo, 2008).

Europe

While the trend in the USA has been to move away from outdoor learning environments, and into more didactic, teacher-orientated lessons, the opposite has been happening in Europe, as indicated by the increase in adventure playgrounds and the development of the Forest School movement. Adventure playgrounds originated in Europe during World War II when Sorensen, a playground designer, noticed that children preferred playing in dirt and lumber more than playing on established playground equipment. After realizing that children had the most fun designing, building, and manipulating their environment, he created the formula for adventure playgrounds to include earth, fire, water, and creative materials (Adventure Playground Association, 2006).

Over the past 10–15 years, adventure playgrounds have regained prominence both on a local community level as well as on a national and policy level in many European countries (Chilton, 2003). Current estimations are that approximately 1,000 adventure playgrounds exist in Europe. These playgrounds are primarily located in Denmark, Switzerland, France, Germany, the Netherlands, England, and Germany. For example, Germany has more than 400 adventure playgrounds and England has more than 80 adventure playgrounds integrated into London's city landscape (Adventure Playground Association, 2006).

Adventure playgrounds function as a meeting place for children, youth, and the whole community by building friendships and skills. They are places that children can easily identify with and call their own because they helped design and build them. In their many forms and applications, adventure playgrounds provide unique opportunities for positive child and youth development (Staempfli, 2009), as well as ample possibilities for service-learning.

In the UK, there are now thousands of Forest School practitioners, offering opportunities in England, Scotland, Wales and Northern Ireland that involve children having regular contact with natural environments over an extended period of time, allowing them to become familiar and have contact with the natural environment (O'Brien, 2009). Forest Schools embrace similar concepts as service-learning pedagogy: Forest School takes place during school hours, occurs regularly, and is linked to national curricula and content standards.

Service-learning

Learn and Serve, America's National Clearinghouse, defines service-learning as 'a teaching and learning strategy that integrates meaningful community service with instruction and reflection to enrich the learning experience, teach civic responsibility, and strengthen communities' (Learn and Serve Clearinghouse, n.d.: 1). Through service-learning, students are challenged to grow as learners and citizens. Service-learning differs from community service or volunteerism in that it involves a mixture of learning objectives, service, and structured reflection. The practice affords students the opportunity to use what they learn in the classroom to make a difference in their community and the world around them (Taylor and Ballengee-Morris, 2004).

Connecting the learning objective to the service experience produces a balanced approach to experiential education, which benefits not only the one being served, but also the service provider (Furco, 1996). Service-learning has seen a rise in both popularity and practice over the past two decades. Each year, thousands of public schools across the USA engage their students in service-learning activities. One survey estimated 4.7 million students from kindergarten through 12th grade participated in service-learning during 2004 (Scales and Roehlkepartain, 2004). The survey further reported that 83 percent of school principals believed service-learning had a positive impact on academic activities, while 92 percent cited positive impacts on civic engagement.

As the practice of service-learning expands, the claims for what it can accomplish increases. What many educators do not realize is that there are service-learning standards. These standards, revised in 2008, include: Meaningful Service, Links to Curriculum, Reflection, Diversity, Youth Voice, Partnerships, Progress Monitoring, and Duration and Intensity (National Youth Leadership Council, 2008).

As comprehensive as the standards are, aligning them with academic standards is the teacher's responsibility. Moreover, these standards do not specify that service-learning is an indoor classroom activity. In fact, it would be difficult to effectively address community needs and work with community partners if children never left their classrooms. Therefore, service-learning activities become an opportunity for increasing outdoor educational experiences.

Standards for learning

The observed decline in outdoor opportunities may be because school districts have been pressured to concentrate on the core academic subjects (Lord, 2006; Lumby, 2010). It also reflects a distinction between *play* and *work* in school settings. Outdoor learning that is fun, interactive, and considered important in the UK (Lord, 2006; Lumby, 2010) and the USA (Winterbottom and Lake, in press), is still not as highly valued as the more direct instruction that takes place indoors.

In June 2010, the National Governors Association Center for Best Practices (NGA Center) and Council of Chief State School Officers (CCSSO) finalized the Kindergarten-12 Common Core State Standards

(CCSS; 2010). These standards, currently adopted by 48 states, two territories, and the District of Columbia, define rigorous skills and knowledge in English Language, Arts and Mathematics that need to be effectively taught and learned. The standards are:

- fewer, clearer, and higher, to best drive effective policy and practice

- aligned with college and work expectations, so that all students are prepared for success upon graduating from high school

- inclusive of rigorous content and applications of knowledge through higher-order skills, so that all students are prepared for the 21st century

- internationally benchmarked, so that all students are prepared for succeeding in our global economy and society

- research and evidence-based.

The Association for Supervision and Curriculum Development (ASCD) endorses the CCSS because they address educating the whole child through a broad and comprehensive curriculum (Carter, 2010). Subsequently, teachers who approach learning by focusing on the concepts of curricular integration and experiential learning (Lake and Jones, 2008, 2012), through thematic teaching (Caine and Caine, 1997), the Project Approach (Katz and Chard, 1989), and other constructivist practices (e.g. Bodrova and Leong, 2007; Copple and Bredekamp, 2009; DeVries and Zan, 1994) may find the CCSS a more natural fit for their classrooms since they espouse curriculum integration and allow teachers to utilize outdoor learning environments.

Typically, academic standards specify what students should know or be able to do and include content, performance, and proficiency descriptors. They require evidence that students have achieved or mastered the standards and to what degree. In order to achieve increased learning and understanding of the academic content, service-learning must be combined with specific subject matter in the school curriculum, match content standards, and utilize active or experiential learning (Billig, 2000). When service-learning is fully integrated with the curriculum, academic outcomes include the improved learning of academic subjects, better grades, and higher standardized test scores. To illustrate how curriculum standards can be taught through service-learning, connections between academic areas and service-learning are explained. However, to maximize the impact of service-learning on student achievement, several academic subjects should be integrated (Roberts, 2002).

Methodology

Program overview

Over the past seven years, a teacher education program located in a large research university in the southeastern USA and the local school district have been collaborating on service-learning. The structure of the program requires a large amount of time to be spent in field-based classrooms. In March of their sophomore year, approximately 60–80 preservice teacher (PST) candidates apply to the early childhood program; 30 applicants are selected and admitted to the program for the following fall semester. Once admitted, the preservice teachers' classes are sequenced and they travel together as a cohort for the next four semesters, or blocks, until graduation. The PSTs are made aware that they are accepted into a program that integrates academic content and service-learning using a cascading knowledge-of-practice model (Lake and Jones, 2008).

A cascading knowledge-of-practice service-learning model is one where the teacher educators teach service-learning pedagogy to the PSTs who are actively involved using service-learning in local schools. The PSTs then teach service-learning to the students in their field placement classrooms via the implementation of service-learning projects. Subsequently, the students teach others about service-learning through their community efforts. The integrated cascading approach offers students an opportunity to learn in a way that is most natural to them, as opposed to a segmented approach stressing isolated skills and concepts (Verducci and Pope, 2001). This model aligns itself with the national reform efforts that emphasize curriculum restructuring and establishes even closer links between curriculum and community.

Participants

The total number of service-learning participants included 132 preservice teachers and 3,500 students, prekindergarten to 2nd grade. Data for this chapter is comprised of the 130 consenting preservice teachers' service-learning lesson plans, questionnaires, and focus group interviews and 563 student responses, which represent five randomly chosen students from each participating classroom. The PST demographic breakdown is as follows: 3 males, 126 females; 115 Caucasians, 7 African Americans, 6 Hispanic Americans, 2 Indian Americans. Child demographic data was incomplete so is not reported.

Procedures

At the end of the spring and fall semesters, all the PSTs provided copies of their service-learning lesson plans that included content and social standards, photos and/or artefacts, self-evaluations (Figure 11.1), and

---

**Evaluation of the Service Learning Projects –
Preservice Teacher Evaluation**

Name:

---

1   Tell us about your Service Learning (SL) project.
2   Describe any involvement of community members or organization.
3   How effective was the SL project for your class?
4   How did your students benefit from the Service Learning project?
5   What changes in students' knowledge and performance have occurred as a result of the SL project?
6   What changes in students' attitudes and behavior have occurred as a result of the SL project?
7   What changes in students' enthusiasm/motivation have occurred as a result of the SL project?
8   Describe any changes in the ways that students talk about their SL project or the subject area of their project.
9   Describe three specific student products and compare the quality of those products with other work by those students.
10   How did the SL project support content standards and the social curriculum?
11   Are you planning to use SL in your own instruction?
12   What have been the major barriers to students participating in this Service Learning project?

Figure 11.1   Self-evaluation

Child Evaluation of the Service Learning Experience

Name:

Children's teacher/PST name:

---

1   Tell me about the _____ [Service Learning] project.
2   What did you learn from this project that you didn't know before?
3   How was your project helpful?
4   How did your project help other people/animals/the environment?
5   What other things have you done to be helpful since working on your project?
6   How did working on the _____ [Service Learning project] compare to the rest of your school work?

Figure 11.2   Student evaluation

student evaluations (Figure 11.2). The evaluation instrument required the PSTs to respond in writing to 11 questions targeting the effectiveness of their projects; the concepts and skills taught; students' academic and social benefits of participating in the project; how the project supported the state standards; and the specific products of the projects. Using a structured questionnaire, data was also collected from five randomly selected children. However, each PST interviewed children in another PST's classroom, thereby reducing *teacher pleasing* answers (Greig et al., 2007).

Qualitative

PSTs were required to identify the state standards, social skills, and service-learning standards in their lesson plans. A doctoral student with a service-learning background identified and counted the standards in each lesson plan. Every 10th lesson plan was then reviewed by one of the professors. Reliability was 100 percent for the content and service-learning standards. The social skills were more complicated to determine reliability because many of the skills are so closely related. For example, one coder identified a social skill as sharing (materials) and the second coder identified the same skill as being helpful (providing materials to a friend). Social reliability ranged from 95 to 100 percent.

The service-learning lesson plans were analysed and coded for curricular themes with similar categories merged. If lesson plans fit in more than one category, the authors made the category decision. Each lesson plan represents only one category. Within each category, lessons plans were further classified by environment: outdoor and indoor. Focus group interviews, conducted at the end of each semester, asked the PSTs to discuss the type of service-learning implemented. These interviews were transcribed, coded, analysed, and triangulated with the emerging results (Hatch, 2007).

Quantitative

The PSTs' lesson plans and student responses were coded by the two authors. Student responses were analysed using SPSS to determine the impact of the outdoor service-learning projects at their schools. Specifically, we wanted to know what content knowledge the students had learned through their service-learning projects. The data analysis was performed using simple cross-tabulations and frequencies (see Figure 11.3: Tables 1 and 2).

Table 1   Cross-tabulation of curriculum themes with academic standards and types of service-learning from preservice teachers' lesson plans

Theme	LA/Reading	Science	Social Studies	Maths	Direct	Indirect	Advocacy	Research
Helping others (33%)	28%	25%	35%	57%	25%	40%	0%	0%
Recycling/ Pollution (22%)	12%	32%	30%	14%	50%	17%	21%	0%
Letter writing (22%)	46%	13%	15%	7%	0%	29%	11%	0%
Endangered species (10%)	12%	15%	5%	21%	0%	5%	58%	0%
Gardening (5%)	0%	8%	1%	0%	8%	4%	0%	50%
Miscellaneous (8%)	2%	6%	14%	7%	17%	6%	11%	0%
Total Number of Lesson Plans (120)	57	71	74	14	24	28	19	1

Table 2   Percentages of academic and social impact responses by students

Service-Learning Type	Academic Learning Comment	Social Learning Comment	No/Non-Learning Comment
Helping those less fortunate	28%	60%	51%
Letter writing	21%	28%	20%
Pollution/Recycling	26%	1%	10%
Gardening	4%	2%	0%
Endangered species	10%	0%	4%
Miscellaneous	11%	9%	14%

Figure 11.3   Tables 1 and 2

Results

The outdoor service-learning projects fell into one of three categories: (1) beautification of the school/gardening; (2) growing plants and flowers to give to family members or people in the community; and (3) recycling/taking care of the environment. Most of the children interviewed (82%) stated that they preferred the outdoor service-learning approach to their regular classroom structure. One student declared: 'You're doing something, it's different. You're communicating to the world ...' The PSTs implementing the service-learning projects with the children discussed how the projects supported their children's content area development:

> This project supported my social studies standard about the students having a sense of responsibility to helping their community by planting a flower garden on their school grounds; they were helping to beautify their school community. This project also supported my science standards about working with others to use what they had learned from their previous experiments

during the week to plant flowers. They had to take the knowledge they learned about plants during the week and use it to successfully plant their flowers. (Lisa)

The PSTs were also cognizant of the fact that the projects helped develop the children's social-emotional development as well as teaching academic standards. More specifically, the PSTs could distinguish how cooperative learning tied in with outdoor learning was strengthening community and school collaborations:

> I expect that the students will walk away from this service-learning project with a new sense of accomplishment for helping their community. They will learn about how plants grow and what supplies are needed to help plants grow. I also expect that the students will learn that when they work cooperatively together, they can accomplish so much more. Working together will also help strengthen the classroom unity and bonds. The students will be evaluated on how effectively they work together through my observational checklist. I will be looking to see if the students were able to correctly plant their flowers, work cooperatively together, and participated in the class discussion following the project. (Becky)

The children in this study seemed to really enjoy the service-learning projects, which specifically focused on planting flowers and plants to give to members of the community. In the project, Sunshine in a Pot, the children learned the value of helping others by spreading a little sunshine through the gift of a potted flower. The PST and children discussed the local hospital, and the reasons why people had to stay there: sickness, injuries, cancer, pregnancy. After lengthy discussions, the children participated in painting flowerpots and planting flowers for someone who was ill or injured in the hospital.

The PST and children worked in small groups. In the morning they painted the pots, and in the afternoon they planted the flowers. In the focus group interviews, the PSTs stated that they were very surprised that no child asked to take his plant home; it was obvious that the children understood the reason for the activity, which was to help others by spreading a little sunshine through the gift of a potted flowering plant.

Indubitably, 86 percent of the children interviewed expressed that they had contributed to helping others in some way after they had finished working on their service-learning projects. More than half of the children, 55 percent, were very specific about ways they were helping and making contributions in their families and communities. Many children still had the passion to tell whoever would listen, the important message of their service-learning project: 'Recycling saves the world; I just learned that!'

Conclusion

The structured and hurried lives that many children in the USA and Europe lead often preclude self-discovery and play in the environment. This chapter has provided evidence that outdoor service-learning benefits children. Therefore, using the outdoor environment as part of the everyday curriculum should encourage practitioners to embrace outdoor learning opportunities and pressure policy-makers to promote outdoor service-learning experiences.

According to Gardner (1999), people have a *naturalist* intelligence that school curricula usually ignore. Naturalists can identify and categorize patterns in nature and are comfortable in the natural world. For individuals with a high naturalist intelligence, the optimal learning environment is one that is centered on environmental themes and issues and is situated in nature. However, the confines of the average western classroom and school building are not conducive to meeting the needs of naturalist learners. Affection for the landscape cannot be developed if students are isolated from it, and such isolation can lead to what Louv (2005) describes as children being nature deficient. Affection for the natural world may eventually protect and save the earth and its inhabitants. Lack of engagement with the practice of restorative processes in daily life exacerbates our disconnection from intuitive responses to environmental changes. Therefore, it is imperative that outdoor learning resumes its historical prominence in schools.

Further reading

Berman, S. (2006) *Service Learning: A Guide to Planning, Implementing, and Assessing Student Projects*, 2nd edn. Thousand Oaks, CA: Corwin Press.
This book was written following years of experience working with teachers in the USA, Canada, the Netherlands, the UK, Eastern Europe, and Australia. It offers practitioners ideas and information about developing service-learning projects with teachers and students in the classroom and beyond.
Lake, V.E. and Jones, I. (2012) *Service Learning in the PreK-3 Classroom: The What, Why, and How to Guide Every Teacher*. Minneapolis, MN: Free Spirit Publishing.
Both authors are highly respected authors on service-learning and have invested time and energy in inspiring and supporting others to develop service-learning in teacher education programs and in school districts across the USA. They have now transferred their shared knowledge into a practical handbook for practitioners.
Thomsen, K. (2013) *Service Learning in Grades K-8: Experiential Learning That Builds Character and Motivation*. Thousand Oaks, CA: Corwin Press.
This book is written for teachers and other educators who believe that their students deserve learning experiences that motivate and engage them, as well as prepare them for their future role as active citizens.

Information for practice

One way to start is by planning an integrated curriculum, for any student level, that offers outdoor participatory and experiential learning activities, incorporates multiple disciplines, facilitates learner decision-making and has developing sensitivity for the environment as the goal. The first step towards designing such a curriculum is to find common themes, goals, and objectives within disciplines. Teachers can examine their curriculum and find natural extensions to outdoor learning. They do not have to implement outdoor service-learning right away, but gradually become more accustomed to moving the learning environment outside the classroom walls. In time, they can add the service-learning components to maximize their children's academic, social, and civic abilities.

References

Adventure Playground Association (2006) Adventure Playgrounds: A Children's World in the City [online]. Available at: http://adventureplaygrounds.hampshire.edu/essence.html (accessed 20 December 2011).

Barros, R.M., Silver, E.J. and Stein, R.E.K. (2009) 'School recess and group classroom behavior', *Pediatrics* 123(2): 431–436.

Billig, S.H. (2000) 'Research on K-12 school-based service-learning: the evidence builds', *Phi Delta Kappan* 81(9): 658–664.

Bodrova, E. and Leong, D.J. (2007) *Tools of the Mind: The Vygotskian Approach to Early Childhood Education*, 2nd edn. Columbus, OH: Merrill/Prentice-Hall.

Caine, R. and Caine, G. (1997) *Education on the Edge of Possibility.* Alexandria, VA: Association for Supervision and Curriculum Development (ASCD).

Carter, G.R. (2010) ASCD Works with CCSSO and NGA on Common Core State Standards Initiative [online]. Available at: http://www.corestandards.org/assets/ccsi_statements/ StatementASCD.pdf

Chilton, T. (2003) 'Adventure playgrounds in the twenty-first century', in F. Brown (ed.) *Playwork: Theory and Practice.* Buckingham: Open University Press, pp. 114–127.

Copple, C. and Bredekamp, S. (2009) *Developmentally Appropriate Practice in Early Childhood Programs: Serving Children from Birth through Age 8*, 3rd edn. Washington, DC: National Association for the Education of Young Children.

DeVries, R. and Zan, B. (1994) *Moral Classrooms, Moral Children: Creating a Constructivist Atmosphere in Early Education.* New York: Teachers College Press.

Doherty, W. (2004) Overscheduled Kids, Under Connected Families: The Research Evidence [online]. Available at: http://www.familylife1st.org/html/research.html (accessed 20 December 2011).

Furco, A. (1996) 'Service learning and school-to-work', *Journal of Cooperative Education* 32(1): 7–14.

Gardner, H. (1999) *Intelligence Reframed: Multiple Intelligences for the 21st Century.* New York: Basic Books.

Greig, A.D., Taylor, J. and MacKay, T. (2007) *Doing Research with Children*, 2nd edn. Newbury Park, CA: Sage.

Hart, C.H. and Sheehan, R. (1986) 'Preschoolers' play behavior in outdoor environments: effects of traditional and contemporary playgrounds', *American Educational Research Journal* 23(4): 668–678.

Hatch, J.A. (2007) 'Assessing the quality of early childhood qualitative research', in J.A. Hatch (eds) *Early Childhood Qualitative Research*. New York: Routledge, pp. 223–244.

Katz, L.G. and Chard, S.C. (1989) *Engaging Children's Minds: The Project Approach.* Norwood, NJ: Ablex.

Lake, V.E. and Jones, I. (2008) 'Service-learning in early childhood teacher education: using service to put meaning back into learning', *Teaching and Teacher Education: An International Journal of Research and Studies* 24(8): 2146–2156.

Lake, V.E. and Jones, I. (2012) *Service Learning in the PreK-3 Classroom: The What, Why, and How-to Guide for Every Teacher.* Minneapolis, MN: Free Spirit Publishing.

Learn and Serve Clearinghouse (n.d.) What is Service-Learning?/What Service-Learning Is [online]. Available at: http://servicelearning.org/what_is_service-learning/service-learning_is/index.php (accessed 15 April 2009).

Lee, S.M., Burgeson, C.R., Fulton, J.E. and Spain, C.G. (2007) 'Physical education and physical activity: results from the School Health Policies and Programs Study 2006', *Journal of School Health* 77: 435–463.

Lord, P. (2006) What Young People Want from the Curriculum [online]. Slough: QCA/NFER. Available at: http://www.qcda.gov.uk/curriculum/434.aspx

Louv, R. (2005) *Last Child in the Woods: Saving our Children from Nature Deficit Disorder.* Chapel Hill, NC: Algonquin Books.

Lumby, J. (2010) 'Enjoyment and learning: policy and secondary school learners' experience in England', *British Educational Research Journal* [online]. Available at: http://www.informaworld.com/smpp/content~content=a919539015~db=all~jumptype=rss

Manzo, K.K. (2008) 'Schools adapting curriculum to the outdoors', *Education Week* 28(15).

National Governors Association Center for Best Practices and Council of Chief State School Officers (2010) *Common Core State Standards.* Washington, DC: National Governors Association Center for Best Practices and Council of Chief State School Officers.

National Youth Leadership Council (2008) *K-12 Service-learning Standards for Quality Practice.* St Paul, MN: National Youth Leadership Council.

O'Brien, L. (2009) 'Learning outdoors: the forest school approach', *Education* 37(1): 45–60.

Olsen, H., Thompson, D. and Hudson, S. (2011) 'Outdoor learning: supervision is more than watching children play', *Dimensions of Early Childhood* 39(1).

Roberts, J.E. (2002) The Relationship of Public Middle School Size, Student Achievement, and Per Pupil Expenditures in South Carolina. Unpublished doctoral thesis, University of South Carolina, Columbia.

Roth, J., Brooks-Gunn, J., Linver, M. and Hofferth, S. (2003) 'What happens during the school day? Time diaries from a national sample of elementary school teachers', *Teachers College Record* 105(3): 317–343.

Scales, P.C. and Roehlkepartain, E.C. (2004) *Community Service and Service-learning in US Public Schools, 2004: Findings from a National Survey.* St Paul, MN: National Youth Leadership Council.

Staempfli, M.B. (2009) 'Reintroducing adventure into children's outdoor play environments', *Environment and Behavior* 41(2): 268–280.

Taylor, P.G. and Ballengee-Morris, C. (2004) 'Service-learning: a language of "we"', *Art Education* 57: 6–12.

Verducci, S. and Pope, D. (2001) 'Rationales for integrating service-learning in teacher education', in J.B. Anderson, K.J. Swick and J. Yff (eds) *Service-learning in Teacher Education: Enhancing the Growth of New Teachers, Their Students, and Communities.* Washington, DC: Aacte.

Winterbottom, C. and Lake, V.E. (in press) '"I alone can make a difference": service-learning for all ages', *Child Care Exchange.*

12

Health Lessons from Nature in the USA

Ithel Jones and Tingting Xu

Chapter overview

The sedentary lifestyle of many young children in the USA has contributed to a rise in children's health disparities. With significant increases in the prevalence of several childhood chronic conditions, pediatric health care providers and others are realizing that exposure to nature can have health benefits. Policymakers, and others, are turning to nature in their effort to develop sustainable methods of promoting healthy lifestyle changes. This chapter examines three promising approaches: the National Environmental Education's (NEE) Children and Nature Initiative, public park physical activity, and children's gardening. Exposure to natural environments and the promotion of outdoor activity in nature can have significant benefits for young children.

During the past few years, here in the USA there has been an increase in the prevalence of several childhood chronic conditions such as childhood obesity, asthma, attention deficit/hyperactivity disorder (ADHD), and vitamin D deficiency (Perrin et al., 2007). One of the major contributors to this disturbing decline in children's health is a shift toward a more sedentary lifestyle (Kaiser Family Foundation, 2005). In addition, it is claimed that children today spend much more time indoors than they do outdoors

(Louv, 2005), and that this has had a significant impact on children's health and well-being. Consequently, educators and researchers in the USA maintain that more emphasis should be placed on promoting outdoor activity in nature for young children (Louv, 2005; McCurdy et al., 2010).

A critical dialogue has emerged in both public health and the environmental education communities about the benefits of nature for children. There is also a growing body of evidence suggesting that exposure to natural environments can improve attention and reduce stress in children (McCurdy et al., 2010). Outdoor play is also considered a practical, cost-effective way to address chronic conditions such as childhood obesity (Potwarka et al., 2008). Thus, in recent years there has been increasing emphasis on learning from nature, or environment-based education in early childhood. Moreover, educators and health care providers are beginning to realize the importance of physical activity in the outdoors, and the importance of providing opportunities for children to engage in learning activities in the natural environment.

Overview of children's health

The prevalence of obesity amongst preschoolers and adolescents in the USA has doubled over the past 30 years, and more than tripled for children aged 6–11. According to the 2007–2008 National Health and Nutrition Examination Survey, obesity affects almost 17 percent of children over the age of 2. Particularly disturbing is the fact that obesity rates for 2- to 5-year-old children have increased from 5 to 10 percent (Ogden and Carroll, 2010), and that one third of low-income preschool children are obese or overweight by the time they are 5 years of age (Pediatric Nutrition Surveillance Report, 2009). Thus, it is hardly surprising that childhood obesity is currently considered one of the most serious health problems affecting children in this country (Dietz, 1998; Hill and Trowbridge, 1998; Schwartz and Puhl, 2003). Childhood obesity is associated with several diseases in adulthood including Type 2 Diabetes, hypertension, and cardiovascular disease. It is estimated that up to 80 percent of obese youth grow up to be obese adults. Furthermore, obese children are more likely to grow up with a negative self-image and lower self-esteem (Dietz, 1998; CDC, 2010).

There is also evidence of vitamin D deficiency in young children. According to government statistics, 9 percent of the pediatric population is vitamin D deficient. Given that the main source of vitamin D comes from exposure to UVB light, it is hardly surprising that researchers have found an association between lifestyle and vitamin D. According to Ohta and colleagues (2009), energy expenditure is positively associated with vitamin D, and a sedentary lifestyle is negatively associated with vitamin D. It seems that vitamin D deficiency in children is a reflection of the modern-day lifestyle. Yet, according to the American Medical Association (2005), children can receive adequate amounts of vitamin D simply through 10–15 minutes of sun exposure twice a week.

There is also concern amongst health care professionals and educators that children and adolescents are increasingly being prescribed medication for depression, anxiety, and behavioral difficulties (Costello et al., 2006). According to the National Health Interview Survey (Pastor and Reuben, 2008), 9 percent of children have ADHD; thus prompting the CDC to describe ADHD as a 'serious health problem'. It is estimated that approximately 5 percent of US children are prescribed medication for emotional or behavioral difficulties (2008).

While there may be many reasons for these health issues in young children, there is increasing evidence that they are related to children's sedentary lifestyles. Recent research findings suggest that children under 13 years spend an average of only about half an hour of unstructured time outdoors each week (Hofferth and Sandberg, 2001). Furthermore, it is reported that children are spending as much as 7.5 hours per day in front of electronic media (Kaiser Family Foundation, 2005). Indeed, many young children spend most of their time in settings and activities that keep them isolated from direct contact with the natural world. This probably leads to declines in children's awareness, knowledge and understanding of the natural environment. Furthermore, young children are less likely to develop positive attitudes and feelings toward the natural environment. The adverse physical, social, and psychological effects of childhood nature deprivation were outlined by Louv in his now classic book *Last Child in the Woods* (2005).

Health benefits of physical activity and natural environments

It is believed that physical activity and increased exposure to the natural environment can improve children's physical health, and reduce stress and attention difficulties. In their physical activity guidelines, the US Department of Health and Human Services (2008) note that physical activity helps children build and maintain healthy bones and muscles, and reduce the risk of obesity. Recent research findings also provide evidence of the health-related benefits of physical activity. For example, in one study increased physical activity was related to a reduction in young children's blood pressure (Hansen et al., 1991). Activity is also considered important in the treatment of type 2 diabetes in children (see, for example, Gahagan and Silverstein, 2003; Shaibibi et al., 2008). It is hardly surprising therefore that there have been calls for the development of programs aimed at maintaining high levels of physical activity in children. The American Academy of Pediatrics (AAP et al., 2006), for example, recommends that children spend as much time outdoors as possible. Furthermore, the AAP recommends promoting lifelong habits of physical activity as opposed to short sessions of aerobic exercise. At the same time, it is claimed that exposure to the natural environment could have significant health benefits.

Recent research suggests that time spent outdoors is associated with increases in physical activity (e.g. Burdette et al., 2004). The finding that for every hour children spend outdoors physical activity increases by 27 percent, and the prevalence of overweight decreases by 14 percent (Cleland et al., 2008) lends support to the premise that school curricula and programs should promote outdoor activities in natural environments. Furthermore, there is increasing recognition of the benefits of making developmentally appropriate nature education an integral part of the daily lives and education of young children.

Recognizing the significant increases in chronic health conditions affecting young children, policymakers and others have focused on developing sustainable methods of promoting healthy lifestyle changes. In recent years, a variety of resources have been developed, and programs and initiatives implemented, all designed to encourage children to be more active, and to connect them with nature. In this chapter, we highlight three promising approaches: the National Environmental Education's (NEE) Children and Nature Initiative, public park physical activity, and children's gardening. In addition, we describe a particularly influential report that will no doubt lead to more children in the USA spending time outside and interacting with nature.

Early childhood environmental education

The *Early Childhood Environmental Education Programs: Guidelines for Excellence* was published in 2010 by the North American Association for Environmental Education (NAAEE) as part of a National Project for Excellence in Environmental Education. Drawing on the expertise of early childhood educators, as well as researchers, the project's *Guidelines* contain a set of recommendations for developing and administering high-quality environmental education programs for young children from birth to age 8, with a focus on ages 3–6. They also serve as a tool for practitioners in developing and improving early childhood environmental education programs. The overall goal of the *Guidelines* was to document an approach, or process, that would enable educators to help children embark on a lifelong journey toward becoming environmentally responsive adults. Throughout the *Guidelines*, the emphasis is on developmentally appropriate activities and settings, as well as appropriate teaching strategies and learning opportunities.

According to the North American Association for Environmental Education (NAAEE, 2010), 'environmental education in early childhood is a holistic concept that encompasses knowledge of the natural world as well as emotions, dispositions, and skills' (NAAEE, 2010: 2). An early childhood environmental education program provides for the development of a sense of wonder, and appreciation of the beauty and mystery of the natural world. For young children, experiences in natural environments provide opportunities for problem solving and developing an interest in the world around them. Of particular importance is the fact that environmental education and early childhood education share several key characteristics, including first-hand experiences and active participation; interdisciplinary, conceptual process development; problem-solving skills; and a holistic approach. In other words, positive interaction with the natural environment is an important part of healthy child development.

Several research studies lend support to the use of environmental education programs with young children. For example, Archie (2003) reported that environmental education helps children build critical thinking and relationship skills. There is also some evidence that the adoption of environmental programs can enhance children's achievement in reading and mathematics (Lieberman and Hoody, 1998). Other benefits include increased self-control (Faber Taylor et al., 2001), the development of positive social skills, (Coffey, 2001), and conservation benefits (NEETF, 2005). More importantly perhaps, children who experience school with diverse natural settings are more physically active and more aware of good nutrition (Bell and Dyment, 2006).

In addition to their early childhood report, the NAAEE developed and published a rating scale for early childhood environmental education. The Early Childhood Environmental Education Rating Scale (ECEERS) is a formative evaluation tool that can be used by teachers to help them evaluate and subsequently improve their environmental education curriculum. This instrument can be used in a variety of centers and programs to reflect on the quality of activities, experiences, interactions, and instruction pertaining to the world of nature.

The rating scale is based on six key characteristics of high quality early childhood environmental education programs (NAAEE, 2010). The procedures for using the rating scale emphasize a collaborative approach in evaluation, through the sharing of different perspectives, and reaching consensus regarding the rating of each specific guideline or recommendation.

Characteristics of early childhood environmental education programs

Early childhood education is 'less about organization of graduated achievements and more about free discovery' (NAAEE, 2010: 3). For young children, environmental education includes activities such as exploration in the natural environment, building with sticks, climbing rocks, running on sand or grass, findings insects, or simply stomping in puddles. In other words, it is a process whereby young children engage in outdoor activities, and develop a relationship with the natural world. In so doing, children learn how to explore and problem solve. Within an early childhood education program, environmental education is learner-centered, and it provides young children with opportunities to construct their own meaning through hands-on investigations.

The early childhood environmental education program also provides exceptional support for the overall healthy growth and development of children. For example, daily explorations can help build valuable skills such as observation, experimentation, and sorting, while allowing for both individual experiences and group sharing. Children's outdoor discoveries also provide excellent subjects for all manner of artistic and verbal expression, and daily walks and outdoor activities help to establish early habits of physical fitness.

The Children and Nature Initiative

While environmental education is an emphasis of the Children and Nature Initiative, an additional focus is on increasing concerns about young children's health and well-being. The main goal of the Children and Nature Initiative is to educate pediatric health care providers about the importance of prescribing outdoor activities for young children. In so doing, the program strives to connect health care providers with local nature sites, so that they can refer families to safe and easily accessible outdoor areas. In short, it is an approach that addresses health concerns by getting children to spend time outdoors.

The Children and Nature Initiative is guided by a committee of experts from diverse fields including health care and education. The primary approach is to educate pediatric health care providers so that they encourage children and families to spend time outdoors. The program also connects health care providers with local parks and nature centers, in an effort to ensure that families are using safe and easily accessible outdoor areas. The program's primary approach is to train a group of pediatric health care professionals in a series of workshops so that they can then educate their colleagues in their own communities, and thereby become 'Nature Champions'. The initiative also provides these individuals with various tools and resources including the *Children's Health and Nature Fact Sheet*, which summarizes the scientific basis for the health-related benefits of nature, as well as the *Pediatric Environmental History Form*, which includes questions for pediatric health care providers to encourage outdoor time for children. Through the Children and Nature Initiative, health care providers, parents, outdoor organizations, schools, federal, state, and local agencies, community groups, and other institutions can work together to encourage children to spend more time outdoors and teach them how to protect their health and the environment. The success of such an initiative, however, depends to a certain extent on the availability of safe, accessible natural places for children and families. Public parks and recreation settings such as playgrounds can potentially provide spaces for children and families to engage in physical activity while interacting with the natural environment. Recently, researchers and others have begun to examine the significance of parks to physical activity and public health (Bedimo-Rung et al., 2005).

Parks, playgrounds and recreation settings

The health benefit of regular physical activity is well established. It is well known, for example, that physical activity decreases heart disease, diabetes, and high blood pressure (US Department of Health and Human Services, 1996). Yet, almost a quarter of the US adult population reported in 2002 that they do not engage in any leisure-time physical activity (Centers for Disease Control and Prevention, 2010). While efforts have been made to change individual behavior, they have not resulted in any significant increases in levels of physical activity. Consequently, there have been calls for environmental-based interventions such as leisure facilities, nature trails, and public parks.

In recent years, there has been an increased emphasis on park-based physical activity as a way of addressing current physical activity requirements (Bedimo-Rung et al., 2005). The benefits of parks and recreation services in the USA are well established (Crompton, 1999). Parks are common community features that provide opportunities for physical activity, for children of all ages, as well as adults. According to Bedimo-Rung and colleagues (2005), however, little is known about the characteristics of public parks that are related to physical activity.

It is proposed that specific park characteristics could be related to park benefits, park use, and physical activity requirements (Bedimo-Rung et al., 2005). Capitalizing on the potential of parks for promoting physical activity requires consideration of park features, condition, access, aesthetics, safety, and policy.

While professionals from health-related professions have been discussing how to design interventions and enhance park-based physical activity levels, others have been addressing the naturalization of playgrounds.

There is a growing movement in North America toward transforming playground designs for preschool and kindergarten from relatively barren areas into naturalized environments for children's play. Guided by Moore and Cosco's Natural Learning Initiative (2000), this movement seeks to modify children's play areas in neighborhoods, urban parks, school grounds, museums, zoos, and botanical gardens so that they do not depend on manufactured equipment. The move toward more natural play areas draws on the concepts of behavior setting, affordance, territorial development, and design as measurable health intervention. That is, there is now greater understanding of how the built environment and its design can motivate higher levels of outdoor physical activity, nutritional awareness, and other health benefits among children in the context of family, neighborhood, and childhood institutions.

Rather than being built, the new play environments are planted and make use of the landscape and its vegetation as both the play settings and the play materials. In other words, the surrounding landscape and its vegetation are incorporated in a way that brings nature to children's daily outdoor play and learning environments. These natural play areas are designed from a child's perspective as informal areas that respond to children's developmental tasks, their sense of place, time, and need to interact with nature. They are designed so that they stimulate children's natural curiosity, as well as their imagination and sense of wonder. Moreover, they are places that promote discovery learning and nurture children's connection with the natural environment (White and Stoecklin, 1998).

Clearly, there are numerous designs that can be used for developing naturalized play environments for young children. The basic components have been effectively summarized by White and Stoecklin (1998) as follows:

- water

- indigenous vegetation including trees, bushes, flowers, and long grasses

- animals, creatures in ponds, butterflies, bugs

- sand

- diversity of color, textures, and materials

- ways to experience the changing seasons, wind, light, sounds, and weather

- natural places to sit in, on, under, lean against, climb, and provide shelter and shade

- different levels and nooks and crannies, places for socialization, places for privacy

- structures, equipment, and materials that can be changed (real or imagined).

There are many benefits of play areas that include the features described above. For example, natural play environments seem to have a positive impact on the development of children's environmental stewardship values and appreciation of nature (Fjortoft, 2001). Other benefits of more natural play areas include developing environmentally responsible behaviors, improved psychological well-being, and improved general behavior. More important perhaps is that there is now some research evidence concerning the health benefits resulting from children interacting and playing in naturalized playgrounds. Children with ADHD seem to have improved concentration following contact with nature (Faber Taylor et al., 2001). Regular play in natural environments also results in more advanced motor fitness, coordination, balance, and agility (Fjortoft, 2001).

The general assumption held by researchers is that variations in pre-school physical activity may be attributable to variations in the form and content of the outdoor environment. Until recently, however, few assessment tools and methods were available that could be used to document the relationship between the physical environment and physical activity. Such tools and data are needed in order to influence early childhood policies concerning children's play areas. This is especially important in North America since policies concerning young children are highly regulated at the state level. A promising approach for measuring the relationship between children's outdoor physical settings and preschool physical activity was developed by Cosco and colleagues (2010).

The *behavior mapping approach* (Cosco et al., 2010) is a direct observation method for simultaneously measuring children's activity levels and their location in the environment. The instrument provides researchers with an efficient, easy-to-use tool, allowing them to document and analyse children's activity in the environment. In turn, this instrument could lead to the identification of specific environmental components that are associated with increased physical activity.

Identifying specific components of parks, and natural playgrounds, should enable policymakers and others to design and develop environments that will encourage young children to be more physically active. Yet, increased physical activity alone is not sufficient to address the health problems affecting young children in this country. This is because many of the health issues described in this chapter are related to poor nutrition.

Nutrition education

Given the disturbing trend in rates of childhood obesity and health-related issues, it is hardly surprising that there have been numerous intervention efforts. The United States Department of Agriculture (USDA), for example, announced the Local Wellness Policy (2004), which was designed to promote student wellness through improved school nutrition education. More recently, the USDA sought to promote healthy eating by developing a new food guide, *My Plate*, to replace the *Food Guide Pyramid* (USDA, 2011). While such interventions may help with obesity prevention (Longley and Sneed, 2009), there is some concern about their success. This is because interventions that focus solely on modifying behaviors concerning healthy eating amongst school-aged children have been shown to have limited long-term effects (Summerbell et al., 2005). This could be because by the time children are in school they have already established food preferences and eating behaviors. Moreover, high-risk eating behaviors, such as a diet containing foods high in fat or sugar, and energy-condensed foods are difficult to change once they have been established (Kelder et al., 1994).

It follows that interventions should start as early as possible (Wojcicki and Heyman, 2010). One promising approach is the movement toward 'greening' schoolyards through gardens at school sites.

School gardens

Several reasons have been put forth concerning the value of school gardens (Ozer, 2007). Some view school gardens as outdoor classrooms or 'learning laboratories', while others see them as aesthetically pleasing areas for children to play in. Recently, however, school gardens have been promoted as a way of encouraging healthy eating habits. The school garden not only helps children learn how to grow plants, but, more importantly, it promotes the consumption of fresh produce.

Drawing on principles of social ecology and community psychology, advocates of school gardens promote their use as a school-level intervention for promoting children's health and well-being across a number of areas. It has been reported that there are more than 200 school gardens in California being used for academic purposes (Graham, 2002). Increasing numbers of such gardens (National Gardening Association, 2012) across the USA suggest that school gardens may be a systemic response to the current obesity crisis. Yet, the evidence concerning the potential effects of school gardens on children's eating habits, nutrition, health and well-being is limited. Anecdotal reports and informal observations suggest, however, that the adoption and use of a school garden is a promising approach for promoting children's healthy eating habits.

Conclusion

In conclusion, there has been a significant increase in the prevalence of several chronic childhood conditions such as obesity in the USA. One possible reason for this dramatic decline in children's health is the shift toward a more sedentary lifestyle. It is generally believed that physical activity can improve children's health. There is now a growing movement in support of the notion that exposure to natural environments can begin to address some childhood health concerns.

From a policy perspective, several national reports and initiatives encourage those who work with young children to provide programs and activities that encourage children to engage with the natural environment. Guidelines for early childhood environmental education developed by the National American Association for Environmental Education (NAAEE, 2010) provide a set of guidelines for developing and administering environmental education programs for young children. Then, programs such as the *Children and Nature Initiative*, help pediatric health care providers connect children and families with the outdoors.

The health lessons from nature are most evident in recent trends concerning children's use of public parks and playgrounds. Park-based physical activity is one approach that is being used to address physical activity requirements. In addition to capitalizing on the potential of parks, there is also increased interest in the naturalization of children's playgrounds. It is hoped that providing such natural play areas will go a long way toward addressing childhood health concerns.

Finally, local and national efforts are seeking to promote children's wellness through nutrition education. The traditional approach has been to focus on modifying behavior through school curricula, and other approaches. Recently, however, using the more naturalistic approach of school gardens is seen as a promising way of promoting healthy eating habits in young children.

Further reading

Louv, R. (2005) *Last Child in the Woods: Saving our Children from Nature Deficit Disorder.* Chapel Hill, NC: Algonquin Books. (Available in the UK as a second edition [2010] from Atlantic Books, London.)

Moore, R. and Marcus, C.C. (2008) 'Healthy planet, healthy children: designing nature into the daily spaces of childhood', in S.R. Kellert, J. Heerwagen and M. Mador (eds) *Biophilic Design: The Theory, Science, and Practice of Bringing Buildings to Life.* Hoboken, NJ: Wiley. Available at: http://naturalearning.org/sites/default/files/MooreCooperMarcus_Healthy.pdf

North American Association for Environmental Education (NAAEE) (2010) *Early Childhood Environmental Education Programs: Guidelines for Excellence.* Washington, DC: NAAEE. Available at: http://resources.spaces3.com/c518d93d-d91c-4358-ae5e-b09d493af3f4.pdf

Information for practice

A multipronged approach to increasing children's engagement with outdoor spaces would seem to be the most beneficial. Developing spaces in settings and in communities is a first step; this can take place alongside information and education programs for parents and practitioners.

References

American Academy of Pediatrics (AAP), Council on Sports Medicine and Fitness and Council on School Health (2006) 'Active healthy living: prevention of childhood obesity through increased physical activity', *Pediatrics* 117: 1834–1842.

Archie, M. (2003) *Advancing Education through Environmental Literacy*. Alexandria, VA: Association for Supervision and Curriculum Development (ASCD).

Bedimo-Rung, A.L., Mowen, A.J. and Cohen, D.A. (2005) 'The significance of parks to physical activity and public health: a conceptual model', *American Journal of Preventive Medicine* 28: 159–168.

Bell, A.C. and Dyment, J.E. (2006) *Grounds for Action: Promoting Physical Activity Through School Ground Greening in Canada*. Almonte, Ontario: Evergreen.

Burdette, H., Whitaker, R.C., Robert, C. and Daniels, S.R. (2004) 'Parental report of outdoor playtime as a measure of physical activity in preschool-aged children', *Archives of Pediatric Adolescent Medicine* 158: 353–357.

Centers for Disease Control and Prevention (CDC) (2010) Physical Activity Guidelines for Americans: Children and Adolescents [online]. Available at: http://www.cdc.gov/healthyyouth/physicalactivity/guidelines.htm

Cleland, V., Crawford, D., Baur, L.A., Hume, C., et al. (2008) 'A prospective examination of children's time spent outdoors, objectively measured physical activity and overweight', *International Journal of Obesity* 32(11), 1685–1693. doi:10.1038/ijo.2008.171

Coffey, A. (2001) 'Transforming school grounds', in T. Grant and G. Littlejohn (eds) *Greening School Grounds: Creating Habitats for Learning*. Toronto: New Society Publishers.

Cosco, N.D., Moore, R.C. and Islam, M.Z. (2010) 'Behavior mapping: a method for linking preschool physical activity and outdoor design', *Medicine and Science in Sport and Exercise*, 513–519.

Costello, E.J., Erkanli, A. and Angold, A. (2006) 'Is there an epidemic of child or adolescent depression?', *Journal of Child Psychiatry* 47: 1263–1271.

Crompton, J.L. (1999) *Financing and Acquiring Park and Recreation Resources*. Champaign, IL: Human Kinetics.

Dietz, W.H. (1998) 'Health consequences of obesity in youth: childhood predictors of adult disease', *Pediatrics* 101: 518–525.

Faber Taylor, A., Kuo, F.E. and Sullivan, W.C. (2001) 'Coping with ADD: the surprising connection to green play settings', *Environment and Behavior* 33: 49–63.

Fjortoft, I. (2001) 'The natural environment and a playground for children: the impact of outdoor play activities in pre-primary school children', *Early Childhood Education Journal* 29: 111–117.

Gahagan, S. and Silverstein, J. (2003) 'Prevention and treatment of type 2 diabetes mellitus in children, with special emphasis on American Indian and Alaska Native children', *Pediatrics*, 112 (4): 970 (1), October.

Graham, H. (2002) *Statewide Principal's School Garden Survey*. Sacramento, CA: Department of Education and Department of Nutrition, University of California at Davis.

Hansen, H.S., Froberg, K., Hydebrandt, N. and Nielsen, J.R. (1991) 'A controlled study of eight months of physical training and reduction of blood pressure in children: the Odense school child study', *British Medical Journal* 303: 682–685.

Hill, J.O. and Trowbridge, F.L. (1998) 'Childhood obesity: future directions and research priorities', *Pediatrics* 101(3): 570–574. Also available at: http://pediatrics.aappublications.org/content/101/3/570

Hofferth, S.L. and Sandberg, J.F. (2001) 'Changes in American children's time', in S.L. Hofferth and T.J. Owens (eds) *Children at the Millennium: Where Have We Come From, Where Are We Going?* New York: JAI, pp. 1–7.

Kaiser Family Foundation (2005) New Study Finds Children Age Zero to Six Spend As Much Time With TV, Computers and Video Games As Playing Outside [online]. Available at: http://www.kff.org/entmedia/entmedia102803nr.cfm

Kelder, S.H., Perry, C.L., Klepp, K.I. and Lytle, L.L. (1994) 'Longitudinal tracking of adolescent smoking, physical activity and food choice behaviors', *American Journal of Public Health* 84(7): 1121–1126.

Lieberman G.A. and Hoody, L.L. (1998) Closing the Achievement Gap: Using the Environment as an Integrating Context for Learning [online]. Available at: http://www.seer.org/extras/execsum.pdf

Longley, C.H. and Sneed, J. (2009) 'Effects of federal legislation on wellness policy formation in school districts in the United States', *Journal of the American Dietetic Association* 109: 95–101.

Louv, R. (2005) *Last Child in the Woods: Saving our Children from Nature Deficit Disorder.* Chapel Hill, NC: Algonquin Books.

McCurdy, L.E., Winterbottom, K.E., Mehta, S.S. and Roberts, J. (2010) 'Using nature and outdoor activity to improve children's health', *Current Problems in Pediatric Adolescent Health Care* 40: 102–117.

Moore, R.D. and Cosco, R.G. (2000) Developing an Earth-bound Culture through Design of Childhood Habitats. Paper presented at the international conference on People, Land and Sustainability, University of Nottingham, UK, 2000.

National Gardening Association (2012) Gardening in Every School Registry [online]. Available at: http://www.kidsgardening.com (accessed 18 August 2012).

North American Association for Environmental Education (NAAEE) (2010) *Early Childhood Environmental Education Programs: Guidelines for Excellence.* Washington, DC: NAAEE.

The National Environmental Education and Training Foundation (NEETF) (2005) Environmental Literacy in America [online]. Washington DC: NEETF. Available at: www.neefusa.org/pdf/ELR2005.pdf (accessed 13 June 2013).

Ogden, C. and Carroll, M. (2010) 'Prevalence of obesity among children and adolescents: United States, trends 1963–1965 through 2007–2008', *National Center for Health Statutes: Health E-Stat* [online]. Available at: http://www.cdc.gov/nchs/data/hestat/obesity_child_07_08/obesity_child_07_08.pdf

Ohta, H., Kuroda, T., Onoe, Y., Orito, S., Ohara, M., and Kume, M. (2009) 'The impact of lifestyle factors on serum 25-hydroxyvitamin D levels: A cross-sectional study in Japanese women aged 19–25 years', *Journal of Bone Mineral Metabolism,* 27, 682–688.

Ozer, E.J. (2007) 'The effects of school gardens on students and schools: conceptualization and considerations for maximizing healthy development', *Health Education and Behavior* 34: 846–863.

Pastor, P.N. and Reuben, C.A. (2008) 'Diagnosed attention deficit hyperactivity disorder and learning disability: United States, 2004–06', *National Center for Health Statistics: Vital Health Stat* 10: 237.

Pediatric Nutrition Surveillance Report (PedNSS) (2009) Obesity among Low-income Preschool Children [online]. Available at: http://www.health.ny.gov/statistics/prevention/nutrition/pednss/2009/

Perrin, J.M., Bloom, S.R., and Gortmaker, S.L. (2007) 'The increase of childhood chronic conditions in the United States', *Journal of the American Medical Association,* 297, 2755–2759.

Potwarka, L.R., Kaczynski, A.T., and Flack, A.L. (2008) 'Places to play: Association of park space and facilities with health weight status among children', *Journal of Community Health,* 33, 344–350.

Schwartz, M.B. and Puhl, R. (2003) 'Childhood obesity: A societal problem to solve', *Obesity Reviews* 4(1), 57–71. doi: 10.1046/j.1467-789X.2003.00093.x

Shaibi, G.,Q., Faulkner, M.,S., Weigensberg, M., J., Fritschi, C., and Goran, M.,I. (2008) 'Cardiorespiratory fitness and physical activity in youth with type 2 diabetes', *Pediatric Diabetes,* 9, 460–3.

Summerbell, C.D., Waters, E., Edmunds, L., Kelly, S.A.M., Brown, T. and Campbell, K.J. (2005) 'Interventions for preventing obesity in children', *Cochrane Database Systematic Review* 20(3): 1–70.

US Department of Agriculture (USDA) (2004) Local Wellness Policy [online]. Available at: http://www.fns.usda.gov/tn/Healthy/wellnesspolicy.html

US Department of Agriculture (USDA) (2011) Choosemyplate.gov: A Brief History of USDA Food Guide [online]. Available at: http://www.choosemyplate.gov/food-groups/downloads/MyPlate/ABriefHistoryOfUSDAFoodGuides.pdf

US Department of Health and Human Services (1996) *A Report from the Surgeon General: Physical Activity and Health.* Atlanta, GA: Centers for Disease Control and Prevention.

US Department of Health and Human Services (2008) 2008 Physical Guidelines for Americans [online]. Available at: http://www.health.gov/PAGuidelines/guidelines/default.aspx

White, R. and Stoecklin, V. (1998) Children's Outdoor Play and Learning Environments: Returning to Nature [online]. Available at: http://www.whitehutchinson.com/children/articles/outdoor.shtml

Wojcicki, J.M. and Heyman, M.B. (2010) 'Let's move: childhood obesity prevention from pregnancy and infancy onward', *The New England Journal of Medicine* 362(16): 1457–1459.

13

Cultivating Canadian Learners – Outside!

Lori Driussi

Chapter overview

This chapter describes the beginning of our school's journey toward maximizing nearby outdoor spaces to promote learning for all students in grades Kindergarten to 7 in an urban location in Burnaby, British Columbia, Canada. Reflecting on adventures in our nearby forest, through the lens of Forest School, the positive benefits of being outside are revealed and plans for meaningful outdoor learning described. It becomes clear that the ethos of Forest School can be cultivated in any school.

Our questions

> I was scared to go in [the large tree stump] before but now I like it! I am not afraid. (Kian, 6 years)

In my 23 years as an educator, I have had the pleasure of planning for and engaging in many outdoor experiences with children in their elementary school years, aged 5 to 13. The above quote is reflective of the excitement and growth students experience when given the opportunity to meaningfully engage with the natural world. Whether it's a formal experience like adventure camp, a less formal forest walk, or spotting a frog on the playground, the sense of wonder is the

Figure 13.1 Kian, Kai and Caroline get inside the tree stump

same. No matter the age, shrieks of 'look at this' and 'look over here' contribute to the outdoor soundscape. What is it about the outdoor experience that generates the engagement that educators dream of observing as students enter the classroom each day? How might we bring this excited observation, spontaneous questioning, natural collaboration and feeling of empowerment to the classroom? How might we more *intentionally* integrate outdoor experiences with the prescribed curriculum? What might happen if we spent more time outside?

Our context

University Highlands Elementary sits atop Burnaby Mountain, next to Simon Fraser University and within a newly developed sustainable community, UniverCity. Aside from the University campus, what was entirely wild just 12 years ago has now been thoughtfully planned to include a town square, a block of merchants, several condominium buildings, a childcare centre and our school. Residents have chosen UniverCity because of its sustainable practices like the award-winning storm water management system, which returns nearly 100 percent of storm water to the ground.

Surrounded by trees and undergrowth native to the area, the school building and grounds were designed to meet Leadership in Energy and Design (LEED) Gold standards, the first in British Columbia. We are fortunate to have a small, forested area next to our school field, along with a drainage pond that services mountain run-off, and an outdoor seating area for gathering in. Venturing a little further allows us access to Burnaby Mountain Park and wilder spaces within the protected Burnaby Mountain Conservation area. With a Reggio Emilia inspired approach, our school, due to the nature of its design and geographical location, is perfectly suited to the notion of the environment as a teacher in its own right.

Box 13.1   Reggio Emilia and Forest School at University Highlands

Reggio Emilia is a pedagogical approach which was developed in northern Italy and is aimed at early learners (see http://earlychildhood.educ.ubc.ca/community/research-practice-reggio-emilia). An important tenant of the Reggio approach is that the environment itself is a teacher, often referred to as the third teacher. That is, the learning space expresses values and encourages particular ways of being. Our LEED Gold School, by virtue of its structure and facilities, is a teacher. For example, a belief in sustainability is demonstrated by the rooftop solar panels that collect and redistribute power, and also by large windows and skylights which minimize energy use for artificial indoor lighting. Classrooms are clustered around central pods inviting the co-construction of knowledge and facilitating inquiry-based learning. The open kitchen and classrooms for preschoolers and beginning teachers suggest a value in welcoming all members of the community into our school and demonstrate that education is a lifelong and collective endeavour. Teachers at University Highlands have been inspired by the Reggio Emilia approach, and intentionally create indoor learning spaces with structures, materials and activities to invite and encourage collaboration, discovery and inquiry.

Our outdoor environment and its features also act as a third teacher. The landscape decorated only with native plants, an outdoor gathering area made with logs cut from on-site trees, and the drainage pond that manages mountain run-off together express a value and belief in the outdoors as having educational capacity. Our goal is to more fluidly incorporate this third teacher

(Continued)

(Continued)

into children's daily experience at school. Using the ethos of Forest School provides helpful signposts along our way to meeting the needs of our students, using the outdoors to enhance their overall development and to address the prescribed curriculum.

Three guiding themes

Three themes: sustainability, community involvement, and inquiry-based learning set the instructional direction for University Highlands' students. We bring these themes to life in a variety of ways, one of which is taking children outside with increasing regularity and purpose.

I will share four forest experiences, making connections with the eight positive outcomes of Forest School (Knight, 2009: 43). Reflecting on these different experiences illuminates the obvious benefits of outdoor play and, more importantly, elicits questions that bring us closer to planning meaningful outdoor learning with clear goals to further student development. While our school does not meet all the criteria that define Forest School (Knight, 2009: 15), we are beginning to bring the ethos of Forest School to our children in conjunction with our three themes.

The positive outcomes outlined in Forest School research describe an educator's wish for all students: confidence, social awareness, an increasingly sophisticated use of language and communication, improved physical skills, knowledge and understanding that leads to care and action, new perspectives about one another and ripple effects that take us beyond the school experience. These outcomes sit within what I have previously described as an aim of education, which is 'to help children become more at home in the world through self-discovery in relation to others' (Driussi, 2008: x).

The positive impact of outdoor learning is well researched, undeniable, and will not be argued here. Rather, I wish to hold open the door, for my own school staff and educators everywhere, to confidently, and with a sense of wonder, step outside holding the hands of children.

Forest adventures

On the edge of our school property, there is a forested area bordered by a municipal park, our school field and the neighbouring condominium development. We have come to think of this tiny forest as our own. Its proximity allows quick access, and there is just enough space to give the illusion of being away from it all. Increased respect for this space has developed as we have come to know and understand it through formal educative experiences such as a visit from an urban ecologist, teacher-scaffolded activities including guided exploration, and natural curiosity like free play and weekend play. Observing students in the forest, engaging in different types of activities, highlights the benefits shown in the Forest School model.

A visit with an urban ecologist

An urban ecologist led each class on a tour of our wooded area and told us about the flora and fauna thriving there and the impact of the infringing construction on the habitat. Learning included how to identify a Hemlock tree by its leaves and bark and the fact that Oregon Grape prefers dry soil and so tends to grow on high ground. Scat was analysed to determine visitors – dog or bear? Formal knowledge ignited curiosity and nurtured a deepening respect as the interdependence of forest life was explained.

This formal outdoor experience does not meet many of the defining characteristics of Forest School, especially that of play-based, child-initiated learning. However, the experience did nurture an interest in the environment, stimulating a desire to learn more (Knight, 2009: 47). Students had new vocabulary and knowledge and thus more precise language for talking and thinking about this environment.

Free play in the forest

There is space outside, space to run, jump, climb, balance and reach. Physical skills are developed in free play as children move under, over and around forest obstacles. Gross motor skills develop as fallen logs, stumps and low hanging branches invite active play. Physical risks are taken, courage is shown and confidence built as children explore the natural world. Watching children during free play allows for new perspectives to develop. Those who show leadership in the classroom become followers outside where their confidence isn't so great.

 Case study 1: Confidence and new perspectives

Nine-year-old Charlie comes alive in the forest. He is confident, careful, insightful and creative here. He scaffolds the risk-taking of his peers as he cautions and offers his hand. Unlike in the classroom, where Charlie spends much of his time avoiding learning and disrupting the class,

(Continued)

(Continued)

here, in this outdoor space, Charlie is a leader. As a teacher and principal, I see more of who Charlie is and who he has the potential to become. I understand him better because I have spent time with him in our forest. Our relationship is strengthened outside and, as a result, we work more productively together when inside. Charlie's expertise and leadership can be accessed and celebrated and allow his peers to relate to him with increased respect and kindness, which in turn increases Charlie's sense of efficacy as a learner. Charlie has new found confidence for intellectual risk-taking in the classroom as a result of his outdoor experiences, as described by Knight (2011: 156).

It is our responsibility as educators to offer all children experiences that allow them to be their very best selves, to realize their potential and to believe in themselves. For some, this means getting outside.

Teacher-scaffolded activities

The teachers at University Highlands have increasingly been taking students into the forest for scaffolded activities. Planned by the teacher, lessons are designed to assist students in engaging with the natural world through guided exploration, recorded observations and art projects. We have noticed that repeated visits to the forest have resulted in increased contentment with the outdoor environment as students develop their strengths and confidence in a familiar environment. They are 'keen to participate in exploratory learning' (Knight, 2009: 46). As with the free play previously discussed, we are getting to know our students more deeply, making us more effective teachers and better able to meet the needs of each of our learners.

 ## Case study 2: Time, motivation and new perspectives

Shayne is a grade 5 boy seemingly disengaged from school life. He claims there is nothing he wishes to learn about and that he has no desire to attend school 'except for seeing my friends'. Several classes, including Shayne's, are participating in Learning in Depth, in which each student engages in a long-term inquiry project about a randomly assigned topic. Shayne's topic is mushrooms, which are abundant around our school and in the nearby forest. On a cool spring day, we took a walk together to collect mushrooms for study, with a shovel and terrarium in hand. Asking Shayne what he thought about mushrooms, he replied, 'I don't like them. I mean to eat.' Asking

(Continued)

(Continued)

Shayne what he knew about mushrooms, he responded there was nothing really that interesting about them. We continued walking, with me wondering about the best way to connect Shayne with a topic to which he seemed indifferent. 'Hey, Ms Driussi, look! Lots of them!' Shayne spotted a meadow of tiny mushrooms in the park grass and bent down to get a closer look. He wondered aloud about what kind they were, whether they were edible, and what happened when the grass was mowed. He very carefully dug several up to put in his terrarium. While a moment before he had claimed disinterest, he was now asking questions and carefully digging. Shayne was motivated to learn. Children need time and in our rush to move through the curriculum we often don't allow the time necessary for children to experience their own curiosity and direct their own learning.

We continued on to the small forest where we discovered larger mushrooms and plants that Shayne collected to enhance the landscape in which he had replanted the found mushrooms. 'I'm going to put them in this grass because they are used to having it around. This rock too because it makes it [the terrarium] look more real.' As he dug into the earth, he exclaimed, 'I love the smell of nature. It clears my head.' What an insight for me. This boy, who struggles to function productively and respectfully in his classroom and who is too insecure about his own ability to learn to maximize his potential, became a different person before my eyes. He shared information with confidence and enthusiasm, he designed a terrarium with intention, his shoulders dropped and his expression softened. He took a breath and so did I. He presented himself, through words and gestures, as capable and engaged. In this space of time and in this place, we found a new relationship and had a new perspective about each other. Neither of us wanted to return to school when the bell called us back. We walked slowly, talked quietly and decided on the best possible locations for the mushroom terrarium.

As Shayne went upstairs to join his class, I wondered how many experiences in the forest it might take to bring the confidence and calm expressed out there into the classroom. How much of Shayne's school day could be outside? How often might we bring the outdoors in?

Box 13.2   'Learning in Depth'

Learning in Depth, developed by Dr Kieran Egan at Simon Fraser University (Egan, 2010), is an innovation in curriculum and instruction designed to ensure that all students become experts about something during their school years. Each child is

(Continued)

(Continued)

randomly assigned a topic to learn about through their school career and builds a portfolio on the topic. The program usually takes about an hour a week, with the students working increasingly outside school time. For more information about Learning in Depth, visit http://www.ierg.net/LiD.

Weekend play

Recent tales of the forest fort that some of the children have been building after school and on the weekend prompted me to investigate. The fort is a large hole dug using hands and shovels. It is covered with small branches to make it a good hiding place but with enough opening exposed 'because we didn't want little kids to fall in', explained 10-year-old Morgan. With repeated visits, Morgan and his friends developed confidence and familiarity using building materials from the forest to create a special, relaxing space for themselves. They had 'freedom, time and space, to learn, grow and demonstrate independence' (Knight, 2009: 46). They also developed social skills as they thoughtfully and cooperatively built the fort and made it visible for the safety of others. This purposeful and fruitful child-initiated exploration reminds us to allow students to direct their own learning, a defining criteria of Forest School.

Reflections

Learning about this small forest space through formal experiences and exploratory play invites children to care about it. They notice the litter and dog feces. They notice when logs have been moved or plants tread upon. They know where the natural nests and birdhouses left by researchers are located. They notice construction debris and wonder why it hasn't been cleaned up. Conversations about social responsibility emerge. Children have an interest in the forest and a desire to spend time there. As they develop their sense of ownership for this small forest they have come to love as their own, their sense of environmental stewardship increases. Rivkin (1995: 37) speaks of children who learn to cherish their own piece of land and who may indeed come to cherish more remote lands. Knight (2009) speaks of the ripple effect of Forest School experiences, which is shown in the examples above.

Looking through the lens of Forest School, it reveals the well-researched importance of outdoor experiences in overall individual human development. More specifically, each of the eight benefits described in Forest School literature are revealed, causing us to notice the possibility and potential of a long-term impact on personal growth, new ways of being and habits of mind, when the Forest School model is formalized. Might we bring children closer to being at home in the world through self-discovery in relation to others?

What do educators need in order to confidently plan outdoor experiences inspired by Forest School? Given that we do not have any trained Forest School leaders (Knight, 2011: 3) in our midst, opportunities to be outside with each other and to collaboratively imagine and plan for outdoor learning and its integration with the prescribed curriculum are needed. Taking students outside initially for teacher-directed or 'scaffolding' (Knight, 2011: 34) lessons has proven to develop confidence and trust: confidence in one's own ability to safely manage a group of children outside and trust in the children's ability to safely participate and enjoy outdoor activities. Taking time to observe children in scaffolded play uncovers a great deal about our students and guides us in planning for future indoor and outdoor learning in all curricular areas. As stated in Knight (2011: 35), 'Learning outside the classroom was most successful when it was an integral element of long-term curriculum planning'. Using the defining criteria of Forest School as a guide, teachers will be inspired to spend purposeful time outside and will readily recognize the cited benefits.

Next steps

We recently spent time outside as a staff to map our school grounds and to make design suggestions for improved access and ease of use. These will be presented to our Board of Education for approval as funding will need to be secured. The teachers have formed a committee to collaboratively design lessons so that children will come to know these outdoor spaces more intimately, initially through scaffolding activities and, then, increasingly, by observing, documenting and reflecting on child-initiated play. A school garden is being planned with a joint committee of students, parents and teachers. We recognize the importance of bringing our families and wider community members together into our planning and eventual implementation.

Bringing the ethos of Forest School to University Highlands, we are clarifying our goals, determining our needs and observing the results of providing regular, student-directed outdoor learning. As we dipped our toes into the outdoor pond, we caught glimpses of increased confidence, concentration, motivation and physical prowess, along with improved social skills, more sophisticated language use, increased concentration and heightened motivation, and deeper knowledge and understanding. New perspectives were developed and ripple effects set in motion. We are on our way.

Further reading

Broda, H.W. *Move the Classroom Outdoors: Schoolyard Enhances Learning in Action.* Portland, ME: Stenhouse.

This text offers a range of practical suggestions and examples for enhancing school grounds to be used as a teaching tool.

Helm, H. and Katz, L. (2011) *Young Investigators: The Project Approach in the Early Years,* 2nd edn. New York: Teachers College Press.

Step-by-step guidance for meaningful project work with young children is provided here, along with ideas for connecting children with nature. Ways of documenting learning are also included.

Schofield, J. and Danks, F. (2012) *The Stick Book: Loads of Things You Can Make or Do with a Stick.* London: Frances Lincoln.

Full of practical ideas for children and adults, this book inspires imaginative play. Activities are safety rated.

Williams, D. and Brown, J. (2012) *Learning Gardens and Sustainability Education: Bringing Life to Schools and Schools to Life.* New York: Routledge.

This text considers school gardens as a teaching tool, placing soil at the centre of the sustainability discussion.

Information for practice

- Take stock of the outdoor experiences currently provided in your setting and set goals for purposeful outdoor experiences. Consider the knowledge and skills you wish to nurture and how this can be done through child-initiated activities.

- Map your location and determine ways to maximize learning in nearby outdoor spaces.

- Ensure adequate resources are available to support outdoor experiences, i.e. clothing, equipment, safety, and classroom materials.

- Research your Ministry or School Board resources to support outdoor learning.

References

Driussi, L. (2008) *Cultivating Risk: A Teacher-Gardener's Journey.* Saarbrucken: VDM.

Egan, K. (2010) *Learning in Depth: A Simple Innovation that Can Transform Schooling.* London, Ontario: Althouse Press.

Knight, S. (2009) *Forest Schools and Outdoor Learning in the Early Years.* London: Sage.

Knight, S. (2011) *Forest School for All.* London: Sage.

Rivkin, M.S. (1995) *The Great Outdoors: Restoring Children's Right to Play Outside.* Washington, DC: National Association for the Education of Young Children.

14

Indian Children's Perceptions of their School Environment

Mallika Kanyal

Chapter overview

The chapter presents a brief overview of Indian education, both in regard to the historical past and the ever-changing present. Reference is made to two main educational philosophies – the nature-based education philosophy of Rabindranath Tagore and the Basic Education (*nai talim*) of Mohandas Karamchand Gandhi, who were both influential politicians as well as intellectual leaders of their time. The current educational experience of our children is analysed using research evidence from a study conducted in a university school in northern India in summer 2009, where 60 5–6-year-old children, their class teachers and 18 parents acted as participants. Children's views in education are vital, especially in the light of ratification of the United Nations Convention on the Rights of the Child (UNCRC) by the Indian government in 1992, raising the social and legal status of children from recipients of knowledge to important stakeholders in education. Equally important are teachers' and parents' views, not only as agents in education but also as agents of mobilising and realising children's rights, especially their rights to participate in education.

Outdoor learning, though not an explicit aim of the research, has become one of the most important aspects of the discussion. Findings from my research constantly show children's attraction to the outdoor environment, urging us to reflect on and attend to the explicit and implicit

(Continued)

(Continued)

expression of children's voices. The representation of their wishes, through various research methods, clearly points toward their perception of an ideal school where the outdoors is an integral part of their education. The chapter, therefore, aims to showcase the historic context as well as children's perception of the current and ideal school experience. The ideals of children's perceptions resonate with the same philosophical principles that were debated decades ago in the 19th century by early education pioneers in India.

Introduction

One of the main debates in early education has been around its curriculum, whether it should be more formal or more play based (Walsh et al., 2006). Walsh et al. (2006) present the views of both the proponents and opponents of a play-based curriculum, with the opponents or formal-model supporters arguing for the skills of reading, writing and arithmetic being taught at an early stage, and the proponents proposing qualitative support for valuing the different ways in which children think. Advocates of the play-based curriculum state that it should be designed with the age and stage of children's development in mind, as pressures from a prescriptive, more formal curriculum not only affect their motivation but can also diminish their experience of childhood.

Tanner et al. (2006) present another contested term in education – quality. They argue for a continuum in our understanding of the term quality, which at one end represents a static and objective idea – portrayed through official definitions, and at the other end represents a more contested and dynamic idea – one which is context-specific and value-based. The former approach makes quality a measurable entity which can be measured through various official mechanisms, such as an audit. The latter approach makes it a more open concept, which can be contested and discussed within a given environment. The dynamic approach accepts the fact that different stakeholders can have varied understandings of the term 'quality'; for example, parents, teachers and children can all have their own unique ways of conceptualising education and the quality of education. It is therefore important to understand the varied perceptions of education as viewed by its stakeholders, of which, I believe, children are the most important. Also, with an acceptance of the United Nations Convention on the Rights of the Child (UNCRC; UN, 1989) as a universal agreement on the protection, provision and participatory rights of children, they (children) are entitled to express their views about the education they receive.

Inspired by these beliefs, the chapter shares the findings of a research study carried out in summer 2009 in a university school in northern

India. Findings from a single school cannot be used to generalise the whole Indian context, but the chapter makes reference to the Indian education system to analyse the data. The text, therefore, in places, makes reference to India, as opposed to the school itself. The research, as stated earlier, was inspired by the UNCRC's participatory rights in understanding children's perceptions of their school experience. Outdoor learning was not an explicit part of the research but the findings strongly indicate children's attraction to the outdoor environment, making outdoor learning an integral part of the work.

The Indian context

Before I discuss the research in detail, it is first important to understand the Indian context in which the concept of education has been contested for decades. The following section begins with a historic consideration of education, starting from pre-independence in the early 19th century, when India made progress under the political leadership of Gandhi and the intellectual leadership of Tagore. Both scholars were deeply interested in educational change and made significant contributions to educational reform. The historic context is therefore illustrated with the help of two examples: (i) Tagore's nature-based education, commonly referred to as *Shantiniketan* – its roots were laid in the pre-independence era but it is still realised in its reincarnated form in the shape of Visva Bharati University in West Bengal (Jain, 2001); and (ii) the programme of Basic Education (BE) undertaken in the first decade of independence, pioneered by Mohandas Karamchand Gandhi as *nai talim* (new education) (Kumar, 2004) but gradually eroded from the Indian education system for various social and political reasons.

These two approaches are included in this chapter because of their explicit links to outdoor, and a more practical and interactional perception of, learning (and therefore teaching). The progressive changes in education thereafter are also included in the discussion, especially the role the Indian government played through its various national and international policies in giving elementary education its current shape and form. Reference is also made to a critical examination of the term 'childhood', from an Indian perspective, as argued by Nieuwenhuys (2009).

(i) Tagore's nature-based philosophy of education
Rabindranath Tagore (1861–1941) was a freedom fighter, a great poet, a profound thinker and a strong school critic (Palmer et al., 2000). Many of his critiques of schooling grew out of his own experiences as a boy and youth. He argued that school (in its *then* current form) alienates the child from nature and also from him- or herself. In striving

for uniform results and averages, the system ignores the value of the 'individual' and promotes dull conformity with its standard curriculum and examinations system. Tagore believed that instead of extrinsic rewards and punishment, children need freedom of thought and freedom of movement, where their whole bodies are free to move and act. These two freedoms can closely be related to the third freedom, the freedom to create, which eventually leads to 'learning'. He believed that forcing children to be stationary, as teachers often do in schools, can actually result in a widening of the gap between the mind and body, where both suffer as a result. Integrating body and mind coordinates ideas and thoughts, facilitating various forms of bodily expressions, resulting in deep learning (Jain, 2001).

Tagore firmly believed in learning through exploration, as openly and actively as nature intended. He strongly felt that activities such as gardening, pruning, animal husbandry and tree planting are essential for children and too much emphasis on indoor learning can cut the child off from community life. He felt that if children are going to care for the community, they need to live deeply within it (Arenas et al., 2006). Tagore finally realised the essence of his philosophy (and poems) in reality by creating a soulful atmosphere in the form of an *ashram* at *Shantiniketan* in 1901 in Bengal, following the model of the forest hermitages of ancient India (Palmer et al., 2000). He called it the 'living temple'. The concept of Shantiniketan therefore started as a radical challenge to the (then-British) government system/model of education, and was heavily influenced by Tagore's own version of de-schooling, de-institutionalizing and building *Swaraj*. It was a place where both children and adults would learn together, drawing upon nature's wonders.

Shilpa Jain (2001) gives a remarkable account of Shantiniketan, envisioned as being surrounded by natural surroundings: open air, solemn rivers, expansive plains of prickly shrubs, red gravel and pebbles, date-palm and sal trees, amalaki and mango groves, the earth stretching its brown arms, the air enveloping everyone in its warmth. Children are free to move about this incredible scenery as they like: to climb trees, swim in rivers, run, dance and skip throughout the vast open country surrounding the ashram. They wear no shoes, socks or slippers, for Tagore believed that they should neither be deprived of their freedom, nor deprived of the learning contexts that nature provided them with – to intimately know the earth by touch (Jain, 2001). As he explained, 'To alienate our sympathy from the world of birds and trees is a barbarity, which is not allowed in my institution' (2001: 126–128).

Today, whilst maintaining some of its uniqueness, Shantiniketan unfortunately is becoming streamlined with the mainstream model of education that Tagore strongly opposed (Jain, 2001). The changes can be linked to external commercial forces as well as internal conformist pressures, which are discussed later in the chapter.

(ii) Nai talim (Basic Education – BE)

BE was inspired by Mohandas Karamchand Gandhi's (1869–1948) proposal for *nai talim* (literally, new education), first announced in 1937, a decade before India won its independence from colonial rule. Although widely known for his political leadership, Gandhi's education and environmental thinking can be seen as largely rooted in his larger philosophical and moral thinking towards a sustained environmental and animal liberation struggle (Palmer et al., 2000).

Immediately after Gandhi's assassination in 1948, BE was adopted as a state policy. The most important change through this policy was the incorporation of manual work or hands-on experience of a productive craft in the core curriculum of primary schools, which challenged the education system of the time, both socially and pedagogically. Socially, it was in direct contradiction to the caste framework of Indian society which believed manual work to be a blue-collar job for the lower castes only. Pedagogically, BE can be seen as inspired by older cultural beliefs about learning in India (Kumar, 1991 in Kumar, 2004). It believed in the integration of knowledge with handicrafts, challenged rote learning and prescriptive textbooks as didactic pedagogical tools. It therefore met resistance from traditionally trained teachers, politicians, bureaucrats and textbook publishers. There were also problems associated with the transition to secondary school. Other political and social changes at that time, such as the two wars that India faced with its neighbours (in the 1960s), the death of its two prime ministers and the break-up of the Congress party under whose leadership India had gained independence, led to a rapid erosion of Gandhi's philosophy. The modernisation and pressure of agricultural productivity in the 1960s paved the way for a reconsideration of the old-style textbook-based curriculum, with the goodness of BE squeezed into a 'work experience' slot in the curriculum (Kumar, 2004). So, towards the end of the 1960s, the primary school returned to what it had known during colonial times – a textbook-based curriculum.

Other national changes

Following independence, development programmes in the country, including those for children and their education were carried out within the framework of the five-year plans, some funded by the central state and some by both central and local governments (Bhakry, 2006). The establishment of the Department of Women and Child Development, set up in the ministry of Human Resource Development in 1985 (Rao, 2007), gave a political direction to children's welfare, including their education. But other integrated social changes, such as the oil crisis in the 1970s and the ensuing debt crisis in the 1980s, frustrated the steps taken by the newly independent government of India to develop an informed debate on childhood, education and child welfare (Nieuwenhuys, 2009).

The early 1990s saw the integration of international policies into domestic laws, the most influential of which was the ratification of the UNCRC (UN, 1989) by the Indian government in 1992 (Bhakry, 2006; Rao, 2007). It has now been 20 years since the implementation of children's rights, but a significant proportion of people are not yet fully aware of the concept of children's rights (Deb and Mathews, 2012). Deb and Mathews (2012) report that there are various rights that conflict with each other in their implementation; for example, the right to protection from inappropriate work (Article 32) and the right to leisure and play (Article 31) are not being fully enjoyed by Indian children. They are deprived of leisure time because of strict routines in life, right from their early childhood, where they often face intense academic pressures from school, family and private tutors. Also, in relation to Article 12, which is about freedom of expression, about one quarter of the research participants in Deb and Mathews' study (75 participants from a total of 300 teachers and parents) do not think children should have rights to freedom of expression and association. The extent of this negative attitude may reflect beliefs around the discipline of children, subservience to parental authorities, and the cultural framework which places a heavy reliance on conformity with the dictates of patriarchy, religion, culture and class (Deb and Mathews, 2012: 257).

Kumar's (2004) work, on a similar note, portrays the distressed state of school education in India. He contests the idea of quality in education in developing countries, especially following post-colonialism, and at the same time urges us not to limit these concerns to developing countries alone. The reason Kumar associates this with the diminishing quality of education is globalisation. Globalisation, with its economic and capitalistic approach, is somewhat responsible for customising education to fulfil the economic demands of the markets, the competitiveness of which gives rise to the commoditisation of knowledge. This, on closer inspection, resembles closely the institutionalisation of education in the industrial economy. The fast pace of globalisation and the shift in global economies put immense pressure on governments, giving rise to policies that widen the gap between the epistemological and the commoditised conception of education (Kumar, 2004).

Kumar further brings our attention to the relationship between *education and work* and *education and culture* in the context of globalisation.

The former dictates the corporate culture of production, taking away the opportunity for self-development, which has traditionally been linked with education. The latter also depicts a weak link where education, whilst ignoring culture, keeps on evolving as a desperate means of coping with the intensely competitive, highly insecure global situation. The weakened relationship between education and work and education and culture, Kumar (2004) believes, has given rise to the insecurities that parents and consequently children face in education today.

Integral to the debate is the general view that we hold about 'childhood' in a given society. Childhood construction can be shaped by the media, research and other social and pedagogical representations that influence policy and, therefore, the everyday experiences of children. Nieuwenhuys (2009) gives an example by making reference to Indian childhood. She diverts our attention to the amount of policy attention children in India have received in the past two decades. These policy changes and national and international publications and interventions bring to the foreground the underdeveloped concept of Indian childhood, which is often represented by the inadequacy of government, the ignorance of parents and the lack of educational opportunities (Nieuwenhuys, 2009). These pathetic representations almost urge us to believe that the Indian childhood is either non-existent or is in such a distressed state that it needs urgent intervention. The intervention work, which is often offered through Non-Government Organisations (NGOs) or international donors and organisations, such as United Nations Children's Fund (UNICEF), International Labour Organisation (ILO) and the World Bank, funds and publishes only that which follows its strict conditions and conforms to set priorities. This can act as a double-edged sword, where researchers and organisations, often in desperate need of funding, conform to the conditions and set priorities of the donors and fall into the vicious cycle of publishing and over-representing the dire condition of childhood in India on an international level. Nieuwenhuys's (2009) critical analysis of the Indian context therefore alerts us to the oversimplification of education and its related problems, and urges us to consider changes in education from the perspective of India's endemic problems and its social structure (Kumar, 2004).

To gather a current view, and from education's most important stakeholders – the children – a research project (outlined below) was conducted in a university school in northern India in summer 2009, with 60 5–6-year-old children from Class 1. The main aim, as inspired by the children's rights movement, was to understand children's perceptions of the school experience. Being mindful of the general criticism of children's rights as undermining adults' rights and authority, the research also draws evidence from teachers, as well as parents' perceptions of children's learning environments. This is believed to give a holistic view of children's education, as perceived by its different stakeholders (the quality issue, as raised earlier by Tanner et al., 2006). Also, as home and school are the two places where children generally spend most of their time, these locales have a large influence on how their rights are realised in practice (Deb and Mathews, 2012).

The research is outlined in the following three boxes, where Box 14.1 gives a general outline of the research and a brief description of the methods used. The findings are then organised into two categories: findings 1 (shown in Boxes 14.2 and 14.3) which are relevant to children and their views; and findings 2 (Box 14.4) which show adults' (teachers' and parents') perceptions of children's education. The research is then discussed in general terms to highlight the importance of the outdoor environment in children's lives.

Box 14.1   Research outline

In summer 2009, a university school in northern India was approached to be involved in a research project to understand young children's perceptions of their school experience. The aim was not explicitly linked to outdoor play but findings from the research reveal a strong wish by children to be outside. The project methods and findings are outlined briefly and discussed in relation to children's desire for outdoor learning experiences.

The project used three qualitative participatory research methods to understand children's perceptions of their learning environment: paired interviews (as used by Evans and Fuller, 1998); photographs and video cameras (inspired by Burke, 2005 – methodology) and research on children's drawings (adapted from Armstrong, 2007).

The first method, children's interviews, was used to understand their perceptions of their school/class, in general. The interviews were carried out in children's everyday education context – their classroom, using a toy telephone as an interview medium. Children were interviewed in pairs and an attempt was made to keep the questions to a minimum of three:

Why do you come to school?

What do you like about coming to school/class?

Is there anything at all that you do not like about your school/class?

(Continued)

(Continued)

In the second method, children were given disposable cameras and simple video cameras to capture their likes and dislikes in the classroom/school environment. The photographs taken were then organised into broad categories of learning environment, depending on the number of times they were shot by the children. The running commentaries (video recordings) were also attended to carefully, aimed at identifying children's likes and dislikes and the reasons behind them.

In the **third and last method**, children were asked to draw two pictures: (i) a picture of their 'actual school experience'; and (ii) a picture of what they anticipate as their 'ideal school experience'. The former picture was supposed to show the day-to-day things they do in their class, and the latter to show the things that they 'would like to see themselves doing in their school/class'.

It was made clear to the children that the two drawings could be similar or different and that in both drawings they had to put themselves, their teacher and a friend or two. They had to make sure that everyone was doing something and also, if possible, label the people in their drawing.

Box 14.2   Research findings 1 – children's perceptions

On the basis of the interviews, children's reasons for coming to school ranged from adult-imposed reasons to reasons which might be of benefit to them (self-gratifying and educational). When making responses concerning what they like about their school, all children mentioned particular activities, such as colouring, drawing, doing maths and English, playing with friends in the playground; some also mentioned the physical comfort, such as fans, big windows, etc. However, when talking about their dislikes, comparatively few mentioned specific activities; instead they were 'satisfied' (liked everything or could not think of anything they disliked), or mentioned factors which might cause them physical or emotional harm (mild aggression and discomfort).

(Continued)

(Continued)

The photographs taken by the children were organised into the categories of learning environment, such as the blackboard area, display area, teacher's sitting area, children's sitting area, outdoor play area, facilities – such as fans, tube lights, windows, etc. They were then asked whether they liked/disliked that area, found it satisfactory or were not sure. The majority of the children liked all these areas in the classroom with a strong favouring of the outside play area. A few were unsure about some areas, like windows, the outside area and fans and tube lights. The reasons they gave for a dislike of windows was their general cleanliness, the outside area as it may become mucky in the rainy season (when the data was collected), and one girl didn't like the outside play area as she did not have friends to play with (she was struggling to make friends being new to the school). There was however no resounding dislike of any of the areas. Video recordings also show a general liking of all the areas, especially the outside play area and the swing. Children's perception of why they liked these areas was a general attraction to activities that underpin the working of these areas, like colouring, reading and writing, playing outside, doing artwork, etc.

Children's drawings of their 'actual school experience' show a majority of them doing class work and the teacher sitting or standing by the blackboard, mainly doing literacy or numeracy related activities. Some view themselves as playing outside with their friends. But a majority perceive themselves as sitting inside the classroom and doing class work.

The 'ideal school experience' drawings depict a very different story. A majority of children see themselves as playing outside with their friends, in the presence or absence of the teacher. A few drew themselves as studying inside with the teacher. A majority drew natural scenic views with their school building, such as the river, trees, ponds, flower beds, etc. They also saw provision of a range of services, such as IT services, snacks (like juice), a fridge, etc. and saw themselves involved in a range of exciting activities like building a tent house, playing with farm animals, being busy in a play area with swings and slides. Some expressed their ideal school as having 'better' fans and tube lights and even an inverter (due to power cuts).

Examples of children's 'actual' and 'ideal school experience' can be found in Box 14.3.

Box 14.3   Children's drawing examples from research

Below are some example drawings. Figures 14.1a and 14.1b show examples of children's 'actual school experience', and

Figure 14.1a Actual school experience drawing by child A

The teacher is teaching us and we are sitting on desks and chairs. My friends are playing in the classroom.

Figure 14.1b Actual school experience drawing by child B

That's my teacher standing by the blackboard. She is teaching us. That's her desk and chair. We are all sitting in the classroom and studying.

Figure 14.2a Ideal school experience drawing by child C

We mostly study in the classroom, but today I am climbing on the swing. My friends are also playing outside in our playground.

Figure 14.2b Ideal school experience drawing by child D

My friend and I are in the school, without our teacher. We are looking outside at the clouds, flowers and trees.

(Continued)

(Continued)

Figures 14.2a and 14.2b show examples of their 'ideal school experience'. The narratives were tape-recorded whilst the children were actively engaged in the process of drawing. The narratives have been translated from Hindi to English.

Box 14.4   Research findings 2 – Teachers' and parents' perceptions of children's school experience

Teachers' views

The teachers (of Class 1 – two class teachers) were interviewed informally to gather their views on young children's education. Semi-structured questions were asked and their views were noted down. Their responses suggest that they would personally prefer to follow a play-based curriculum for this age group (birth–8), but it is the conflict between their own philosophy of education and the demands of the prescriptive curriculum (from the Central Board of Secondary Education – CBSE) that makes them feel under pressure to follow a highly structured programme of work. They view the present curriculum as being more theoretical and assessment-based but are satisfied with the way things are organised at the moment. They however indicate that they would like to see some changes, such as the introduction of more practical activities, the use of more interactive resources, etc.

It is the changing economic conditions in India that, they believe, contribute to the ever-demanding curriculum. The growth of India's economic capital has had an impact on the experiences children go through in school – for example, children are being put under enormous pressure to meet the demands of a highly competitive workforce. This could also be correlated with the pressures that some aspiring parents put on school for their children's academic achievements. The teachers believe that this indirect impact of economy contributes by making the curriculum more didactic and prescriptive.

Parents' views on early years education

Parents of the children (from both sections of Class 1) were approached during a parent/teacher meeting and interviewed in

(Continued)

(Continued)

small groups. A total of 18 parents were interviewed. Their views can be classified as 'mixed views' and are organised into the following three categories. They said that they wanted their child's education to be:

1 More academic-based: a small minority (mainly mothers) expressed that they would like to see more engagement with academic activities and less with creative activities, like drawing and colouring. They said that the school should spend less time on creative activities.

2 More play-based: a majority (especially fathers) said that the curriculum should be more play-based and that children should be spending less time reading and writing. They said that children are forced to learn by rote rather than through creative approaches. They view the curriculum as assessment (exam) based, barely stimulating children's capacity to learn. They would like to see more opportunities for teacher training and professional development (using the latest learning and teaching approaches) and the school's more active engagement in interactive learning processes. Parents said that they would like to see less homework being given to their children so they can spend more quality time at home.

3 More ability-based: a minority said that education should be more 'ability-based' and differentiated according to children's abilities. Children with stronger academic ability should be encouraged to learn at a faster pace and the ones who need more help should be provided with extra support rather than being forced to match their counterparts.

The findings from the research can be interpreted on two different levels. First, it is important to listen to children's views, as the changing ideas of childhood regard them not only as receivers but also as important stakeholders in education. They are entitled to express their views and have their voices heard, as is evident from Article 12 of the UNCRC, to which India became a signatory in 1992. There may be difficulties, however, in the translation of such aspirational policies into practice. It may be hard for the teacher to attend to multiple voices at one time. Also, the teacher might not be aware of the appropriate tools to capture children's views, which could be expressed in multiple ways. Therefore, it is vital not only to consider children's participation from a rights perspective but also from a relational perspective, where children are given the time and freedom to establish a relationship with the teacher and are also given the interactional space, both mental and physical, to feel comfortable and confident in sharing their ideas, ideas which they know will be valued. Bae (2010) also simplifies the implementation of participatory rights to practice and argues that they cannot be applied in isolation from other rights – for example, 'Article 12, as a general principle, is linked to the other general principles of the Convention, such as Article 3 (primary consideration of the best interests of the child), Article 13 (the right to freedom of expression) and Article 17 (the right to information)' (Bae, 2010: 207).

Second, it is vital to see what children are trying to say. Here, we may need to scratch beneath the surface and keep our eyes and minds open to both the explicit and implicit voices of children. As is evident from the research example above, children are happy coming to school and love spending time with their friends and teachers. This explicit expression by the children is worth celebrating as it surely is an indication of positive school experiences. However, on closer inspection, it becomes apparent that they want to spend more time outside. The outside space is mostly perceived to be children's space as the majority of them do not want the teacher to be there with them. They also perceive it to be a playful space, with appropriate resources and facilities. Interestingly enough, the drawings also show their desire to be close to nature. This is evident from most of the 'ideal school drawings', where children have included trees, flowers, rivers, mountains, clouds, forests, etc. in their pictures. The children's desire to be close to nature reminds us of ancient Indian times, when *gurus* (teachers) used to educate children in mother nature, in the woods in *gurukuls* (educational dwellings in the forests, at the outskirts of villages). Tagore's observation that it was the forest and not the town that was the fountain head of Indian civilisation is undoubtedly true (cited in Altekar, 2009: 96). A detailed description of ancient Indian education is beyond the scope of this chapter, but parallels can be drawn with children's perceptions of their ideal school experience (as shown in Box 14.3).

Reflecting on what children 'want' from education as opposed to what they 'get' in reality, I wonder if there is a need for education leaders in India to pause and look back on the rich tradition laid by Tagore and Gandhi, and other equally important contributors. The roots appear to be strong and it may only be a matter of reviving those philosophies which have always given attention to the rich, meaningful experiences that nature has to offer both children and adults. Indoor experiences and their educational value cannot be underestimated but can be restricting at times. Looking at the research example above, the majority of children depict a monotonous indoor routine for the 'actual' school experience where they are being taught by the teacher, who mostly stands at the blackboard. The drawings overwhelmingly represent an academically driven, traditional view of the classroom, where the teacher takes the position of authority and the children attend to their instructions (Lodge, 2007; Weber and Mitchell, 1995).

The drawings of the ideal school experience, on the other hand, depict a very different perception of school. Here, children see themselves as being given the freedom to explore a range of activities, such as playing in a tent; playing football; seeing farm animals; playing games with their friends; running around; watching clouds, rivers and mountains; playing around a pond; feeding the ducks; and even studying literacy and numeracy outside. The outdoors therefore can be seen to lend itself to a range of activities, which may not necessarily be realised indoors. I do not deny the importance of the indoor learning environment, but, as rightly said by Parker (2008, in Bilton, 2010), similar experiences can happen inside, but the outside explodes the potential of them.

Considering the perspectives of these three important stakeholders of education – children, teachers and parents – who unanimously prefer a play-based curriculum, it becomes apparent that there is a need for change in the education system. The current system in India is going through a phase of change through the implementation of the National Curriculum Framework (NCF) (2005), under the strong academic leadership of Professor Krishna Kumar, who took over as the director of the National Council of Educational Research and Training in September 2004. This was the time when concern was being raised about a lot of curricular trends. Kumar has been trying to bring a fresh child-centred perspective to the Council through a series of reforms that are believed to make learning more meaningful for children (Srinivasan, 2010). But like any new approach, the framework dissemination is not going without criticism. Deepa (2005) questions the translation of this framework into reality with weak infrastructure and a culture of para-teachers (appointed on a contractual basis). Also, to revive a child-friendly education, it is not just the textbooks but also the schoolteachers who need to become child-friendly (Thapar, 2005). Despite all the criticism, Professor Kumar (2005) says that the National Council for

Teacher Education, a statutory body that lays down guidelines for regulating teachers' education in the country, has welcomed the NCF 2005. The Council is in the process of revising the Bachelor of Education (B.Ed) programmes on the basis of the NCF. Overall, although still in its conception stage, the NCF seems to be a welcoming and promising framework which has the potential to overtake and shift the current didactic processes into a more inclusive and interactive methodology towards education (Kanyal and Cooper, 2010).

Going forward

As is evident from the research findings, children prefer an outdoor learning environment to that of an indoor learning environment. There is a need to develop creative approaches to listen to young children, so that their views can be taken into account when planning and designing responsive learning environments. The answer may lie in the adoption of participatory approaches. The findings from the research, however, do not come as a surprise, as learning from outdoors, and from mother nature, was the traditional approach in ancient as well as pre-independence India. It can be seen from this chapter that India has come a long way from pre-independence in achieving and debating its education provision. The country, however, needs to revive and revisit its roots, whilst considering modern approaches to educating its new generations.

Further reading

Deb, S. and Mathews, B.P. (2012) 'Children's rights in India: parents' and teachers' attitudes, knowledge and perceptions', *The International Journal of Children's Rights* 20(2): 241–264.
This is useful reading to get an outline of the status of children's rights in India, especially from teachers' and parents' perspectives. It shows how securely and efficiently (or not) these rights are applied in practice.
Kumar, K. (2004) Quality of Education at the Beginning of the 21st Century: Lessons from India [online]. Available at: http://unesdoc.unesco.org/images/0014/001466/146663e.pdf (accessed 20 June 2012).
This is useful reading for understanding quality-related concerns in education from a socio-cultural perspective. It discusses the complex impact of globalisation on education and shares some case studies from India to demonstrate the challenges that come with the mainstreaming of innovative practices in education.
Nieuwenhuys, O. (2009) 'Is there an Indian childhood?', *Childhood* 16(2): 147–153.
This critical read raises questions on the generalised (academic) construction of the 'Indian childhood'. The author challenges the idea of (International) NGO-induced childhood services and programmes that claim to be saving the Indian childhood, and urges the reader to have a critical eye while engaging with any such literature.

Information for practice

In order to provide more responsive learning environments for children, we must think of ways of encouraging children to participate in learning and research. It not only provides children with greater opportunities for participation, but also helps the practitioner co-construct and learn along with the child, thus creating a shared pedagogical environment. This can be done by adopting participatory approaches in practice which may include visual representations, such as drawings, mapping, photography, and also more traditional approaches such as group discussions. For ideas on using participatory approaches with children, see Alison Clark's work on the use of the 'Mosaic Approach', and for ideas on how children and young people can get involved in research, see Mary Kellett's work at the Children's Research Centre, Open University (online). The Centre trains and supports children and young people to investigate issues identified as important to them. These ideas can easily be adapted to plan an engaging outdoor environment using children's views and, where possible, with the help of children as researchers.

References

Altekar, A.S. (2009) 'Student life', in *Education in Ancient India* [online: Google books]. Delhi: Isha Books, Chapter 3. Arenas, A., Bosworth, K. and Kwandayi, H.P. (2006) 'Civic service through schools: an international perspective', *British Association for International and Comparative Education* 36(1): 23–40.

Arenas, A., Bosworth, K. and Kwandayi, H.P. (2006) 'Civic service through schools: an international perspective', *British Association for International and Comparative Education*, 36(1): 23–40.

Armstrong, D. (2007) Classroom Visions: Efficient and Effective Ways to Differentiate Education, April [online]. Available at: www.classroomvisions.com (accessed 10 January 2009).

Bae, B. (2010) 'Realizing children's right to participation in early childhood settings: some critical issues in a Norwegian context', *Early Years* 30(3): 205–218.

Bhakry, S. (2006) *Children in India and their Rights*. New Delhi: National Human Rights Commission.

Bilton, H. (2010) *Outdoor Learning in the Early Years: Management and Innovation*, 3rd edn. London: Routledge.

Burke, C. (2005) 'Play in focus: children researching their own spaces and places for play', *Children, Youth, Environments* 15(1): 27–53.

Deb, S. and Mathews, B.P. (2012) 'Children's rights in India: parents' and teachers' attitudes, knowledge and perceptions', *The International Journal of Children's Rights* 20(2): 241–264.

Deepa, A. (2005) New Curriculum Framework: A Few Chapters Short [online]. Available at: http://www.indiatogether.org/2005/dec/edu-ncf2005.htm (accessed 14 November 2009).

Evans, P. and Fuller, M. (1998) 'Children's perceptions of their nursery education', *International Journal of Early Years Education* 6(1): 58–75.

Jain, S. (2001) The Poet's Challenge to Schooling: Creative Freedom for the Human Soul [online]. Available at: http://www.swaraj.org/shikshantar/resources.html (accessed 20 July 2012).

Kanyal, M. and Cooper, L. (2010) 'Young children's perceptions of their school experience: a comparative study between England and India', *Procedia: Social and Behavioral Sciences* 2(2): 3605–3613.

Kellett, M., Children's Research Centre, Open Univeristy, see http://www.open.ac.uk/education-and-languages/main/people/mary.kellett

Kumar, K. (2004) Quality of Education at the Beginning of the 21st Century: Lessons from India [online]. Available at: http://unesdoc.unesco.org/images/0014/001466/146663e.pdf (accessed 20 June 2012).

Kumar Sharma, S. (2005) New Curriculum Framework: A Few Chapters Short [online]. Available at: http://www.indiatogether.org/2005/dec/edu-ncf2005.htm (accessed 14 November 2009).

Lodge, C. (2007) 'Regarding learning: children's drawings of learning in the classroom', *Learning Environment Research* 10: 145–156.

National Curriculum Framework (2005) *National Council of Educational Research and Training* [online]. Available at: http://www.ncert.nic.in/html/pdf/schoolcurriculum/framework05/prelims.pdf (accessed 15 November 2009).

Nieuwenhuys, O. (2009) 'Is there an Indian childhood?', *Childhood* 16(2): 147–153.

Palmer, J., Cooper, D. and Corcoran, P.B. (2000) *Fifty Key Thinkers on the Environment* [online: Google books]. London: Routledge, pp. 142–146.

Rao, J. (2007) UNICEF India – The Children: The History of Child Rights in India [online]. Available at: http://www.unicef.org/india/children_3220.htm (accessed 20 July 2012).

Srinivasan, M. (2010) 'Interview – It was remarkable experience protecting academic integrity from political attacks', *The Hindu*, 4 March [online]. Available at: http://www.thehindu.com/opinion/interview/article139044.ece (accessed 30 July 2012).

Tanner, E., Welsh, E. and Lewis, J. (2006) 'The quality-defining process in early years services: a case study', *Children & Society* 20: 4–16.

Thapar, R. (2005) 'National curriculum framework and the social sciences', *The Hindu*, 5 November [online]. Available at: http://www.hinduonnet.com/thehindu/thscrip/print.pl?file=2005090501141000.htm&date=2005/09/05/&prd=th& (accessed 11 November 2009).

United Nations (UN) (1989) United Nations Convention on the Rights of the Child [online]. Available at: http://www.unicef.org/rightsite/237_202.htm (accessed 1 June 2010).

Walsh, G., Sproule, L., McGuinness, C., Trew, K., Rafferty, H. and Sheehy, N. (2006) 'An appropriate curriculum for 4–5-year-old children in Northern Ireland: comparing play-based and formal approaches', *Early Years* 26(2): 201–221.

Weber, S. and Mitchell, C. (1995) *That's Funny, You Don't Look Like a Teacher: Interrogating Images and Identity in Popular Culture*. Abingdon: RoutledgeFalmer. Also available at: Anglia Ruskin University [online], http://site.ebrary.com/lib/anglia/Doc?id=10058250&ppg=17 (accessed 10 February 2010).

Index

Added to a page number 'f' denotes a figure.